KOREAN Picture Dictionary

Written by : Kang Hyoun-hwa Kyunghee University
Translated by : Peter Schroepfer English **Piao Wenzi** Chinese **Ogoshi Naoki** Japanese

DARAKWON

Introduction

처음 이 책을 만들겠다고 생각하게 된 것은 우연히 대형 서점의 외국 서적 코너에서 영어판 그림 사전을 접한 후부터이다. 깔끔하게 만들어진 영어판 그림 사전을 보면서 왜 한국어판 그림 사전은 아직 나오지 않았을까 하는 생각이 들었다. 그러나 막상 그림 사전을 만들기로 마음을 먹기 시작하면서부터 곧 그 이유를 알 수 있었다. 우선 상대적으로 적은 수요를 가진 한국어 학습시장에서 많은 정성과 경비가 소요되는 그림 사전을 만드는 작업은 만만치 않았다. 또한 외국의 것과 차별화되는 우리의 독특한 생활환경 설정이나 그에 따른 어휘 선정 작업도 쉽지 않았다. 그러나 일을 진행하면서 많은 외국인 학습자들이나 외국어 전공자들이 한국어 학습을 위한 그림 사전의 필요성에 대해 조언해 주었고 그런 호응 덕분에 한동안 접어두었던 이 책의 작업을 마무리 지을 수 있는 용기를 가지게 되었다.

외국어로서의 한국어 학습 목적은 학습자에 따라 다양할 수 있으며, 그 목적에 따라 목표로 하는 습득 어휘의 수나 질이 달라질 수 있다. 관광, 단기 연수의 경우 일상생활에 꼭 필요한 기초 어휘 몇 백 개 정도만 필요하며, 유학생, 주재원 등의 장기 체류자의 경우는 훨씬 더 많은 수의 어휘 습득이 요구된다고 하겠다. 그러나 기존의 한국어 교재는 교육기관에서의 교육을 전제로 한 급별(단계별) 언어 학습에 주안점을 두고 편찬되어 이런 다양한 요구를 반영할 수 없었다. 또한 사전을 참고하려 해도 일반 국어사전은 단어 수도 많고 한국어로 기술되어 있어서 한국어를 전혀 모르는 외국인이 접할 수 없는 문제점이 있었다. 따라서 생활에 필요한 기초 어휘를 쉽게 알 수 있는 주제별 그림 사전이 반드시 필요함을 절감하게 되었다.

이 책은 이해가 쉬운 그림을 이용한 사전이므로 정규적 언어학습 없이도 한국에서 단기 체류하는 외국인이나 한국 입국을 준비하는 외국인을 위한 생활 안내 사전으로 활용될 수 있다. 또한 정규 수업 과정에서의 주제별 어휘 보충학습 자료로 활용될 수 있으며, 국내 거주 외국인(단기 체류자, 외국인 노동자, 주재원)들에게도 실제 한국 생활을 위한 기초 생활 어휘 사전의 역할을 하게 될 것이다.

이 책은 약 13 section의 주제로 이루어져 있고 각 section마다 4~5개의 하위 주제로 구성되어 있다. 각각의 주제에서는 단기 체류자가 가장 많이 접하는 환경(주거, 교통, 쇼핑, 음식점, 은행 등)에서 주로 쓰이는 기초 어휘를 주제별로 선정하고 실생활에서 사용되는 필수어휘를 다루고 있다. 장면별로 제시되는 구체적인 삽화 제시는 한국어나 한국 문화에 대한 사전 이해가 없는 사람도 쉽게 접근 가능하다. 아울러 이 사전은 해당 지역의 한국어 전문가들이 대역한 영어, 중국어, 일본어의 3개 언어를 제공하고 있다는 것이 장점이다.

끝으로 어려운 제작 환경에도 불구하고 흔쾌히 출판을 허락해 주신 다락원의 사장님과 실무진께 진심으로 감사드리며 훌륭한 대역을 제공해 주신 서반석 선생님(영어), 오고시 나오키 선생님(일본어), 박문자 선생님(중국어)에게도 감사를 드린다. 끝으로 본 사전이 나오기까지 함께 고생한 도우미 김유미에게도 감사의 뜻을 전한다.

2006년 11월
강현화

I first had the idea of this book after seeing an English picture dictionary in the foreign publications section in one of Seoul's large bookstores. It was well made, and I wondered why Korean picture dictionary has not been produced. Soon, I realized why. The demand for Korean language learning materials is still relatively small, and producing a picture dictionary would require a lot of effort and expense. Also, the work of creating uniquely Korean environments with the drawings and selecting the appropriate vocabulary for inclusion was not going to be easy. But in the course of putting the book together there were many foreign learners of Korean and teachers of foreign languages who told me of the need for one. For a time I had set the work aside, but, thanks to their support, I had the courage to finish.

Different people will have different goals in studying Korean as a foreign language, and so the number and character of the words each student needs can vary. Someone needing Korean as a tourist or for a short period of professional training in a Korean context will need only a few hundred basic words, while long-term residents such as foreign students or people stationed in Korea will need to learn a far larger vocabulary. So far, however, Korean language learning materials have been developed for mostly for step-by-step, formal classroom education in language institutes, and so have been unable to meet such diverse demands. Furthermore, most regular Korean dictionaries include a lot of words, and the definitions are in Korean, making it problematic for foreigners who speak no Korean at all to use them. Subsequently I came to be keenly aware of the absolute necessity of a picture dictionary of basic vocabulary needed in daily life and organized by theme.

This book uses pictures to promote easy understanding, and can be used as a daily vocabulary guide for foreigners preparing to come to Korea or who are here for a short time, even if they do not take formal language classes. It can be used in regular courses as well, to supplement the learning of vocabulary specific to different areas, and it will serve as a dictionary of basic practical vocabulary for foreigners (shot-term residents, migrant workers, and persons relocated for professional reasons) actually living in Korea.

This book is organized into approximately thirteen subject areas, each of which has four or five subsections. Vocabulary was chosen for each subject for being words that short-term residents frequently come into contact with. The focus was actual use in everyday life, and what has been included is essential daily vocabulary. The illustrations in each scene are easy for persons with no prior knowledge of Korean or Korean culture to understand. Another advantage of this dictionary is that it has English, Chinese, and Japanese definitions as well, translated by Korean language experts from the areas those languages are spoken.

Finally I would like to extent my heartfelt thanks to the president of Darakwon and the staff there, for agreeing to publish this despite a difficult publishing environment. I also thank Peter Schroepfer, Ogoshi Naoki, and Piao Wenzi for their fine translations, in English, Japanese, and Chinese, respectively. Thanks finally to assistant Kim Yu-mi, who suffered with me until the very end.

November 2006
Kang Hyoun-hwa

How to Use This Book

This book was designed for easy use by new foreign learners of Korean. It covers a total of approximately 3,800 words chosen from the 50,000 vocabulary words found on the National Academy of the Korean Language's (NAKL) list of most frequently used words in Korean and the Yonsei Korean Dictionary, as well as from textbooks used in teaching Korean as a foreign language at the university level. 2,400 words are accompanied by individual drawings in the main section of the book and an additional 1,400 are listed in the appendix. Each word is followed by its equivalent in English, Chinese, and Japanese.

Thirteen categories cover a diverse range of vocabulary from everyday life, in subjects from home to school and from nature to the galaxy.

> **Each category in the main section is divided into Pictures & Vocabulary, More Vocabulary, and Phrases & Expressions.**

- In Pictures & Vocabulary items in each picture is identifiable by numbered vocabulary.

- Related words that are not represented in the pictures provided may be found under More Vocabulary.

- Examples of how to use the vocabulary in each section are provided under Phrases & Expressions.

> **Appendix:** In the Appendix you will find "Verbs & Adjectives," "Practical Vocabulary," and "Phrases & Expressions." The overwhelming number of words included in the book's main section are nouns. Frequently used verbs and adjectives are provided in Verbs & Adjectives. In Practical Vocabulary you will find basic words not included in the main section. Phrases & Expressions covers the Chinese and Japanese not included in each category of the main section for reasons of space.

> **Index:** All vocabulary provided in the book's main section are listed in English, Chinese, and Japanese for ease of use.

Contents

Introduction 2
How to use this book 4

01 일상 — Everyday Terms | 日常 | 日常 10

달력	Calendar Terms ｜ 日历 ｜ 暦	10
날씨	Weather ｜ 天气 ｜ 天気	12
상태 · 성질 묘사	Descriptions of Status, Character ｜ 描述状态, 性质 ｜ 状態, 性質描写	13
색깔	Colors ｜ 颜色 ｜ 色彩	14
위치 및 방향	Location and Direction ｜ 位置及方向 ｜ 位置、方向	15
숫자 (수)	Numbers ｜ 数字 ｜ 数字	16
물건을 세는 단위	Units for Counting Objects ｜ 数量单位 ｜ ものを数える単位	18
시간	Time ｜ 时间 ｜ 時間	20
화폐 (돈)	Currency ｜ 货币 ｜ 貨幣(お金)	22

02 사람들 — People | 人(们) | 人 24

얼굴	Face ｜ 脸 ｜ 顔	24
신체와 기관	Body and Organs ｜ 身体与器官 ｜ 身体, 器官	26
나이 (연령)	Age ｜ 年龄 ｜ 年齢	28
가족	Family ｜ 家庭 ｜ 家族	30
사람의 일생	Events in a Lifetime ｜ 人的一生 ｜ 人の一生	32
느낌표현 1	Feelings 1 ｜ 表达感觉 1 ｜ 感情表現1	34
느낌표현 2	Feelings 2 ｜ 表达感觉 2 ｜ 感情表現2	36

03 의복류 — Clothing | 服装类 | 衣服類 38

의류 1	Clothing 1 ｜ 服装 1 ｜ 衣類1	38
의류 2	Clothing 2 ｜ 服装 2 ｜ 衣類2	40
속옷	Underwear ｜ 内衣 ｜ 下着	42
신발	Footwear ｜ 鞋 ｜ 履物	43
모자, 가방	Hats, Bags ｜ 帽, 箱包 ｜ 帽子、鞄	44
액세서리	Accessories ｜ 首饰 ｜ アクセサリー	45
화장품	Cosmetics ｜ 化妆品 ｜ 化粧品	46
의복 · 액세서리 관련동사구	Phrase about Clothing, Accessories ｜ 有关衣服-首饰动词句 ｜ 衣服、アクセサリー関連の動詞句	47
세탁	Laundry ｜ 洗涤 ｜ 洗濯	48

04 음식 | Food | 饮食 | 食べ物 — 50

야채	Vegetables ｜ 蔬菜 ｜ 野菜	50
과일	Fruits ｜ 水果 ｜ 果物	51
생선 및 해산물	Fish and Marine Products ｜ 鲜鱼及海产物(水产品) ｜ 魚、海産物	52
육류	Meats ｜ 肉类 ｜ 肉類	53
음료	Beverages ｜ 饮料 ｜ 飲み物	54
전통차와 술	Traditional Teas and Alcoholic Drinks ｜ 传统茶与酒 ｜ 伝統茶、酒	55
한식	Korean Food ｜ 韩餐 ｜ 韓国料理	56
분식	Snack Food ｜ 小吃 ｜ 軽食	57
중식	Chinese Food ｜ 中餐 ｜ 中国料理	58
일식	Japanese Food ｜ 日餐 ｜ 日本料理	59
양식	Western Food ｜ 西餐 ｜ 洋食	60
과자류	Confectionaries ｜ 饼干类 ｜ 菓子類	61
식료품	Foodstuff ｜ 食品 ｜ 食料品	62
패스트푸드	Fast Food ｜ 快餐 ｜ ファーストフード	64
김치 담그기	Making Kimchi ｜ 做泡菜 ｜ キムチを作る	66
상 차림	Table Items ｜ 摆桌 ｜ お膳の用意	67
식당 (음식점)	Restaurant ｜ 餐厅 ｜ 食堂(飲食店)	68

05 주거 | Living Space | 居住 | 住居 — 70

주거 형태	Forms of Domicile ｜ 居住形态 ｜ 住居の形態	70
주방	Kitchen ｜ 厨房 ｜ キッチン	72
거실	Livingroom ｜ 大厅 ｜ 居間	74
침실	Bedroom ｜ 卧室 ｜ 寝室	75
욕실	Bathroom ｜ 浴室 ｜ 浴室	76
청소용구	Cleaning Devices ｜ 清扫工具 ｜ 掃除用具	78
공구	Tools ｜ 工具 ｜ 工具	80

06 학교 | School | 学校 | 学校 — 82

교실	Classroom ｜ 教室 ｜ 教室	82
학교시설	School Facilities ｜ 学校设施 ｜ 学校の施設	84
도서관	Library ｜ 图书馆 ｜ 図書館	86
시험	Test(s) ｜ 考试 ｜ 試験	88
한국의 학제	Korean School System ｜ 韩国的学制 ｜ 韓国の学校制度	89

07 일 Work | 工作 | 仕事 90

사무실 1 Office 1 | 办公室 1 | 事務室 1 ... 90
사무실 2 Office 2 | 办公室 2 | 事務室 2 ... 92
전화 Telephone | 电话 | 電話 ... 93
컴퓨터 Computer | 电脑 | コンピューター ... 94
E-mail E-mail | 电子邮件 | E-mail ... 96
공장 Factory | 工厂 | 工場 ... 98

08 생활 Service & Retailers | 生活 | 生活 100

병원 Hospital | 医院 | 病院 ... 100
증상 및 질병 Symptoms & Diseases | 症状及疾病 | 症状,疾病 ... 102
약국 및 응급처치 Pharmacy and Emergency Care | 药店及急救措施 | 薬局、応急処置 ... 104
은행 Bank | 银行 | 銀行 ... 106
우체국 Post Office | 邮局 | 郵便局 ... 108
미용실 / 이발소 Beauty Salon / Barbershop | 美容店 / 理发店 | 美容室 / 理髪店 ... 110
백화점 / 쇼핑센터 Department Store / Shopping Center | 百货商场 / 购物中心 | デパート / ショッピングセンター ... 112

09 교통 Transportation | 交通 | 交通 114

버스와 택시 Bus and Taxi | 公交车与出租车 | バス、タクシー ... 114
지하철 Subway | 地铁 | 地下鉄 ... 116
교차로 Intersections | 交叉路 | 交差点 ... 118
교통표지판 Traffic Signs | 交通标志 | 交通標識板 ... 120
자동차 운전 Driving Automobiles | 汽车驾驶 | 自動車運転 ... 122
자동차 부품 Automobile Parts | 汽车零部件 | 自動車部品 ... 124
공항 Airport | 机场 | 空港 ... 126

10 레크리에이션 Leisure & Recreation | 娱乐 | レクリエーション 128

취미와 놀이 Hobbies and Games | 兴趣与游戏 | 趣味、遊び ... 128
스포츠 Sports | 体育 | スポーツ ... 130
음악 Music | 音乐 | 音楽 ... 132
미술, 영화와 공연 Art, Movies, Performances | 美术, 电影与演出 | 美術、映画、公演 ... 134
TV와 오디오 Television and Audio | 电视与音响 | TV、オーディオ ... 136
여행 Travel | 旅行 | 旅行 ... 138

11 식물과 동물 — Plants & Animals | 植物与动物 | 植物、動物 — 140

나무	Trees ∣ 树 ∣ 木	140
꽃	Flowers ∣ 花 ∣ 花	141
가축	Livestock, Domestic Animals ∣ 牲畜 ∣ 家畜	142
야생동물	Wild Animals ∣ 野生动物 ∣ 野生動物	143
새	Birds ∣ 鸟 ∣ 鳥	144
파충류, 양서류, 곤충	Reptiles, Amphibia and Insects ∣ 爬虫类, 两栖类, 昆虫 ∣ 爬虫類, 両生類, 昆虫	145

12 우주와 세계 — The universe & The world | 宇宙与世界 | 宇宙、世界 — 146

우주	Cosmos ∣ 宇宙 ∣ 宇宙	146
자연	Nature ∣ 自然 ∣ 自然	147
세계	World ∣ 世界 ∣ 世界	148

13 한국 — Korea | 韩国 | 韓国 — 150

행정구역과 지리	Administrative Districts and Geography ∣ 行政区域与地理 ∣ 行政区域, 地理	150
역사와 문화	History and Culture ∣ 历史与文化 ∣ 歷史, 文化	152
정치와 법률	Politics and Law ∣ 政治与法律 ∣ 政治, 法律	154
산업과 경제	Industry and Economy ∣ 产业与经济 ∣ 産業, 経済	156
종교	Religion ∣ 宗教 ∣ 宗教	157
군사와 무기	Military and Weaponry ∣ 军事与武器 ∣ 軍事, 武器	158

Appendix — 161

Phrases & Expressions — 162
Practical Vocabulary — 167
Verbs & Adjectives — 178
Index — 184

KOREAN
Picture
Dictionary

Everyday Terms	日常	日常	일상
People	人(们)	人	사람들
Clothing	服装类	衣服類	의복류
Food	饮食	食べ物	음식
Living Space	居住	住居	주거
School	学校	学校	학교
Work	工作	仕事	일
Service & Retailers	生活	生活	생활
Transportation	交通	交通	교통
Leisure & Recreation	娱乐	レクリエーション	레크리에이션
Plants & Animals	植物与动物	植物、動物	식물과 동물
The universe & The world	宇宙与世界	宇宙、世界	우주와 세계
Korea	韩国	韓国	한국

01 달력 Calendar Terms | 日历 | 曆

2010 CALENDAR

3 March

SUN	MON	TUE	WED	THU	FRI	SAT
	1	2	3	4	5	6
7	8	9	10	11	12	13
14	15	16	17	18	19	20
21	22	23	24	25	26	27
28	29	30	31			

1 해 (년)
year
年
年

2 달 (월)
month
月
月

3 주
week
星期(周)
週

4 일
day
日
日

5 주말
weekend
周末
週末

6 주중
during the week
本周内
週の半ば

7 평일
weekday
平日
平日

8 요일
days of the week
星期(周)
曜日

9 일요일
Sunday
星期日
日曜日

10 월요일
Monday
星期一
月曜日

11 화요일
Tuesday
星期二
火曜日

12 수요일
Wednesday
星期三
水曜日

13 목요일
Thursday
星期四
木曜日

14 금요일
Friday
星期五
金曜日

15 토요일
Saturday
星期六
土曜日

달력 Calendar Terms | 日历 | 曆

01

Everyday Terms

계절 seasons | 季节 | 季節

16 **봄** spring | 春 | 春   17 **여름** summer | 夏 | 夏   18 **가을** fall | 秋 | 秋   19 **겨울** winter | 冬 | 冬

월 months | 月 | 月

20 **1월**
January
一月
1月

21 **2월**
February
二月
2月

22 **3월**
March
三月
3月

23 **4월**
April
四月
4月

24 **5월**
May
五月
5月

25 **6월**
June
六月
6月

26 **7월**
July
七月
7月

27 **8월**
August
八月
8月

28 **9월**
September
九月
9月

29 **10월**
October
十月
10月

30 **11월**
November
十一月
11月

31 **12월**
December
十二月
12月

More Vocabulary

오늘	today	今天	今日
내일	tomorrow	明天	明日
어제	yesterday	昨天	昨日
모레	the day after tomorrow	后天	あさって
글피	two days after tomorrow	大后天	しあさって

그제 (그저께)	the day before yesterday	前天	おととい
이번 주 (금주)	this week	这星期	今週
지난주	last week	上星期	先週
다음 주 (내주)	next week	下星期	来週

11

01 날씨 Weather | 天气 | 天気

1 해 (태양)
sun
太阳
太陽

2 구름
cloud
云彩
雲

3 안개
fog, mist
雾
霧

4 비
rain
雨
雨

5 홍수
flood
洪水
洪水

6 폭풍
storm
暴风
嵐

7 번개
lightening
闪电
稲妻

8 눈
snow
雪
雪

9 고드름
icicle
冰柱
つらら

10 맑음
clear
晴天
晴れ

11 흐림
cloudy
阴天
曇り

12 더위
hot
酷热
暑さ

상태 · 성질 묘사 Descriptions of Status, Character | 描述状态-性质 | 狀態、性質描写

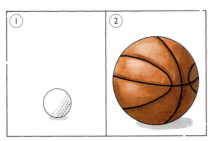

1 작은
small
小小的
小さい

2 큰
large
大大的
大きい

3 빠른
fast
快
早い

4 느린
slow
慢
遅い

5 딱딱한
hard
硬硬的
固い

6 부드러운
soft
软软的
柔らかい

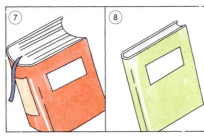

7 두꺼운
thick
厚厚的
厚い

8 얇은
thin
薄薄的
薄い

9 가득한
full
满满的
いっぱいの

10 빈
empty
空空的
空の

11 무거운
heavy
重重的
重い

12 가벼운
light
轻轻的
軽い

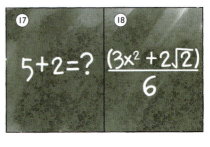

13 착한
good (character)
善良的
良い

14 나쁜
bad
邪恶的
悪い

15 비싼
expensive
昂贵的
高い

16 싼
inexpensive
低廉的
安い

17 쉬운
easy
容易的
易しい

18 어려운
difficult
艰难的
難しい

13

01 색깔 Colors | 颜色 | カラー

1. **주황색**
orange
朱黄色
だいだい色

2. **초록색**
green
绿色
緑色

3. **갈색**
brown
棕色（褐色）
茶色

4. **청록색**
blue green
青绿色
黄緑色

5. **흰색/하얀색**
white
白色
白

6. **하늘색**
azure
天蓝色
空色

7. **검은색**
black
黑色
黒

8. **회색**
gray
灰色
灰色

9. **보라색**
purple
紫色
紫色

10. **빨간색**
red
红色
赤

11. **노란색**
yellow
黄色
黄色

12. **파란색**
blue
蓝色
青

13. **분홍색**
pink
粉红色
ピンク

위치 및 방향 Location and Direction | 位置及方向 | 位置、方向

1 **동**
east
东
東

2 **서**
west
西
西

3 **남**
south
南
南

4 **북**
north
北
北

5 **앞**
front
前
前

6 **뒤**
rear
后
後ろ

7 **왼쪽**
left
左
左

8 **오른쪽**
right
右
右

9 **안**
inside
里
中

10 **밖**
outside
外
外

11 **아래**
below
下
下

12 **밑**
below
底下
底

13 **위**
above
上
上

14 **가운데**
middle
中间
真ん中

15 **사이**
between
之间
間

More Vocabulary

옆　next to｜旁边｜橫
양쪽　both sides｜两边｜両側
안쪽　the inside｜里边｜内側
바깥쪽　the outside｜外边｜外側

숫자(수) Numbers | 数字 | 数字

0 영 (공)
zero
零
0

1 일 (하나)
one
一
一 (一つ)

2 이 (둘)
two
二
二 (二つ)

3 삼 (셋)
three
三
三 (三つ)

4 사 (넷)
four
四
四 (四つ)

5 오 (다섯)
five
五
五 (五つ)

6 육 (여섯)
six
六
六 (六つ)

7 칠 (일곱)
seven
七
七 (七つ)

8 팔 (여덟)
eight
八
八 (八つ)

9 구 (아홉)
nine
九
九 (九つ)

10 십 (열)
ten
十
十 (とお)

11 십일 (열하나)
eleven
十一
十一

12 십이 (열둘)
twelve
十二
十二

13 십삼 (열셋)
thirteen
十三
十三

14 십사 (열넷)
fourteen
十四
十四

15 십오 (열다섯)
fifteen
十五
十五

16 십육 (열여섯)
sixteen
十六
十六

17 십칠 (열일곱)
seventeen
十七
十七

18 십팔 (열여덟)
eighteen
十八
十八

19 십구 (열아홉)
nineteen
十九
十九

20 이십 (스물)
twenty
二十
二十

30 삼십 (서른)
thirty
三十
三十

40 사십 (마흔)
forty
四十
四十

50 오십 (쉰)
fifty
五十
五十

60 육십 (예순)
sixty
六十
六十

70 칠십 (일흔)
seventy
七十
七十

80 팔십 (여든)
eighty
八十
八十

90 구십 (아흔)
ninety
九十
九十

숫자(수) Numbers | 数字 | 数字

01 Everyday Terms

100 백
one hundred
一百
百

1,000 천
one thousand
一千
千

10,000 만
ten thousand
一万
一万

100,000 십만
one hundred thousand
十万
十万

1,000,000 백만
one million
一百万
百万

1,000,000,000 십억
one billion
十亿
十億

1st 첫째
first
第一
1番目

2nd 둘째
second
第二
2番目

3rd 셋째
third
第三
3番目

4th 넷째
fourth
第四
4番目

5th 다섯째
fifth
第五
5番目

6th 여섯째
sixth
第六
6番目

7th 일곱째
seventh
第七
7番目

8th 여덟째
eighth
第八
8番目

9th 아홉째
ninth
第九
9番目

10th 열 번째
tenth
第十
10番目

20th 스무 번째
twentieth
第二十
20番目

17

01 물건을 세는 단위 Units for Counting Objects | 数量单位 | ものを数える単位

밥 한 그릇
a bowl of rice
一碗米饭
ご飯1杯

맥주 한 병
a bottle of beer
一瓶啤酒
ビール1本

콜라 한 캔
a can of coke
一听可乐
コーラ1缶

사과 한 상자 (박스)
a box of apples
一箱苹果
りんご1箱

밀가루 한 봉지
a bag of flour
一袋面粉
小麦粉1袋

달걀 한 판 (30개)
a box of eggs (30 eggs)
一盘鸡蛋 (30个)
卵1箱（30個入り）

우유 한 팩
a carton of milk
一袋牛奶
牛乳1パック

빵 한 조각
a piece of bread
一块面包
パン一切れ

떡 한 접시
a plate of tteok
一碟年糕
餅一皿

휴지 한 두루마리
a roll of tissue paper
一卷卫生纸
トイレットペーパー1ロール

치약 한 통 (튜브)
a tube of toothpaste
一支牙膏
歯磨き粉1つ(チューブ)

기름 한 숟가락
a spoon of oil
一勺油
油1さじ

물건을 세는 단위 | Units for Counting Objects | 数量単位 | ものを数える単位 01

분수 fractions | 分数 | 分数

 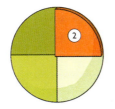 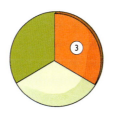 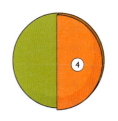 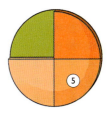

1. 1/8 (8분의 1)
one eighth
八分之一
8分の1

2. 1/4 (4분의 1)
one fourth
四分之一
4分の1

3. 1/3 (3분의 1)
one third
三分之一
3分の1

4. 1/2 (2분의 1)
one half
二分之一
2分の1

5. 3/4 (4분의 3)
three fourths
四分之三
4分の3

퍼센트 percent | 百分比 | パーセント

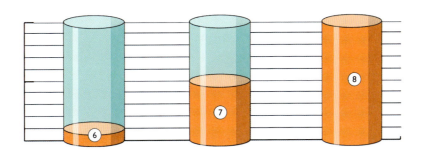

6. 10% (10퍼센트)
ten percent
百分比十
10パーセント

7. 50% (50퍼센트)
fifty percent
百分比五十
50パーセント

8. 100% (100퍼센트)
one hundred percent
百分比百
100パーセント

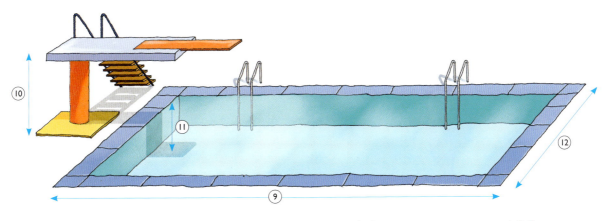

9. 길이
length
长度
長さ

10. 높이
height
高度
高さ

11. 깊이
depth
深度
深さ

12. 너비
width
宽度
幅

19

01 시간 Time | 时间 | 時間

1 정오
noon
中午
正午

2 자정
midnight
午夜
夜中の12時

3 오전
morning
上午
午前

4 오후
afternoon
下午
午後

5 새벽
dawn
凌晨
明け方

6 아침
morning
早晨
朝

7 낮
day
白天
昼

8 저녁
evening
晚上
夕方

9 밤
night
夜
夜

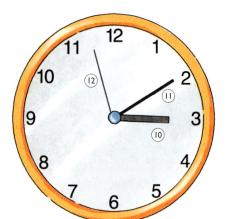

10 시
hour
点
時

11 분
minute
分
分

12 초
second
秒
秒

시간 Time | 时间 | 時間

1시 (한 시)
one o'clock
一点
1時

2시 5분 (두 시 오 분)
five past two
两点五分
2時5分

3시 10분 (세 시 십 분)
ten past three
三点十分
3時10分

4시 15분 (네 시 십오 분)
fifteen past four
四点十五分
4時15分

5시 20분 (다섯 시 이십 분)
twenty past five
五点二十分
5時20分

More Vocabulary

02:20 a.m. (새벽 두 시 이십 분)	two twenty in the morning	凌晨两点二十分	明け方の2時20分
07:10 a.m. (오전 일곱 시 십 분)	seven ten in the morning	上午七点十分	午前7時10分
01:50 p.m. (한 시 오십 분 /두 시 십 분 전)	one fifty p.m.	下午一点五十分	午後1時 50分/2時10分前
08:30 p.m. (여덟 시 삼십 분/여덟 시 반)	eight thirty p.m.	下午八点半	午後8時 30分/8時半
6시 25분 (여섯 시 이십오 분)	twenty five past six	六点二十五分	6時25分
7시 30분 (일곱 시 삼십 분)	seven thirty	七点三十分	7時 30分
8시 35분 (여덟 시 삼십오 분)	thirty five past eight	八点三十五分	8時 35分
9시 40분 (아홉 시 사십 분)	forty past nine	九点四十分	9時40分
10시 45분 (열 시 사십오 분)	forty five past ten	十点四十五分	10時45分
11시 50분 (열한 시 오십 분)	fifty past eleven	十一点五十分	11時50分
12시 55분 (열두 시 오십오 분)	fifty five past twelve	十二点五十五分	12時55分

01 화폐(돈) Currency | 货币 | 貨幣(お金)

동전 coin | 硬币 | 硬貨

1. **10원 (십원)**
   10 won
   十元
   10ウォン

2. **50원 (오십원)**
   50 won
   五十元
   50ウォン

3. **100원 (백원)**
   100 won
   一百元
   100ウォン

4. **500원 (오백원)**
   500 won
   五百元
   500ウォン

지폐 paper money | 纸币 | 紙幣

5. **1,000원 (천원)**
   1,000 won
   一千元
   1,000ウォン

6. **5,000원 (오천 원)**
   5,000 won
   五十元
   5,000ウォン

7. **10,000원 (만원)**
   10,000 won
   一万元
   10,000ウォン

화폐(돈) Currency | 货币 | 貨幣(お金)

Everyday Terms 01

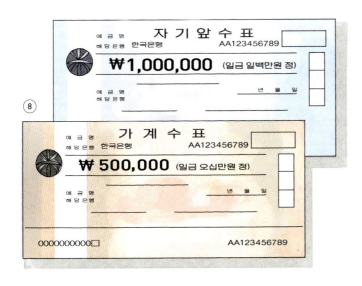

8 수표
Bank Checks
支票
小切手

9 신용카드
Credit Card
信用卡
クレジットカード

10 현금카드
Cash Card
储蓄卡 (现金卡)
キャッシュカード

More Vocabulary

현금	cash	现金	現金	더치 페이	paying separately	AA制	割り勘
잔돈	small change	零钱	おつり	결제	payment	结算	決済
계산(서)	bill, check	清单	計算(書)	일시불	payment in full	一次付清	一回払い
영수증	receipt	发票	領収書	할부	installment	分期付款	分割払い
지갑	wallet	钱包	財布	신용불량	bad credit	信用不良	カード破産

Appendix p.162

Phrases & Expressions

- 한턱 내다 to treat someone
- 수표 뒷면에 이서하다 to endorse the back side of a check
- 카드 영수증에 사인하다 (서명하다) to sign a credit card receipt
- 카드를 제시하다 to show one's credit card
- 신분증을 제시하다 to show identification

- 돈을 주다 (지불하다) to pay (using money)
- 돈을 세다 to count money
- 잔돈을 받다 to receive change
- 영수증을 받다 to receive a receipt
- 팁을 주다 to give a tip

02 얼굴 Face | 脸 | 颜

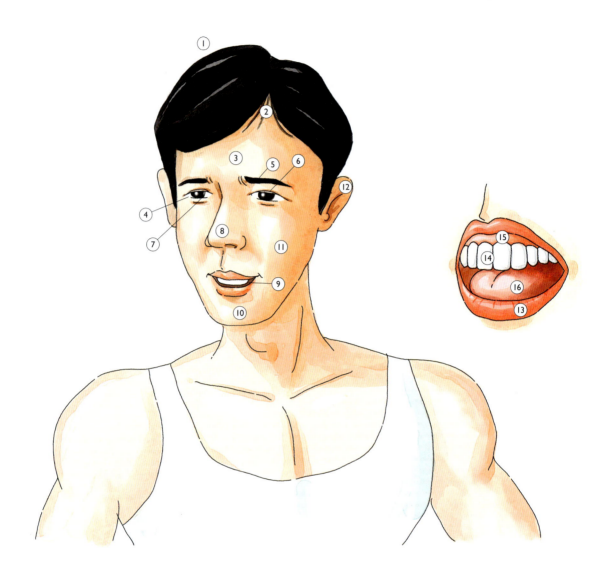

1. **머리**
   head
   头
   頭

2. **머리카락**
   hair
   头发
   髪の毛

3. **이마**
   forehead
   额头
   額

4. **눈**
   eyes
   眼睛
   目

5. **눈썹**
   eyebrow
   眉毛
   眉

6. **쌍꺼풀**
   a double-edged eyelid
   双眼皮
   二重まぶた

7. **눈동자**
   pupil
   眼珠
   瞳

8. **코**
   nose
   鼻子
   鼻

얼굴 Face | 脸 | 顔

9 **입**
mouth
嘴
口

10 **턱**
chin
下颌
あご

11 **뺨 (볼)**
cheek
腮
頬

12 **귀**
ear
耳朵
耳

13 **입술**
lips
嘴唇
唇

14 **이**
teeth
牙齿
歯

15 **잇몸**
gums
牙龈
歯茎

16 **혀**
tongue
舌头
舌

More Vocabulary

여드름	pimple	粉刺	にきび		머리모양	hair style	发型	ヘアースタイル
털	(facial) hair	毛	毛		짧은 머리	short hair	短发	ショートヘアー
주근깨	freckle	雀斑	そばかす		긴 머리	long hair	长发	ロングヘアー
점	mole	痣	ほくろ		생머리	straight hair	直发	ストレートヘアー
턱수염	beard	三羊胡子	あごひげ		대머리	bald	秃头	はげ頭
콧구멍	nostril	鼻孔	鼻の穴		파마 머리	perm	卷发 (烫发)	パーマヘアー
귓불	earlobe	耳垂儿	耳たぶ					

Appendix p.162

Phrases & Expressions

- 얼굴을 씻다 (세수하다) to wash one's face
- 손을 닦다 (손을 씻다) to wash one's hands
- 이를 닦다 (양치질하다) to brush one's teeth
- 입안을 헹구다 to rinse one's mouth
- 머리를 감다 to wash one's hair
- 머리를 헹구다 to rinse one's hair
- 머리를 말리다 to dry one's hair

- 코를 풀다 to blow one's nose
- 눈을 뜨다 / 감다 to open / close one's eyes
- 입을 벌리다 / 다물다 to open / close one's mouth
- 고개를 숙이다 / 들다 to lower / raise one's head
- 머리를 빗다 to comb one's hair
- 머리를 묶다 to tie one's hair

신체와 기관 Body and Organs 身体与器官 身体と器官

1 목
neck
脖子
首

2 어깨
shoulder
肩膀
肩

3 가슴
chest
胸脯
胸

4 팔
arm
胳膊
腕

5 손
hand
手
手

6 손가락
finger
手指头
手の指

7 손목
wrist
手腕
手首

8 손등
back of the hand
手背
手の甲

9 등
back
后背
背中

10 엉덩이
buttocks
臀部
尻

11 허리
waist
腰
腰

12 다리
leg
腿
脚

13 발
foot
脚
足

신체와 기관 Body and Organs | 身体与器官 | 身体と器官

14 **허벅지**
inside of the thigh
大腿
内もも

15 **무릎**
knee
膝盖
膝

16 **종아리**
calf
小腿
ふくらはぎ

More Vocabulary

목구멍	throat	喉咙	喉
겨드랑이	armpit	腋窝	わき
팔꿈치	elbow	胳膊肘儿	肘
손톱	fingernail	手指甲	手の爪
손바닥	palm	手心	手のひら
발톱	toenail	脚指甲	足の爪
발꿈치	heel	脚后跟	かかと
발바닥	sole of the foot	脚心	足の裏
발목	ankle	脚腕	足首
발등	the instep of the foot	脚背	足の甲
발가락	toe	脚指头	足の指
배	abdomen	肚子	腹
배꼽	navel	肚脐	へそ
피부	skin	皮肤	皮膚
뼈	bone	骨头	骨
동맥	artery	动脉	動脈
정맥	vein	静脉	静脈

손가락의 명칭	finger names	手指头的名称	指の名称
엄지	thumb	拇指	親指
검지	index finger	食指	人差し指
중지	middle finger	中指	中指
약지	ring finger	无名指	薬指
새끼손가락	little finger	小拇指	小指

내부기관	internal organs	内脏器官	内部器官
뇌	brain	脑	脳
심장	heart	心脏	心臓
허파	lung	肺	肺
간	liver	肝	肝
쓸개	gallbladder	胆囊	胆囊
위	stomach	胃	胃
장	intestines	肠	腸
신장	kidney	肾脏	腎臓
방광	bladder	膀胱	膀胱

나이 (연령) Age | 年龄 | 年齢

1 **아기**
baby
婴儿
赤ちゃん

2 **유아**
infant
幼儿
乳児

3 **어린이, 아이**
child
儿童, 小孩
子供

4 **청소년**
juvenile
青少年
青少年

More Vocabulary

소년	boy	少年	少年
소녀	girl	少女	少女
성인	adult	成人	成人
여자	woman	女人	女
남자	man	男人	男
어린	(very) young (child age)	年少的	幼い
젊은	young	年轻的	若い
중년의	middle aged	中年的	中年の
늙은	old	年迈的	年取った
연상	older	年长	年上
연하	younger	年少	年下

동갑	of the same age	同岁	同い年
나이	age	岁数	歳
생일	birthday	生日	誕生日
유부남	married man	有妇之夫	既婚男性
유부녀	married woman	有夫之妇	既婚女性
임산부	pregnant woman	孕妇	妊婦
독신	single	独身	独身
가정	family, home, household	家庭	家庭
신혼부부	newlywed couple	新婚夫妇	新婚夫婦
신랑	groom	新郎	新郎
신부	bride	新娘	新婦

나이 (연령) Age | 年龄 | 年齢

5 아가씨
unmarried woman
小姐
未婚の若い女性

6 청년
young man
青年
青年

7 아줌마
ajumma, middle aged woman
阿姨
おばさん

8 아저씨
ajeossii, adult man
大叔
おじさん

9 노인
old person
老人
老人

Appendix p.162

Phrases & Expressions

- 나이가 많다 be old (of many years)
- 연세가 많다 be old (honorific form)
- 나이가 적다 be young (of few years)
- 연세가 적다 be young (of few years)

- 젊어 보이다 to look young
- 늙어 보이다 to look old
- 나이 들어 보이다 to look old (of many years)

02 가족 Family | 家族 | 家族

1. **할아버지 (조부)**
   grandfather
   爷爷（祖父）
   おじいさん（祖父）

2. **할머니 (조모)**
   grandmother
   奶奶（祖母）
   おばあさん（祖母）

3. **외할아버지 (외조부)**
   maternal grandfather
   姥爷
   母方の祖父

4. **외할머니 (외조모)**
   maternal grandmother
   姥姥
   母方の祖母

5. **아빠 (아버지)**
   father
   爸爸
   お父さん

6. **엄마 (어머니)**
   mother
   妈妈
   お母さん

7. **형**
   elder brother of a man
   哥哥
   兄

8. **오빠**
   elder brother of a woman
   哥哥
   兄

9. **누나**
   elder sister of a man
   姐姐
   姉

10. **언니**
    elder sister of a woman
    姐姐
    姉

11. **나**
    I, me, myself
    我
    私

12. **남동생**
    younger brother
    弟弟
    弟

30

가족 Family | 家族 | 家族

13 여동생
younger sister
妹妹
妹

14 삼촌 (숙부)
uncle, younger brother of one's father
叔叔（叔父）
父の兄弟

15 고모
(paternal) aunt
姑姑
父の姉妹

16 고모부
husband of one's (paternal) aunt
姑父
父の姉妹の夫

17 이모
(maternal) aunt
姨妈
母の姉妹

18 외삼촌
(maternal) uncle
舅舅
母方のおじ

More Vocabulary

부모	parents	父母	両親
형제	brothers	兄弟	兄弟
자매	sisters	姐妹	姉妹
남매	brother and sister	兄妹	兄と妹、姉と弟
부부	married couple	夫妇	夫婦
남편	husband	丈夫	夫
부인(아내, 마누라)	wife	夫人 (妻子, 老婆)	妻
자식(자녀)	child	儿女 (子女)	子供
딸	daughter	女儿	娘
아들	son	儿子	息子
장남(큰아들)	first son	长子	長男
막내	lastborn	老幺	末っ子
손자	grandson	孙子	(男の)孫
손녀	granddaughter	孙女	孫娘
사촌	cousin	堂兄弟	いとこ
조카	nephew, niece	侄子	甥、姪
시부모	parents of one's husband	公婆	夫の父母
시아버지	woman's father-in-law	公公	舅
시어머니	woman's mother-in-law	婆婆	姑
장인	man's father-in-law	岳父	義父
장모	man's mother-in-law	岳母	義母
사위	son-in-law	女婿	婿
며느리	daughter-in-law	儿媳妇	嫁
친척	relative	亲戚	親戚
큰아버지	uncle, elder brother of one's father	伯父	伯父
큰어머니	aunt, wife of the elder brother of one's father	伯母	伯母
숙모	aunt, wife of the younger brother of one's father	婶婶 (叔母)	叔母
이모부	husband of one's (maternal) aunt	姨夫	母の姉妹の夫
외숙모	wife of one's (maternal) uncle	舅妈	母方のおじの妻

Appendix p.162

Phrases & Expressions

- 약혼하다 to become engaged to marry
- 결혼하다 to marry
- 장가가다 to marry (a woman, as a man)
- 시집가다 to marry (a man, as a woman)
- 이혼하다 to divorce
- 재혼하다 to remarry

02 사람의 일생 Events in a Lifetime 人的一生 人の一生

1 **출생**
birth
出生
出生

2 **돌잔치**
party marking a baby's first birthday
周岁宴
一歳の誕生日

3 **입학식**
ceremony marking entrance to a new school
入学典礼
入学式

4 **생일 파티**
birthday party
生日宴
誕生パーティー

5 **제대**
discharge from the military
退伍
除隊

6 **졸업식**
graduation ceremony
毕业典礼
卒業式

7 **입사**
entering a company
进公司
入社

8 **결혼식**
marriage ceremony
婚礼
結婚式

9 **집들이**
housewarming party
乔迁宴
引っ越し祝い

사람의 일생 Events in a Lifetime 人的一生 人の一生

10 출산
giving birth
分娩
出産

11 승진
promotion
晋升
昇進

12 사망
death
过世
死亡

More Vocabulary

입대	entering the military	当兵	入隊	장례식	funeral	葬礼	葬式
약혼식	engagement ceremony	订婚礼	婚約の式	제사	ancestral rites	祭礼	祭祀
신혼여행	honeymoon	蜜月旅行	新婚旅行	성년식	coming-of-age ceremony	成年仪式	成人式
환갑, 회갑	60th birthday	花甲	還曆				

02 느낌 표현1 | Feelings 1 | 表达感觉 1 | 感情表现 1

느낌 표현 1 | Feelings 1 | 表达感觉 1 | 感情表現 1

1. 기쁘다
to be happy
高兴
嬉しい

2. 슬프다
to be sad
悲哀
悲しい

3. 좋다
to be good
好
良い

4. 싫다
to be disagreeable
不要 / 不喜欢
嫌いだ

5. 웃다
to smile
笑
笑う

6. 울다
to cry
哭
泣く

7. 자랑스럽다
to be proud
骄傲
誇らしい

8. 부끄럽다
to be shameful
惭愧
恥ずかしい

9. 즐겁다
to be pleasant
愉快
楽しい

10. 화나다
to get angry
生气
腹が立つ

11. 상쾌하다
to be refreshing
爽快
爽快だ

12. 불쾌하다
to be unpleasant
不快
不快だ

13. 기분 좋다
to be in a good mood
心情好
気持ちが良い

14. 기분 나쁘다
to be in a bad mood
心情坏
不愉快だ

15. 재미있다
to be interesting
有趣儿
面白い

16. 재미없다
to be uninteresting
没趣儿
つまらない

17. 편하다
to be comfortable
方便
便利だ

18. 불편하다
to be uncomfortable
不便
不便だ

19. 만족하다
to be satisfactory
满足
満足だ

20. 불만스럽다
to be dissatisfactory
不满
不満だ

More Vocabulary

미워하다	to hate	讨厌	憎む
감사하다	to thank	感谢	感謝する
수줍다	to be shy	害羞	内気だ
대견하다	to be admirable	了不起	感心だ
창피하다	to be embarrassed	羞愧	恥ずかしい
혐오하다	to hate	厌恶	嫌う
무관심하다	to be indifferent	无动于衷 (漠不关心)	無関心だ
질투하다	to be jealous	嫉妒	嫉妬する
든든하다	to be strong, reliable	踏实	心強い
억울하다	to feel mistreated	冤枉	悔しい

02 느낌 표현2 Feelings 2 | 表达感觉 2 | 感情表現 2

느낌 표현2 Feelings 2 | 表达感觉 2 | 感情表現 2

1 **고맙다**
to be thankful
谢谢
ありがたい

2 **미안하다**
to be sorry
抱歉
申し訳ない

3 **좋아하다**
to like
喜欢
好む

4 **사랑하다**
to love
爱
愛する

5 **염려하다**
to worry
担心
心配する

6 **부러워하다**
to be envious of
羡慕
うらやましがる

7 **외롭다**
to be lonely
孤单
寂しい

8 **우울하다**
to be depressed
忧郁
憂鬱だ

9 **당황하다**
to be confused
惊慌
あわてている

10 **피곤하다**
to be tired
疲倦
疲れている

11 **신나다**
to get in high spirits
开心, 兴致勃勃
夢中になる

12 **졸리다**
to feel sleepy
困 (倦)
眠い

13 **무섭다**
to be scary
害怕
怖い

14 **놀랍다**
to be surprising
惊人
驚くべきだ

More Vocabulary

안심하다	to be relieved	放心	安心する
초조하다	to feel anxious	焦急	いらだっている
편안하다	to be peaceful	舒服	安らかだ
불안하다	to be insecure	不安	不安だ
생기 있다	to be animated, lively	有朝气	生き生きとしている
행복하다	to be happy	幸福	幸せだ
불행하다	to be unfortunate	不幸	不幸だ
침착하다	to be composed	沉着	落ち着いている
만만하다	to be easy	小看	くみしやすい
지루하다	to be boring	乏味	退屈だ
자신 있다	to be confident	有信心	自信がある
두렵다	to be afraid of	怕	恐ろしい
짜증나다	to become annoyed	烦躁	苛立つ
심심하다	to be bored from inactivity	无聊	退屈だ
통쾌하다	to be gratifying	痛快	痛快だ
답답하다	to be stuffy	烦闷	もどかしい
반갑다	to be pleased	(见到您)很高兴	嬉しい

의류 1 Clothing 1 | 服装1 | 衣類1

1. **점퍼**
   jumper
   夹克
   ジャンパー

2. **바지**
   pants, trousers
   裤子
   ズボン

3. **남방**
   buttondown shirt
   衬衫
   開襟シャツ

4. **와이셔츠**
   (dress) shirt
   男衬衫
   ワイシャツ

5. **조끼**
   vest
   坎肩
   チョッキ

6. **원피스**
   one-piece dress
   连衣裙
   ワンピース

7. **칠부 바지**
   knickers
   七分裤
   七分ズボン

8. **블라우스**
   blouse
   女式衬衫
   ブラウス

9. **멜빵바지**
   pants with suspenders
   背带裤
   つりズボン

10. **티셔츠**
    T-shirt
    T血衫
    Tシャツ

11. **반바지**
    short pants
    短裤
    半ズボン

12. **웨딩드레스**
    wedding dress
    婚纱
    ウエディングドレス

의류 1 Clothing 1 | 服装1 | 衣類1

13 턱시도
tuxedo
(男) 礼服
タキシード

14 스웨터
sweater
毛衣
セーター

15 면 바지
cotton pants
棉裤
綿パン

16 치마
skirt
裙子
スカート

More Vocabulary

상의	coat, upper garment	上衣	上着
투피스	two-piece dress	套装	ツーピース
청바지	blue jeans	牛仔裤	ジーンズ
니트	knit	针线衣	ニット

03 의류 2 Clothing 2 | 服装2 | 衣類2

1 코트
coat, overcoat
大衣
コート

2 모피코트
fur coat
毛皮大衣
毛皮コート

3 트렌치코트
trench coat
防水衣
トレンチコート

4 카디건
cardigan
开襟毛线衣
カーディガン

5 무스탕
Mustang
羊皮半大衣
羊皮コート

6 파카
parka
派克
パーカー

7 가죽코트
leather coat
皮大衣
レザーコート

8 한복
Korean clothing, hanbok
韩服
韓服

More Vocabulary

바바리	trench coat	风雨衣	バーバリーコート
신사복	(man's) suit	男装	紳士服
숙녀복	(woman's) suit, dress wear	女装	婦人服
아동복	children's wear	童装	子供服
유아복	clothing for infants	婴儿服装	乳児服
양복	suit	西服	洋服
정장	formal wear	正装	正装
캐주얼	casual wear	便装	カジュアル

파자마	pajamas	睡衣裤	パジャマ
가운	gown, robe	睡袍	ガウン
무늬	pattern(s)	纹儿	柄
줄무늬	striped	条纹	縞柄
물방울무늬	polka dotted	水珠纹	水玉模様
체크무늬	checkered	格纹	チェック
꽃무늬	flower pattern	花纹	花柄

의류 2 Clothing 2 服装2 衣類2

9 비옷
rain clothes
雨衣
雨着

10 수영복
swimsuit
泳装
水着

11 스키복
ski suit
滑雪运动服
スキーウェアー

12 작업복
work clothes
工作服
作業服

13 교복
school uniform
校服
(学校の)制服

14 트레이닝복 (운동복)
sweat suit, sportswear
运动服
トレーニングウェア、運動着

15 유니폼
uniform
制服
ユニホーム

16 잠옷
sleepwear
睡衣
寝巻き

More Vocabulary

사이즈	size	型号	サイズ
XL (특대)	extra large	特大	XL(特大)
L (대)	large	大	L(大)
M (중)	medium	中	M(中)
S (소)	small	小	S(小)
XS (특소)	extra small	特小	XS(極小)

옷감	cloth types, textures	衣料	生地
면	cotton	棉	綿
마	hemp	麻	麻
모	fur	毛	毛
견	silk	绢	絹
레이온	rayon	人造纤维	レーヨン
나일론	nylon	尼龙	ナイロン
울	wool	毛	ウール

03 속옷 Underwear | 内衣 | 下着

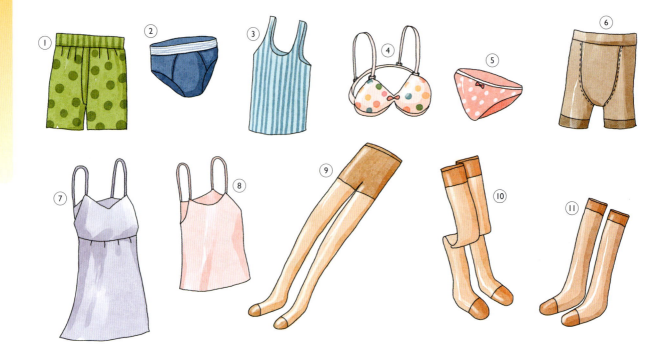

1. **트렁크 팬티 (사각팬티)**
   boxer shorts
   平口内裤
   トランクス

2. **삼각팬티**
   briefs
   三角内裤
   ブリーフ

3. **메리야스**
   undershirts
   针织品
   メリヤス

4. **브래지어**
   bra
   胸罩
   ブラジャー

5. **팬티**
   underpants
   内裤
   パンツ

6. **거들**
   girdle
   腹带
   ガードル

7. **슬립**
   slip
   衬裙
   スリップ

8. **캐미솔**
   camisole
   背心式女内衣
   キャミソール

9. **팬티스타킹**
   pantyhose
   连裤丝袜
   パンティーストッキング

10. **밴드스타킹**
    stockings
    长统袜
    ガーターストッキング

11. **판탈롱 스타킹**
    knee-highs
    短袜
    ショートストッキング

More Vocabulary

페티코트 petticoat | 衬裙 | ペチコート

신발 Footwear 鞋 履物

03 Clothing

1. **구두**
   (usually) leather shoes
   皮鞋
   靴

2. **하이힐**
   high heels
   高跟鞋
   ハイヒール

3. **운동화**
   sneakers, sports shoes
   运动鞋
   運動靴

4. **등산화**
   mountain-climbing boots
   登山鞋
   登山靴

5. **부츠**
   boots
   靴子
   ブーツ

6. **샌들**
   sandals
   凉鞋
   サンダル

7. **고무신**
   rubber shoes
   胶皮鞋
   ゴム靴

8. **장화**
   boots
   长筒鞋
   長靴

9. **밑창**
   sole
   鞋底
   靴底

10. **굽**
    heel
    鞋跟
    かかと

11. **끈**
    shoestrings
    鞋带
    紐

12. **구둣주걱**
    shoehorn
    鞋拔
    靴べら

More Vocabulary

슬리퍼　　slippers　｜拖鞋　｜スリッパ

03 모자, 가방 Hats, Bags | 帽，箱包 | 帽子、鞄

1 야구모자
baseball cap
棒球帽
野球帽子

2 중절모
soft hat, felt hat
礼帽
中折れ帽子

3 털모자
fur hat
毛线帽
毛皮の帽子

4 숄더백
shoulder bag
挂肩式皮包
ショルダーバッグ

5 핸드백
handbag
手提包
ハンドバッグ

6 서류가방
briefcase
文件包
ブリーフ鞄

7 배낭
backpack
背嚢
リュックサック

More Vocabulary

| 등산모자 | mountain climbing hat | 登山帽 | 登山帽 |
| 썬 캡 | visor | 太阳帽 | サンキャップ |

액세서리 Accessories | 首饰 | アクセサリー

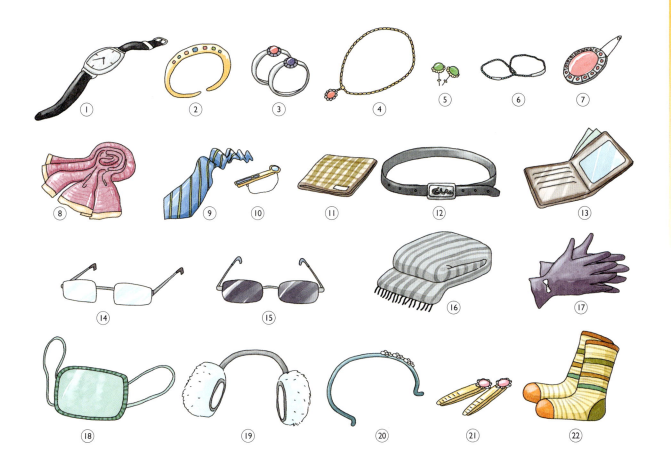

1	시계	watch	手表	時計
2	팔찌	bracelet	手镯	腕輪
3	반지	ring	戒指	指輪
4	목걸이	necklace	项链	ネックレス
5	귀걸이	earring	耳环	イヤリング
6	발찌	ankle bracelet	脚镯	足輪
7	브로치	brooch	胸针	ブローチ
8	스카프	scarf	丝巾	スカーフ
9	넥타이	necktie	领带	ネクタイ
10	넥타이핀	tie pin	领带夹	ネクタイピン
11	손수건	handkerchief	手绢	ハンカチ
12	벨트 (혁대)	belt	腰带	ベルト
13	지갑	wallet	钱包	財布
14	안경	eyeglasses	眼镜	眼鏡
15	선글라스	sunglasses	墨镜（太阳镜）	サングラス
16	목도리	winter scarf	围巾	マフラー
17	장갑	gloves	手套	手袋
18	마스크	mask	口罩	マスク
19	귀마개	earplugs	耳盖	耳あて
20	머리띠	headband	发带	ヘアバンド
21	머리핀	hairpin	发夹	ヘアピン
22	양말	socks	袜子	靴下

03 화장품 Cosmetics 化妆品 化粧品

1. **스킨 (화장수)**
   skin conditioner
   化妆水
   スキン（化粧水）

2. **로션**
   lotion
   乳液
   ローション

3. **크림**
   cream
   面霜
   クリーム

4. **파운데이션**
   foundation
   粉底液
   ファンデーション

5. **파우더**
   powder
   散粉
   パウダー

6. **콤팩트**
   compact (case)
   粉饼
   コンパクト

7. **마스카라**
   mascara
   睫毛膏
   マスカラ

8. **아이섀도**
   eye shadow
   眼影
   アイシャドー

9. **아이브로펜슬**
   eyebrow pencil
   眼线笔
   アイブロウペンシル

10. **립스틱**
    lipstick
    口红
    リップスティック

11. **매니큐어**
    manicure
    指甲油
    マニキュア

12. **손톱깎이**
    nail cutter
    指甲刀
    爪切り

13. **향수**
    perfume
    香水
    香水

14. **팩**
    pack
    面膜
    パック

15. **화장솜**
    cotton
    化妆棉
    コットン

16. **자외선 차단제**
    sun block
    防晒霜
    紫外線カット剤

의복, 액세서리 관련동사구 Phrases about Clothing, Accessories | 有关衣服-首饰动词句 | 衣服、アクセサリー関連の動詞句

옷이 헐렁하다 / 끼다	clothes are loose / tight	衣服肥 / 紧	服が緩い / きつい
바지 기장이 길다 / 짧다	pant legs are long / short	裤腿长 / 短	ズボンの丈が長い / 短い
옷이 크다 / 작다	clothes are big / small	衣服大 / 小	服が大きい / 小さい
허리가 크다 / 작다	waist is big / small	腰肥 / 瘦	ウエストが大きい / 小さい
옷을 갈아입다 / 벗다	to change / remove clothes	换衣服 / 脱	服を着替える / 脱ぐ
윗옷을 걸치다 / 벗다	to put on / remove upper garment	披外套 / 脱	上着をひっかける / 脱ぐ
단추를 채우다 (잠그다)	to fasten a button	扣扣子	ボタンをかける
단추를 풀다 (끄르다)	to undo a button	解扣子	ボタンを外す

| 안경을 쓰다 / 벗다 | to wear / remove eyeglasses | 戴眼镜 / 摘 | 眼鏡をかける / 取る |
| 모자를 쓰다 / 벗다 | to wear / remove hat | 戴帽子 / 摘 | 帽子を被る / 取る |

| 시계를 차다 / 풀다 | to wear / remove wristwatch | 带手表 / 摘 | 時計をはめる / 外す |
| 벨트를 차다 / 풀다 | to wear / remove belt | 扎腰带 / 解 | ベルトをつける / 外す |

| 스카프를 매다 / 풀다 | to wear / remove scarf | 戴围巾 / 摘 | スカーフを巻く / 外す |
| 넥타이를 매다 / 풀다 | to wear (tie) / remove (untie) necktie | 系领带 / 解 | ネクタイを結ぶ / 外す |

| 가방을 들다 | to carry a bag | 拿包 | 鞄を持つ |
| 가방을 매다 | to wear a bag | 背包 | 鞄を担ぐ |

머리핀을 꽂다 / 빼다	to wear / remove a hairpin	戴发夹 / 摘	ヘアピンを挿す / 外す
머리띠를 하다 / 빼다	to wear / remove a headband	系发带 / 摘	ヘアバンドをする / 取る
귀걸이를 하다 / 빼다	to wear / remove an earring	戴耳环 / 摘	イヤリングをする / 外す
목걸이를 하다 / 빼다	to wear / remove a necklace	戴项链 / 摘	ネックレスをする / 外す
팔찌를 하다 / 빼다	to wear / remove a bracelet	带手镯 / 摘	腕輪をする / 外す

| 반지를 끼다 / 빼다 | to wear / remove a ring | 带戒指 / 摘 | 指輪をはめる / 外す |
| 장갑을 끼다 / 벗다 | to wear / remove gloves | 戴手套 / 摘 | 手袋をはめる / 取る |

스타킹을 신다 / 벗다	to wear / remove stockings	穿丝袜 / 脱	ストッキングを履く / 脱ぐ
양말을 신다 / 벗다	to wear / remove socks	穿袜子 / 脱	靴下を履く / 脱ぐ
구두를 신다 / 벗다	to wear / remove (leather) shoes	穿皮鞋 / 脱	靴を履く / 脱ぐ
신발을 신다 / 벗다	to wear / remove footwear, shoes	穿鞋 / 脱	履物を履く / 脱ぐ

03 세탁 Laundry | 洗涤 | 洗濯

세탁 Laundry | 洗涤 | 洗濯

1. **건조대** clothes rack 晾衣架 物干し台
2. **옷걸이** hanger 衣架 ハンガー
3. **빨래집게** clothes pin 晾衣夹 洗濯バサミ
4. **빨랫비누** laundry soap (bar form) 肥皂 洗濯せっけん
5. **섬유유연제** fabric conditioner 纤维柔软剂 繊維柔軟剤
6. **세제** detergent 洗衣粉 洗剤
7. **탈수기** drying machine 甩干机 脱水機
8. **세탁기** laundry machine 洗衣机 洗濯機
9. **빨랫감** laundry 洗涤物 洗濯物
10. **빨래 바구니** laundry basket 洗衣筐 洗濯かご
11. **다리미판** ironing board 熨斗架 アイロン台
12. **다리미** iron 熨斗 アイロン
13. **분무기** sprayer 喷水器 噴霧器

More Vocabulary

| 세탁 망 | laundry net | 护衣网 | 洗濯ネット |
| 빨랫줄 | clothes line | 晾衣绳 | 洗濯物の干しひも |

세탁 기호	laundering symbols	洗涤说明	洗濯マーク
드라이할 것	dry clean	需干洗	ドライすること
짜지 말 것	do not wring, squeeze	不要拧	絞ってはいけない
색깔 있는 옷과 같이 빨지 말 것	do not wash with colored clothes	不可有色衣物同洗	色柄物と一緒に洗わないこと
염소계 표백제는 안 됨	do not use chlorine-based bleach	不可氯漂	塩素系漂白剤使用不可
그늘진 곳에 말릴 것	dry in shade	阴凉处晾干	陰干しすること
다리미 온도	iron temperature	熨烫温度	アイロンの温度
다리지 말 것	do not iron	不可熨烫	アイロン不可

Appendix p.162

Phrases & Expressions

- **탈수를 하다, 옷을 짜다** to drain, to wring out
- **옷을 털다** to shake clothes out
- **옷을 널다** to hang clothes (to dry)
- **옷을 말리다** to dry clothes
- **옷을 개다** to fold clean clothes
- **옷걸이에 걸다** to hang on a hanger
- **빨래를 삶다** to boil clothes
- **비누칠하다** to apply soap
- **옷을 비비다** to rub clothes
- **옷을 헹구다** to rinse
- **다리다** to iron
- **얼룩을 제거하다** to remove stain(s)
- **물이 빠지다 (탈색되다)** to lose color
- **옷이 줄어들다** clothes shrink

야채 Vegetables | 蔬菜 | 野菜

1. **감자**
   potato
   土豆
   ジャガイモ

2. **고구마**
   sweet potato
   地瓜
   さつまいも

3. **오이**
   cucumber
   黄瓜
   きゅうり

4. **호박**
   squash
   南瓜
   かぼちゃ

5. **토마토**
   tomato
   番茄
   トマト

6. **배추**
   Chinese cabbage, pe-tsai
   白菜
   白菜

7. **옥수수**
   corn
   玉米
   とうもろこし

8. **당근**
   carrot
   胡萝卜
   人参

9. **양배추**
   cabbage
   卷心菜
   キャベツ

10. **마늘**
    garlic
    大蒜
    にんにく

11. **고추**
    red (hot) pepper
    辣椒
    唐辛子

12. **콩**
    bean
    豆
    豆

13. **양파**
    onion
    洋葱
    玉ねぎ

14. **파**
    green onion
    葱
    ネギ

15. **상추**
    lettuce
    生菜
    サンチュ

16. **콩나물**
    bean sprouts
    大豆芽
    豆もやし

과일 Fruits 水果 果物

04 Food

1 **사과**
apple
苹果
りんご

2 **배**
pear
梨
梨

3 **귤**
mandarin orange
橘子
みかん

4 **오렌지**
orange
橙子
オレンジ

5 **포도**
grape
葡萄
ブドウ

6 **딸기**
strawberry
草莓
イチゴ

7 **수박**
watermelon
西瓜
スイカ

8 **참외**
chamoe, "oriental melon"
香瓜
マクワウリ

9 **감**
persimmon
柿子
柿

10 **복숭아**
peach
桃
桃

11 **레몬**
lemon
柠檬
レモン

12 **바나나**
banana
香蕉
バナナ

51

04 생선 및 해산물 Fish and Marine Products | 鲜鱼及海产物(水产品) | 魚、海産物

1 문어
octopus
章鱼
タコ

2 오징어
cuttlefish
鱿鱼, 墨斗鱼
イカ

3 꽁치
mackerel pike
秋刀鱼
サンマ

4 갈치
hairtail
带鱼
タチウオ

5 고등어
mackerel
青鱼
サバ

6 장어
eel
鳗鱼
ウナギ

7 새우
shrimp, prawn
虾
エビ

8 게
crab
螃蟹
カニ

9 멍게
ascidian
海囊
ホヤ

10 해삼
trepang
海参
ナマコ

11 굴
oyster
牡蛎
カキ

12 조개
shellfish
贝
貝

13 꼬막
ark shell
泥蚶
ハイガイ

14 홍합
sea mussel
贻贝
イガイ

52

육류 Meats | 肉类 | 肉類

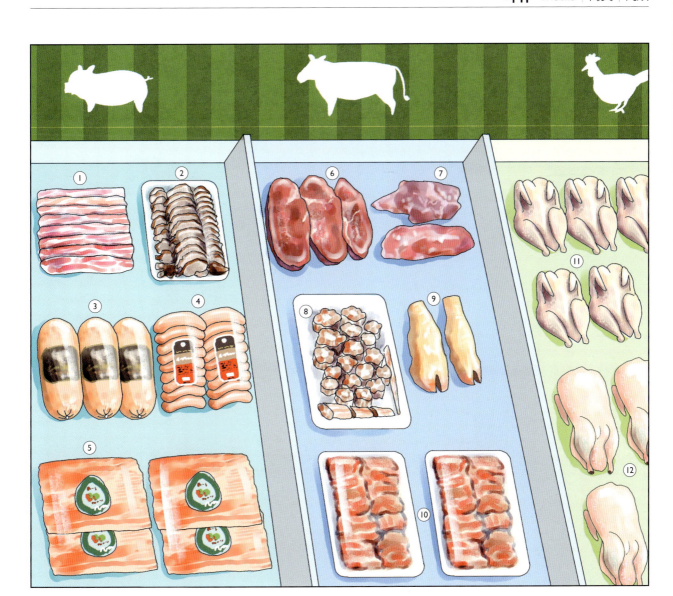

돼지고기 pork | 猪肉 | 豚肉

1. **삼겹살**
boned rib of pork
五花肉
三枚肉

2. **족발**
pettitoes
猪蹄
豚足

3. **햄**
ham
火腿
ハム

4. **소시지**
sausage
香肠
ソーセージ

5. **베이컨**
bacon
腊肠
ベーコン

소고기 (쇠고기) beef | 牛肉 | 牛

6. **안심**
lead beef
牛筋间肉
ロース

7. **등심**
sirloin
里脊肉
ヒレ

8. **꼬리**
oxtail
牛尾
尾

9. **우족**
beef feet
牛蹄
牛の脚

10. **갈비**
ribs
牛排
カルビ

11. **닭고기**
chicken (meat)
鸡肉
鶏肉

12. **오리고기**
duck (meat)
鸭肉
カモ肉

04 음료 Beverages | 饮料 | 飲み物

1. **생수**
spring water
矿泉水
水

2. **우유**
milk
牛奶
牛乳

3. **요구르트**
yogurt
酸奶
ヨーグルト

4. **커피**
coffee
咖啡
コーヒー

5. **팥빙수**
red bean sherbet
冰粥
カキ氷

6. **오렌지주스**
orange juice
橙汁
オレンジジュース

7. **포도주스**
grape juice
葡萄汁
ブドウジュース

8. **복숭아주스**
peach juice
桃汁
ピーチジュース

9. **딸기주스**
strawberry juice
草莓汁
イチゴジュース

10. **토마토주스**
tomato juice
番茄汁
トマトジュース

11. **당근주스**
carrot juice
胡萝卜汁
キャロットジュース

전통차와 술 Traditional Teas and Alcoholic Drinks | 传统茶与酒 | 伝統茶、酒

차 tea | 茶 | お茶

1 **인삼차**
ginseng tea
人参茶
人参茶

2 **녹차**
green tea
绿茶
緑茶

3 **홍차**
black tea, Western tea
红茶
紅茶

술 alcoholic drinks | 酒 | 酒

4 **소주**
soju
烧酒
焼酎

5 **맥주**
beer
啤酒
ビール

6 **막걸리**
makgeoli
米酒
マッカリ

More Vocabulary

생강차	ginger tea	生姜茶	生姜茶
대추차	jujube tea	枣茶	ナツメ茶
칡차	arrowroot tea	葛茶	くず茶
유자차	citron tea	柚子茶	ゆず茶

과일주	fruit wine	果子酒	果実酒
포도주	grape wine	葡萄酒	葡萄酒
매실주	apricot / plum brandy	杨梅酒	梅酒

04 한식 | Korean Food | 韩餐 | 韓国料理

불고기
bulgogi
烤肉
プルゴギ

삼겹살
samgyeopsal
五花肉
三枚肉

갈비
galbi
排骨
カルビ

비빔밥
bibimbap
拌饭
ビビンバ

냉면
naengmyeon
冷面
冷麺

국수
noodles
面条
麺類

칼국수
kalguksu
切面
カルグクス(韓国式手打ちうどん)

만둣국
dumpling soup
饺子汤
マンドゥクック(餃子入りスープ)

떡국
rice cake soup
米糕汤
トックック（お雑煮）

김치찌개
kimchi jjigae
泡菜汤
キムチチゲ

된장찌개
doenjang jjigae
大酱汤
テンジャンチゲ

부대찌개
budae jjigae
什锦汤（锅）
プデチゲ

순두부찌개
sundubu jjigae
嫩豆腐汤
スンドゥブチゲ (豆腐チゲ)

갈비탕
galbitang
排骨汤
カルビタン

삼계탕
samgyetang
参鸡汤
サムゲタン

설렁탕
seolleongtang
牛杂碎汤
ソルロンタン

육개장
yukgaejang
细丝牛肉汤
ユッケジャン

버섯전골
beoseot (mushroom) jeongol
蘑菇火锅
キノコ鍋

분식 Snack Food | 小吃 | 軽食

김밥
gimbap
紫菜卷饭
のり巻き

떡볶이
tteokbokki
炒米糕
トッポッキ

어묵
eomuk
鲜鱼凉粉
かまぼこ

순대
sundae
米肠
スンデ（豚の腸詰め）

라면
ramyeon
拉面
ラーメン

쫄면
jjolmyeon
劲道面
チョルミョン

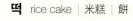
떡 rice cake | 米糕 | 餅

인절미
injeolmi
糯米糕
インヂョルミ

시루떡
sirutteok
蒸糕
シルトック

무지개떡
mujigaetteok
彩虹糕
ムジゲトック

송편
songpyeon
松糕
ソンピョン

가래떡
garaetteok
条糕
カレトック

More Vocabulary

수제비	sujebi	面片汤	すいとん	
라볶이	rabokki	拉面炒年糕	ラポッキ	
절편	jeolpyeon	切糕	チョルピョン	

백설기	baekseolgi	白蒸糕	ペクソルギ
약과	yakgwa	药果	ヤッカ
호떡	hotteok	烙饼	ホットック

04 중식 Chinese Food | 中餐 | 中国料理

자장면
jajangmyeon
炸酱面
ジャージャー麺

짬뽕
jjamppong
大杂烩面
チャンポン

울면
ulmyeon
温面
五目あんかけソバ

군만두
toasted dumplings
煎饺子
焼きギョーザ

물만두
water-boiled dumplings
水饺子
水ギョーザ

탕수육
sweet-and-sour pork
糖醋肉
酢豚

팔보채
ba bao cai
八宝菜
八宝菜

마파두부
ma po bean curd
麻婆豆腐
マーボ豆腐

꽃빵
steamed twisted roll
花卷
中国蒸しパン

고추잡채
chilli chop suey
辣椒杂菜
コチュチャプチェ

해파리냉채
cold dish of jellyfish
凉拌海蜇
クラゲの冷菜

깐풍기
fried chicken in garlic sauce
干烹鸡
乾烹鶏 (鶏の唐揚げにピリ辛ソースをかけた料理)

More Vocabulary

양장피	liang zhang pi	凉皮	両張皮 (両張皮と野菜などをカラシソースで和えた前菜料理)
유산슬	sea cucumber with shrimp and beef	溜三丝	溜三絲 (豚肉を中心に肉、海産物、野菜をあんかけで炒めた料理)
잡탕밥	rice mixed with fish and vegetables	汤泡饭	チャプタンパプ
잡채밥	chop suey rice	什锦饭	チャプチェパプ

일식 Japanese Food | 日餐 | 日本料理

생선회
sashimi
生鱼片
刺身

생선초밥 (스시)
sushi
寿司
寿司

김초밥
nori maki
紫菜饭卷
のり巻き

유부초밥
inari sushi
油腐寿司
いなり寿司

알밥
rice topped with fish roe
鱼仔拌饭
丼

돈가스
pork cutlet
猪排
豚カツ

생선가스
fish cutlet
鱼排
魚フライ

장어구이
broiled eel
烤鳗鱼
ウナギの蒲焼

우동
udon
乌冬面
うどん

메밀국수
soba noodles
荞麦面
ざるそば

59

04 양식 Western Food | 西餐 | 洋食

비프 스테이크 (비후 스테이크)
beef steak
牛排
ビーフステーキ

비프커틀릿 (비후가스)
beef cutlet
炸牛排
ビーフカツレツ

스프
soup
汤
スープ

샐러드
salad
沙拉
サラダ

스파게티
spaghetti
意大利面
スパゲッティー

카레라이스
curry rice
咖喱饭
カレーライス

샌드위치
sandwich
三明治
サンドイッチ

피자
pizza
比萨饼
ピザ

프라이드치킨
fried chicken
炸鸡
フライドチキン

More Vocabulary

| 바비큐폭찹 | barbecue pork chop | 烤猪排 | ポークチョップ |

과자류 Confectionaries | 饼干类 | 菓子類

쿠키
cookie
饼干
クッキー

빵
bread (pastry)
面包
パン

케이크
cake
蛋糕
ケーキ

사탕
candy
糖果
飴

초콜릿
chocolate
巧克力
チョコレート

아이스크림
ice cream
冰淇淋
アイスクリーム

More Vocabulary

비스킷	biscuit	饼干	ビスケット
파이	pie	派	パイ
껌	gum	口香糖	ガム

04 식료품 Foodstuff 食品 食料品

1. **쌀**
rice
米
米

2. **보리**
barley
麦
麦

3. **밀가루**
flour
白面
小麦粉

4. **두부**
tofu
豆腐
豆腐

5. **미역**
brown seaweed
海带
わかめ

6. **당면**
Chinese noodles
粉丝
春雨

7. **국수**
noodles
面条
麺類

8. **김**
dry laver
海苔
海苔

9. **스파게티 면**
spaghetti noodles
意大利面
スパゲッティー（の麺）

10. **마요네즈**
mayonnaise
沙拉酱
マヨネーズ

11. **케첩**
ketchup
番茄酱
ケチャップ

12. **버터**
butter
黄油
バター

식료품 Foodstuff | 食品 | 食料品

13 마가린
margarine
人造黄油
マーガリン

14 치즈
cheese
奶酪
チーズ

15 꿀
honey
蜂蜜
蜂蜜

16 잼
jam
果酱
ジャム

17 된장
doenjang
大酱
みそ

18 고추장
gochujang
辣椒酱
唐辛子みそ

19 깨
sesame
芝麻
ゴマ

20 고춧가루
chilli powder
辣椒粉
唐辛子粉

21 후춧가루
ground pepper
胡椒粉
コショウ

22 설탕
sugar
(食用) 糖
砂糖

23 소금
salt
盐
塩

24 간장
soy sauce
酱油
醤油

25 참기름
sesame oil
香油
ごま油

26 식초
vinegar
醋
酢

27 식용유
cooking oil
食用油
食用油

More Vocabulary

컵 라면	cup ramyeon	杯装拉面	カップラーメン
양념	seasonings, marinades, condiments	调料	薬味
조미료	artificial seasoning	调味料	調味料
젓갈	salted fish	鱼籽浆	塩辛
통조림	canned foods	罐头	缶詰
참치 캔	canned tuna	金枪鱼罐头	シーチキンの缶詰
꽁치 캔	canned mackerel pike	秋刀鱼罐头	サンマの缶詰
과식	overeating	过食	食べ過ぎ
과음	overdrinking	酗酒	飲み過ぎ
금식	fasting	禁食	断食
후식	dessert	甜食	デザート
군것질	snacking between meals	零食	間食
다이어트	diet	减肥	ダイエット

Appendix p.162

Phrases & Expressions

- 짜다 to be salty
- 맵다 to be hot (spicy)
- 달다 to be sweet
- 쓰다 to be bitter
- 시다 to be sour
- 싱겁다 to be insipid, taste flat

- 칼칼하다 to be thirst-causing
- 텁텁하다 to be tasteless
- 매콤하다 to be somewhat spicy-hot
- 얼큰하다 to be rather spicy-hot
- 시원하다 to be refreshing
- 느끼하다 to be greasy

패스트푸드 Fast Food | 快餐 | ファーストフード

| 1 | **메뉴**
 menu
 菜单
 メニュー | 2 | **불고기버거**
 bulgogi burger
 烤肉汉堡
 プルゴギバーガー | 3 | **치즈버거**
 cheese burger
 奶酪汉堡
 チーズバーガー | 4 | **새우버거**
 shrimp burger
 虾肉汉堡
 エビバーガー |

패스트푸드 Fast Food | 快餐 | ファーストフード | 04

5 **치킨버거**
chicken burger
鸡肉汉堡
チキンバーガー

6 **주문대 (계산대)**
counter
收银台
カウンター

7 **컵**
cup
杯子
コップ

8 **스트로 (빨대)**
straw
吸管
ストロー

9 **딸기잼**
strawberry jam
草莓酱
イチゴジャム

10 **물 티슈**
wet tissue
湿巾
ウェットティッシュ

11 **프렌치프라이**
French fries
炸署条
フライドポテト

12 **팥빙수**
patbingsu, red-bean sherbet
冰粥
カキ氷

13 **콘 샐러드**
corn salad
玉米沙拉
コーンサラダ

14 **치킨**
chicken
炸鸡
チキン

15 **핫도그**
hot dog
热狗
ホットドッグ

16 **치즈스틱**
cheese stick
奶酪条
チーズスティック

More Vocabulary

세트메뉴	set menu	套餐	セットメニュー
햄버거	hamburger(s)	汉堡包	ハンバーガー
애플파이	apple pie	苹果派	アップルパイ
아르바이트생	person working temporary, part-timer	打工生	アルバイト
유니폼	uniform	制服	制服
이름표	name tag	名签	名札
회원카드	membership card	会员卡	会員カード
포장	wrapping	包装	包装
분리수거 함	garbage can for different classifications of garbage	分装垃圾桶	分別ゴミ回収箱

Appendix p.162

Phrases & Expressions

- 메뉴를 고르다 / 결정하다 to choose / decide from the menu
- 세트메뉴를 주문하다 to order one of the sets
- 회원카드를 제시하다 to present a membership card
- 햄버거를 먹다 to eat a hamburger
- 소스를 뿌리다 to spread some sauce
- 음료수를 마시다 to drink a beverage
- 음료수를 리필하다 to get a beverage refill
- 음식을 흘리다 to spill one's food
- 휴지로 닦다 to wipe with napkin
- 테이블을 치우다 to clear a table
- 테이블이 더럽다 / 깨끗하다 to mess up / clean up a table
- 음식을 포장하다 to wrap food

65

04 김치 담그기 Making Kimchi | 做泡菜 | キムチを作る

1. **배추를 2~4 등분하다** to cut Chinese cabbage into 2 or 4 pieces | 把白菜分成2~4等分 | 白菜を2~4等分する

2. **배추를 소금물에 절이다** to soak Chinese cabbage in salted water | 用盐水腌白菜 | 白菜を塩水に漬ける

3. **무를 채(를) 썰다** to cut and slice radish | 把萝卜切丝 | 大根を千切りにする

4. **마늘 / 생강을 다지다** to chop garlic / ginger | 捣大蒜 / 姜 | にんにく / 生姜をつぶす

5. **무채에 고춧가루를 넣어 버무리다**
   to mix sliced radish and powdered red pepper | 用辣椒粉拌萝卜丝 | 大根の千切りに唐辛子粉を入れてあえる

6. **배추포기에 소를 넣다** to put a mixture inside a each leaf | 腌好的白菜里拌调料 | 白菜の株に薬味を入れる

7. **독(용기, 김치냉장고)에 담다**
   to store in a kimchi pot | 装在缸里(容器，泡菜冰箱) | 甕(容器，キムチ冷蔵庫)に入れる

More Vocabulary

총각김치	chonggak kimchi	小萝卜泡菜	チョンガーキムチ
파김치	pa kimchi	葱泡菜	ネギのキムチ
오이소박이	oi sobagi	黄瓜泡菜	キュウリの中に具を詰めたキムチ
깍두기	kkakdugi	萝卜快儿泡菜	カクテギ
백김치	baek kimchi	白泡菜	唐辛子を使わずに漬ける白いキムチ
동치미	dongchimi	萝卜水泡菜	トンチミ

상 차림 Table Items 摆桌 お膳の用意 04

1. **밥상**
   (eating) table
   饭桌
   食膳

2. **김치**
   kimchi
   泡菜
   キムチ

3. **젓가락**
   chopsticks
   筷子
   箸

4. **숟가락**
   spoon
   勺子
   スプーン

5. **국그릇**
   soup / broth bowl
   汤碗
   吸い物椀

6. **밥그릇**
   rice bowl
   饭碗
   茶碗

7. **접시**
   plate, dish
   盘子
   皿

8. **종지**
   small bowl
   小碗
   調味料容器

9. **뚝배기**
   earthenware bowl
   沙锅
   土鍋

10. **밥**
    rice
    饭
    ご飯

11. **국**
    soup, broth
    汤
    汁

12. **냄비받침**
    pot stand
    锅垫儿
    鍋敷き

13. **국자**
    lade, dipper
    汤勺
    しゃくし

14. **반찬그릇**
    banchan (side dish) plate
    小碟子
    おかずの皿

15. **밥주걱**
    rice scoop
    饭勺
    しゃもじ

67

04 식당 (음식점) Restaurant | 餐厅 | 食堂 (飲食店)

1 **차림표 (메뉴)**
menu
菜单
メニュー

2 **냅킨**
napkin
餐巾纸
ナプキン

3 **양념통**
condiment jar
调料盒
調味料容器

4 **개인접시**
dish
个人用碟子
銘々皿

5 **컵**
cup
杯子
コップ

6 **쟁반**
tray
盘子
お盆

7 **수저통**
spoon stand
餐具盒
箸入れ

8 **테이블**
table
餐桌
テーブル

식당 (음식점) Restaurant | 餐厅 | 食堂 (飲食店)

9 정수기
water purifier
净水器
浄水器

10 물수건
wet towel
湿巾
おしぼり

11 살균소독기
sterilization device
杀菌消毒器
殺菌消毒機

12 휴대용 가스레인지
portable gas stove
携帯用煤气灶
携帯用ガスコンロ

13 종업원
employee
服务员
店員

More Vocabulary

가격표	price list, price tag	价格表	価格表
재떨이	ashtray	烟灰缸	灰皿
예약석	reserved seat	预约席	予約席
금연석	no smoking seat	禁烟席	禁煙席
주방장	head chef	厨师长	コック長
주인	owner	主人	主人
계산서	check, bill	清单	計算書
영수증	receipt	发票	領収書
이쑤시개	toothpick	牙签	爪楊枝
셀프서비스	self service	无服务员餐厅	セルフサービス
유아놀이방	children's play area	幼儿房	お遊戯広場
커피자판기	coffee vending machine	自动饮料机	コーヒー自動販売機

Phrases & Expressions

- 주문을 받다 to take an order
- 음식을 주문하다 / 시키다 to order food
- 반찬을 더 주문하다 to order more banchan (side dishes)
- 개인접시에 음식을 덜다 to put food on one's plate
- 냅킨으로 입을 닦다 to wipe one's lips with a napkin
- 계산하다, 돈을 내다 to pay
- (돈을) 각자 내다 to pay separately
- 예약하다 to make a reservation
- 예약을 취소하다 to cancel a reservation
- 친절하다 / 불친절하다 be friendly / unfriendly
- 자리가 없다 to have no seats available
- 배달하다 to deliver

05 주거 형태 Forms of Domicile | 居住形态 | 住居の形態

아파트 apartment | 公寓 | マンション

1 **1층**
first floor
一楼
1階

2 **2층**
second floor
二楼
2階

3 **3층**
third floor
三楼
3階

4 **4층**
fourth floor
四楼
4階

5 **비상구**
emergency exit
安全出口
非常口

6 **계단**
stairs
楼梯
階段

7 **엘리베이터 (승강기)**
elevator
电梯
エレベーター

8 **관리실 (경비실)**
guard box
门卫
管理室（警備室）

70

주거 형태 | Forms of Domicile | 居住形态 | 住居の形態

9 **주차장**
parking lot
停车场
駐車場

10 **놀이터**
playground
儿童游乐场, 游乐场
遊び場

단독주택 single-unit housing | 单独住宅 | 1戸建ての家

11 **집**
house, home
房子
家

12 **정원**
garden
庭园
庭

13 **대문**
gate
大门
門

14 **초인종 (벨)**
doorbell
门铃
呼び鈴 (ベル)

15 **우편함**
mailbox
邮件箱
郵便受け

More Vocabulary

연립주택	row houses │ 连排住宅 │ テラスハウス		어린이집	day care center │ 托儿所 │ 子供の家
빌라	villa │ 公寓 │ (高級な)マンション		아파트 관리비	apartment management fees │ 公寓管理费 │ アパート管理費
가옥	house (building, structure) │ 房屋 │ 家屋		전기세	electricity fees │ 电费 │ 電気代
문패	doorplate │ 门牌 │ 表札		수도세	water fees │ 水费 │ 水道代
마당	yard │ 院子 │ 中庭		전화세	telephone fees │ 电话费 │ 電話代
뜰	yard │ 庭 │ 庭		재산세	roperty tax │ 财产税 │ 財産税
옥상	rooftop │ 楼顶 │ 屋上		자동차세	auto tax │ 汽车税 │ 自動車税
양로원	retirement home │ 养老院 │ 老人ホーム		보험료	insurance fee │ 保险费 │ 保険料
유치원	kindergarten │ 幼儿园 │ 幼稚園			

Appendix p.163

Phrases & Expressions

- 엘리베이터를 타다 to take an elevator
- 계단을 올라가다 / 내려가다 to go up / go down stairs
- 주차장에 차를 주차시키다 (주차하다) to park a car in the parking area

05 주방 | Kitchen | 厨房 | キッチン

	1 **찬장** pantry, cupboard 厨具柜 食器棚	4 **식기세척기** dishwashing machine 洗碗机 食器洗い機	7 **도마** cutting board 菜板 まな板
	2 **그릇** vessel, container, bowl, dish 餐具 食器	5 **싱크대** sink 水池子 シンク台	8 **믹서** blender 搅拌机 ミキサー
	3 **선반** shelf 搁板 棚	6 **칼** knife 菜刀 包丁	9 **커피메이커** coffee maker 咖啡机 コーヒーメイカー

주방 Kitchen | 厨房 | キッチン

Living Space

10 냉장고
refrigerator
冰箱
冷蔵庫

11 쌀통
rice container
米桶
米びつ

12 전기밥솥
electric rice cooker
电饭锅
電気炊飯器

13 환풍기
ventilation fan
排气扇
換気扇

14 주전자
kettle
水壶
やかん

15 가스레인지
gas stove, gas oven
煤气炉
ガスレンジ

16 전자레인지
microwave oven
微波炉
電子レンジ

17 오븐
oven
烤箱
オーブン

18 종이타월
paper towel
厨房纸巾
紙タオル

19 토스터
toaster
烤面包机
トースター

20 식탁
dining table
饭桌
食卓

21 냄비
pot
锅
鍋

22 거품기
eggbeater
泡沫机
泡だて器

23 김치냉장고
kimchi refrigerator
泡菜冰箱
キムチ冷蔵庫

More Vocabulary

냄비집게	pot lifter	取物夹	鍋つかみ
조리대	kitchen table	烹调台	調理台
팬	pan	平锅	ファン
체	strainer	筛子	ふるい

식탁보	tablecloth	饭桌布	テーブルクロス
식탁의자	table chairs	饭桌椅子	食卓椅子
가스밸브	gas valve	煤气阀门	ガスバルブ

Appendix p.163

Phrases & Expressions

- (야채를) 볶다 to fry (vegetables), roast
- (시금치를) 데치다 to boil (spinach)
- (나물을) 무치다 to season (greens)
- (콩나물을) 삶다 to boil (bean sprouts)
- (호박전을) 부치다 to pan fry (panfried pumpkin)
- (오징어를) 튀기다 to fry (cuttlefish)
- (국 / 찌개를) 끓이다 to boil (soup, stew)
- (콩을) 졸이다 to parch (beans)
- 밥상을 펴다 / 접다 to prepare / meal table
- 밥을 푸다 to scoop rice from container it was cooked in

- 국을 뜨다 to scoop soup (with ladle, from pot)
- 숟가락질을 / 젓가락질을 하다 to use spoon / use chopsticks
- 생선 가시를 바르다 to remove bones from fish
- 간장에 찍다 to dip into soy sauce
- 숭늉을 마시다 to drink water boiled in pot rice was cooked in
- 빈 그릇을 치우다 to remove empty plates
- 그릇을 씻다 to wash a dish
- 그릇을 말리다 to dry the dishes
- 설거지를 하다 to do the dishes

05 거실 Livingroom | 大厅 | 居間

1 천장 ceiling 天花板 天井	**4 벽** wall 墙壁 壁	**7 커튼** curtain 窗帘 カーテン	**10 탁자** table 茶桌 テーブル	**13 에어컨** air conditioner 空调 エアコン
2 형광등 fluorescent lamp 日光灯 蛍光灯	**5 창문** window 窗户 窓	**8 쿠션** cushion 软垫儿 クッション	**11 카펫** carpet 地毯 カーペット	**14 오디오** stereo 音响 オーディオ
3 전구 light bulb 电灯泡 電球	**6 책장** bookcase 书柜 本棚	**9 소파** sofa 沙发 ソファー	**12 마룻바닥** wooden floor 地板 板の間	**15 화분** flowerpot 花盆 植木鉢

More Vocabulary

베란다 | veranda | 阳台 | ベランダ

침실 Bedroom | 卧室 | 寝室

1 화장대
makeup stand, dressing table
化妆台
化粧台

2 거울
mirror
镜子
鏡

3 옷장
wardrobe
衣柜
洋服ダンス

4 시계
clock
表
時計

5 램프
lamp
煤油灯
ランプ

6 침대
bed
床
ベッド

7 베개
pillow
枕头
枕

8 시트
sheet
床单
シーツ

9 이불
(Korean) bedclothes, quilt
被子
布団

10 매트리스
mattress
床垫
マットレス

11 방바닥
(bare) floor
地面
部屋の床

More Vocabulary

| 침대커버 | bedspread | 床罩 | ベッドカバー |
| 담요 | blanket | 毯子 | 毛布 |

| 전등 | electric light | 电灯 | 電気 |

05 욕실 Bathroom | 浴室 | 浴室

1. **수건**
   towel
   毛巾
   タオル

2. **화장지**
   toilet paper
   卫生纸
   トイレットペーパー

3. **면도기**
   shaver
   剃须刀
   みそり

4. **샴푸**
   shampoo
   洗发精
   シャンプー

5. **린스 (컨디셔너)**
   conditioner
   护发素
   リンス (コンディショナー)

6. **치약**
   toothpaste
   牙膏
   歯磨き粉

7. **칫솔**
   toothbrush
   牙刷
   歯ブラシ

8. **수도꼭지**
   faucet
   水龙头
   蛇口

욕실 Bathroom 浴室 浴室

9 세면대
washstand
洗面台
洗面台

10 비누
soap
香皂
石鹼

11 샤워커튼
shower curtain
浴帘
シャワーカーテン

12 샤워기
shower head
淋浴器
シャワー

13 변기
toilet
马桶
便器

14 타일
tile
瓷砖
タイル

15 배수구
drain
排水口
排水口

16 욕조
bathtub
浴缸
浴槽

More Vocabulary

타월장	towel cabinet	毛巾柜	タオル棚
목욕가운	bathrobe	浴衣	風呂用ガウン
욕실 슬리퍼	bathroom slippers	浴室拖鞋	風呂用スリッパ
체중계	scale	体重称	体重計
콘택트렌즈	contact lenses	隐形眼镜	コンタクトレンズ
헤어 드라이기	hair dryer	吹风机	ドライヤー
때수건	plastic "towel" for scrubbing	搓澡巾	かすりタオル
거품	bubbles, foam	泡沫	泡
비데	bidet	便洁器	ビデ
가글	gargle	漱口水	うがい薬
양치 컵	cup for toothbrushing	漱口杯	うがいコップ
세숫대야	washbasin, washbowl	洗脸盆	洗面器
바가지	dipper, scoop	瓢儿 (葫芦)	ひょうたんで作ったひしゃく
세척솔	toilet brush	洗涤刷子	洗浄ブラシ

Appendix p.163

Phrases & Expressions

- 용변을 보다 to relieve oneself
- 물을 내리다 to flush
- 물을 틀다 / 잠그다 to turn on / off the water (faucet)
- 비누를 칠하다 to apply soap
- 세수를 하다 to wash one's face
- 수건으로 닦다 to wipe with a towel
- 수건을 걸다 to hang up a towel
- 치약을 짜다 to squeeze (apply) toothpaste
- 면도하다 to shave
- 샤워를 하다 to shower
- 욕조에 물을 받다 to fill a bathtub with water
- 목욕을 하다 to bathe
- 체중을 달다 to weigh oneself
- 렌즈를 끼다 / 빼다 to put on / remove contacts

05 청소용구 Cleaning Devices | 清扫工具 | 掃除用具

1	청소기	3	물걸레	5	먼지떨이	7	쓰레기봉투
	vacuum cleaner		wet floorcloth		duster		garbage bag
	吸尘器		湿布		掸子		垃圾袋
	掃除機		濡れ雑巾		はたき		ゴミ袋

2	소형청소기	4	마른걸레	6	고무장갑	8	빗자루
	porterable vacuum		dry floorcloth		rubber gloves		broom
	小型吸尘器		干布		橡皮手套		扫把
	小型掃除機		乾いた雑巾		ゴム手袋		ほうき

청소용구 Cleaning Devices | 清扫工具 | 掃除用具

9 **쓰레받기**
dustpan
垃圾铲
ちり取り

10 **스펀지**
sponge
海绵
ポンジ

11 **양동이**
(metal) bucket
白铁罐
バケツ

12 **자루걸레**
mop
拖把
モップ

13 **쓰레기통**
garbage can, trash can
垃圾桶
ゴミ箱

14 **앞치마**
apron
围裙
プロン

15 **수세미**
scrubber
碗刷子
たわし

16 **두건**
head towel
头巾
頭巾

More Vocabulary

사닥다리 (사다리)	ladder	梯子	はしご
방충제	insecticide	防虫剂	防虫剤
방향제	aromatic substance	芳香剂	芳香剤
욕실용 세제	restroom cleanser	卫浴洁净剂	浴室用洗剤
곰팡이 제거제	mold removal solution	防蛀剂	カビ取り(剤)
습기 제거제	dampness remover	除潮剂	湿気取り(剤)
유리 세정제	window washing fluid	玻璃清洁剂	ガラスクリーナー
가구 광택제	furniture brightener	家具亮洁剂	家具光沢剤
소독	disinfectant	消毒	消毒
파출부 / 가정부	maid	小时工 / 帮佣手	派出婦 / 家政婦

Appendix p.163

Phrases & Expressions

- 침대를 정돈하다 to make one's bed
- 시트를 갈다 to change the sheets
- 이불을 개다 / 펴다 to put away / unfold (Korean) bedclothes
- 환기시키다 to let fresh air in
- 장난감을 치우다 to clean up one's toys
- (카펫을) 진공청소하다 to vacuum (a carpet)
- 마룻바닥을 쓸다 / 닦다 to sweep / wipe a floor
- 걸레질하다 to wipe (a floor) with a damp cloth
- 책장을 정리하다 to organize a bookshelf
- 가구의 먼지를 털다 to knock the dust off the furniture
- 창문을 닦다 to clean a window
- 쓰레기통을 비우다 to empty a trash can
- 쓰레기를 버리다 to throw trash away
- 화분에 물주다 to water a (plant in a) flowerpot
- 정원을 가꾸다 to grow a garden

05 공구　Tools｜工具｜工具

1 **삽**	3 **망치**	5 **너트**	7 **못**
shovel	hammer	nut	nail
铲子	锤子	螺丝母	钉子
シャベル	かなづち	ナット	釘

2 **도끼**	4 **볼트**	6 **줄자**	8 **나사**
ax	bolt	measuring tape	screw
斧头	螺栓	卷尺	螺丝钉
斧	ボルト	卷尺	ねじ

공구 Tools | 工具 | 工具

9 **톱**
saw
锯
のこぎり

10 **드릴**
drill
钻孔机
ドリル

11 **드라이버**
screw driver
改锥
ドライバー

12 **스패너**
wrench
扳手
スパナー

13 **펜치**
pliers
铁钳
ペンチ

14 **페인트붓**
paint brush
油漆刷子
ペイント筆

15 **페인트**
paint
油漆
ペイント

16 **페인트롤러**
paint roller
油漆滚棒
ペイントローラー

17 **흙손**
trowel
泥刀
こて

18 **끌**
chisel
凿子
鑿(のみ)

19 **손수레**
handcart
手推车
手押し車

More Vocabulary

전선	electric wire	电线	電線
배터리	battery	电池	バッテリー
파이프	pipe	钢管	パイプ
전기테이프	electric tape	绝缘胶布	電気用絶縁テープ
플래시라이트	flashlight	手电筒	フラッシュライト
수도계량기	water gauge	自来水计量器	水道計量器
두꺼비집	fuse box	熔断器	安全器
가스	gas	煤气	ガス
계량기	gauge	计量器	計量器
물뿌리개	sprinkling can	洒水器	じょうろ
호스	hose	胶皮管(水龙)	ホース

Appendix p.163

Phrases & Expressions

- 고장 나다 to malfunction
- 전원이 나가다 to have electricity go off
- 지붕이 새다 to have a roof leak
- 벽에 금이 가다 to crack appear in a wall
- 유리창이 깨지다 to have glass window break
- 자물쇠가 부러지다 to have a lock break
- 계단이 부서지다 to have a staircase break
- 보일러가 고장 나다 the boiler breaks
- 수도꼭지가 새다 to have a faucet leak
- 싱크대 물이 새다 to have a sink leak
- 배수구가 / 변기가 막히다 to have the drain / toilet get clogged
- 파이프가 얼다 to have a pipe freeze

06 교실 Classroom 教室 教室

| 1 | 화이트보드
white board
白板
ホワイトボード | 3 | 칠판
blackboard
黑板
黑板 | 5 | 탁자
table
写字台
テーブル | 7 | 책상
desk
书桌
机 |

| 2 | 선생님
teacher
教师
先生 | 4 | 지구본
globe
地球仪
地球儀 | 6 | 의자
chair
椅子
椅子 | 8 | 학생
student
学生
学生 |

교실 Classroom | 教室 | 教室

9 지도
map
地图
地図

10 복도
hallway
走廊
廊下

11 분필
chalk
粉笔
チョーク

12 칠판지우개
blackboard eraser
黑板擦儿
黒板消し

13 지시봉
pointer
指挥棒
指示棒

14 책가방
book bag
书包
学生かばん

15 책
book(s)
书
本

16 공책
notebook
笔记本
ノート

17 필통
pencil case
笔筒
筆箱

18 보드 마카
board marker
白板笔
ボードマーカー

More Vocabulary

국기	national flag	国旗	国旗
게시판	bulletin board	公告栏	掲示板
스피커	(electric) speaker	喇叭 / 扩音机	スピーカー
출석	attendance	考勤	出席
결석	absence	缺席	欠席
조퇴	leaving early	早退	早退
지각	arriving late	迟到	遅刻
휴강	(a teacher) skipping a lecture	停课	休講

교과서	textbook	教科书	教科書
연습장	notebook	练习本	練習帳
사전	dictionary	词典	辞典
전자사전	electric dictionary	电子词典	電子辞典
입학	school admittance	入学	入学
졸업	graduation	毕业	卒業
전학	transfer schools	转学	転校
짝	desk mate	伴儿	ペア

Appendix p.163

Phrases & Expressions

- 앉으세요 please be seated
- 일어나세요 please stand up
- 다시 한 번 설명해 주세요 please explain one more time
- 읽어보세요 please read (it)
- 써보세요 please write (it)
- 따라 하세요 please repeat after me
- 잘 들으세요 listen carefully
- 숙제가 있습니다 there is homework
- 토론하다 to debate
- 발표하다 to announce
- 공책에 쓰다 to write in a notebook

- 지우개로 지우다 to erase with an eraser
- 질문하다 to ask a question
- 학생들이 떠들다 students make a disturbance
- 수업이 시작되다 / 끝나다 to start / finish class
- 교실로 / 교실에 들어오다 to enter a classroom
- 출석을 부르다 to call roll
- 대답하다 to answer
- 사전을 빌려주다 to lend a dictionary
- 단어를 찾다 to find a word (in the dictionary)
- 단어를 암기하다 to memorize a word
- 숙제를 제출하다 to submit homework

06 학교 시설 School Facilities 学校设施 学校の施設

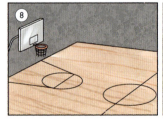
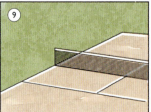
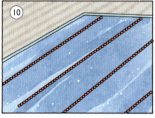

1 **강의실**
classroom
教室
講義室

2 **도서관**
library
图书馆
図書館

3 **기숙사**
dormitory
宿舍
学生寮

4 **학생 식당**
student cafeteria
学生食堂
学生食堂

학교 시설 | School Facilities | 学校设施 | 学校の施設

5 **체육관**
gymnasium
体育馆
体育館

6 **강당**
lecture hall
礼堂
講堂

7 **운동장**
playground
操场
運動場

8 **농구 코트**
basketball court
篮球场
バスケットコート

9 **테니스 코트**
tennis court
网球场
テニスコート

10 **수영장**
swimming pool
游泳馆
プール

11 **야외음악당**
outdoor music venue
露天音乐堂
野外音楽堂

12 **정문**
main gate
正门
正門

More Vocabulary

본관	main building	主楼	本館
학생회관	student center	学生会馆	学生会館
학생 상담소	student counseling	学生咨询处	学生相談所
학교 신문사	school newspaper	校报社	学校の新聞社
동아리 방	club room	活动小组房	サークル室
교수 연구실	professor's office	教授研究室	教授研究室
학과 사무실	department office	教研室	学科事務室
세미나실	seminar room	会议室	セミナー室
실험실	laboratory	实验室	実験室
미술실	art room	美术室	美術室
음악실	music room	音乐室	音楽室
무용실	dance room	舞蹈室	舞踊室
탈의실	changing room, locker room	脱衣室	脱衣室
샤워실	shower room	洗浴室	シャワー室
서점	bookstore	书店	書店
문방구	stationery store	文具店	文房具店
셔틀버스 승차장	shuttle bus stop	班车站	シャトルバス乗り場
공중전화(기)	public phone	公用电话	公衆電話
자동판매기	automatic vending machine	自动售饮机	自動販売機
증명서 자동 발급기	automated document-issuing machine	电脑开证机	証明書発給機
분수대	fountain	喷水台	噴水
벤치	bench	长椅	ベンチ
후문	rear gate	后门	裏門

도서관 Library 图书馆 図書館

1 도서 / 책 book 图书 図書 / 本	**3 저자명** author's name 著作名 著者名	**5 휴게실** lounge 休息室 休憩室
2 도서명 book title 图书名 書名	**4 출판사명** publisher's name 出版社名 出版社名	**6 자료실** data (material) room 资料室 資料室

86

도서관 Library | 图书馆 | 図書館

7 서가
bookstack
书架
書架

8 신문
newspaper
报纸
新聞

9 잡지
magazine
杂志
雜誌

10 백과사전
encyclopedia
百科全书
百科事典

More Vocabulary

사서	librarian | 图书管理员 | 司書		바코드	bar code | 条形码 | バーコード
단행본	monograph | 单行本 | 単行本		열람실	reading room | 阅览室 | 閲覧室
주제어	keyword | 主题词 | キーワード		복사실	(photo)copy room | 复印室 | 複写室
검색어	search word | 搜索词 | 検索語		전자정보실	computer room | 电子信息室 | 電子情報室
학생증	student identification | 学生证 | 学生証		정기 간행물실	periodicals room | 期刊阅览室 | 定期刊行物室
구입 신청	request for purchase | 申请购买 | 購入申請		학위 논문실	dissertation room | 学位论文室 | 学位論文室
대출	book borrowing | 借书 | 貸し出し		참고 열람실	reference bookstack room | 参考阅览室 | 参考閲覧室
반납	book return(ing) | 还书 | 返却			

Appendix p.164

Phrases & Expressions

- 책을 신청하다 to apply for a book
- 도서를 예약하다 to reserve a book
- 목차를 보다 to look at the table of contents
- 컴퓨터로 (도서를 / 책을) 검색하다 to search for a book by computer
- 책을 찾다 to find a book
- 대출 중이다 on loan
- 연체료를 지불하다 to pay an overdue fee
- 복사하다 to photocopy
- 책을 빌리다 / 반납하다 to borrow / return a book

시험 Test(s) | 考试 | 試験

필기시험 written test | 笔试 | 筆記試驗

1. **시험지**
test paper
试卷
試験用紙

2. **답안지**
answer sheet
答卷
解答用紙

3. **이름**
name
姓名
名前

4. **번호**
number
学号
番号

5. **문제**
question
考题
問題

듣기시험 listening test | 听力考试 | 聞き取り試験

6. **랩실 (어학실)** language laboratory | 语音室 | LL教室

필기도구 writing utensils | 笔记用具 | 筆記用具

7. **연필**
pencil
铅笔
鉛筆

8. **볼펜**
ball pen
圆珠笔
ボールペン

9. **지우개**
eraser
橡皮
消しゴム

10. **컴퍼스**
compas
圆规
コンパス

11. **자**
ruler
尺子
物差し

12. **삼각자**
set square, triangle
三角尺
三角定規

13. **각도기**
protractor
半圆规
分度器

한국의 학제 Korean School System | 韩国的学制 | 韓国の学校制度

유치원 kindergarten | 幼儿园 | 幼稚園

초등학교 (6년) elementary school (six years) | 小学 (六年) | 小学校 (6年)

중학교 (3년) middle school (three years) | 初中 (三年) | 中学校 (3年)

고등학교 (3년) high school (three years) | 高中 (三年) | 高校 (3年)

대학교 (4년) university (four years) | 大学 (四年) | 大学 (4年)

대학원 graduate school | 研究生院 | 大学院

학생활동 student activities | 学生活动 | 学生活動

학생회 student association | 学生会 | 学生会

동아리 clubs | 社団 | サークル

축제 festival | 联欢节 | 大学祭

MT group retreat | MT | 合宿

야유회 picnic party | 郊游 | ピクニック

스터디 study group | 小组学习 | 勉強会

수학여행 school excursion | 修学旅行 | 修学旅行

졸업여행 graduation trip | 毕业旅行 | 卒業旅行

소풍 picnic | 郊游 | 遠足

예술제 (학예회-초등학교) art festival (called 학예회 in elementary school) | 艺术节 | 文化祭(学芸会-小学校)

체육대회(운동회-초등학교) clubs sports tournament (called 운동회 in elementary school) | 运动会 | 体育大会 (運動会-小学校)

수련회 training gathering | 修炼活动 | 心身鍛錬キャン

More Vocabulary

여름 방학	summer vactaion	暑假	夏休み	1학기	the first semester	一学期	一学期
겨울 방학	winter vacation	寒假	冬休み	2학기	the second semester	二学期	二学期

사무실 1 Office 1 | 办公室 1 | 事務室 1

1. **블라인드**
   blind
   遮帘
   ブラインド

2. **캐비닛**
   cabinet
   橱柜
   キャビネット

3. **서류함**
   filing cabinet
   文件箱
   書類箱

4. **책꽂이**
   bookstand
   书架
   本立て

5. **파티션**
   partition
   隔板
   パーティション

6. **컴퓨터**
   computer
   电脑
   パソコン

7. **책상**
   desk
   办公桌
   机

8. **의자**
   chair
   椅子
   椅子

9. **서랍**
   drawer
   抽屉
   引き出し

90

사무실 1 Office 1 | 办公室 1 | 事務室 1

10 휴지통
wastepaper basket
垃圾桶
ゴミ箱

11 전화기
telephone
电话机
電話機

12 원형 테이블
round table
圆桌
円形テーブル

13 팩스
fax machine
传真机
ファックス

14 회의실
meeting room
会议室
会議室

More Vocabulary

주식회사	stock company	股份公司	株式会社
대기업	conglomerate	大企业	大企業
중소기업	medium-sized company	中小企业	中小企業
사장실	president's office	经理办公室	社長室
비서	secretary	秘书	秘書
신입사원	employee without person's first job	新职员	新入社員
경력사원	employee with previous experience	资深职员	中途採用社員
공개채용	"open hiring"	公开录用	公開採用
특별채용	"special hiring"	特别录用	特別採用
이력서	resume	履历表	履歴書
자기소개서	written personal introduction	自我介绍书	自己推薦書

연봉	annual salary	年薪	年俸
월급	monthly salary	月薪	月給
휴가	vacation	休假	休暇
연차	annual paid hoilday	年休	年次
월차	monthly day off	月休	月次
출장	business trip	出差	出張
야근	night duty, working late	夜班	夜勤
회식	eating out with coworkers	公司聚餐	会食
거래처	client, customer	客户	取引先
매출액	(amount of) sales	销售额	売上高
비품 보관함	supply cabinet	办公用品保管箱	備品保管箱
파일 폴더	file folder	文件夹	ファイルホルダー
결재함	"to be approved" box	批准文件架	決裁箱
결재파일	file "to be approved"	批准文件	決裁ファイル

Appendix p.164

Phrases & Expressions

- 인사하다 to greet (someone)
- 명함을 주고받다 to exchange name cards
- 악수하다 to shake hands
- 자신을 소개하다 to introduce oneself
- 사무실을 안내하다 to show someone around an office
- 업무를 설명하다 to explain the work / office duties
- 회의하다 to have a meeting
- 협상하다 to negotiate
- 접대하다 to entertain (a customer)

사무실 2 Office 2 | 办公室 2 | 事務室 2

1. **명함**
   name card
   名片
   名刺

2. **다이어리**
   date book
   记事本
   ダイアリー

3. **계산기**
   calculator
   计算器
   計算機

4. **인주**
   red stamping ink for traditional seals
   印泥
   朱肉

5. **도장**
   seal, stamp
   印章
   印鑑

6. **탁상용 달력**
   desktop calendar
   台式月历
   卓上カレンダー

7. **포스트잇**
   post-it
   便条
   ポストイット

8. **메모지**
   scratch paper
   便笺
   メモ用紙

9. **가위**
   scissors
   剪刀
   はさみ

Appendix p.164

Phrases & Expressions

- 출근하다 to go to work
- 퇴근하다 to leave work
- 전화하다 to telephone (someone)
- 서류에 사인하다 to sign a document
- 보고서를 작성하다 to draft a report
- 결재를 올리다 to submit a document for approval
- 도장을 찍다 to stamp with a seal

전화 Telephone | 电话 | 電話

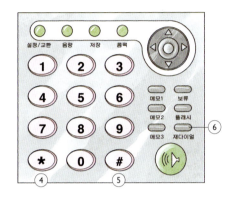

1 **유선전화기**
wired telephone
有线电话
有線電話機

2 **발신자표시창**
(display window that shows) caller identification
来电显示窗
発信者表示窓

3 **무선전화기**
cordless phone
无线电话机
無線電話機

4 **별표**
star (on telephone dial)
星号键
星印

5 **우물정**
pound button (on telephone dial)
井字键
シャープ

6 **재다이얼**
redial
重播
リダイアル

7 **핸드폰**
mobile phone
手机
携帯 (電話)

More Vocabulary

자동응답기	answering machine	电话留言机	留守番電話
메시지	message	信息	メッセージ
문자메시지	text message	短信	文字メッセージ
음성메시지	voice message	留言	音声メッセージ
부재중 통화	call received while away	未接电话	発信者番号表示
통화중	busy, call in progress	通话中	通話中
디카폰	phone with digital camera	数码手机	デジタルフォン
MP3폰	phone with MP3 function	MP3手机	MP3フォン

Appendix p.164

Phrases & Expressions

- 전화를 걸다 / 끊다 to call / hang up telephone
- 전화를 잘못 걸다 to call the wrong number
- 응답기를 확인하다 to listen to message machine
- 전화번호부를 찾다 to search the phone book
- 114에 문의하다 to ask (call) 114

컴퓨터 Computer | 电脑 | コンピューター

1. **데스크탑 컴퓨터**
   desktop computer
   台式电脑
   デスクトップパソコン

2. **디스크 드라이브**
   disk drive
   磁盘驱动器
   ディスクドライブ

3. **전원 스위치**
   power switch
   电源开关
   電源スイッチ

4. **모니터 / 화면**
   monitor
   显示器
   モニター / 画面

5. **키보드 / 자판**
   keyboard
   键盘
   キーボード

6. **마우스**
   mouse
   鼠标
   マウス

7. **마우스 패드**
   mouse pad
   鼠标垫
   マウスパッド

8. **모뎀**
   modem
   调制解调器
   モデム

9. **멀티 탭**
   multi tab
   多用分接头
   マルチタップ

컴퓨터 Computer | 电脑 | コンピューター

10 **플로피 디스크**
floppy disk
软盘
フロッピーディスク

11 **시디 (CD)**
CD
CD
CD

12 **PDA**
PDA
掌上电脑
PDA

13 **프린터**
printer
打印机
プリンター

14 **스캐너**
scanner
扫描仪
スキャナー

15 **노트북 컴퓨터**
laptop
笔记本电脑
ノートパソコン

More Vocabulary

초고속 인터넷	high speed internet	超速因特网	超高速インターネット
바이러스	virus	病毒	ウイルス
백신	vaccine	疫苗	ワクチン
컴퓨터 기사	computer technician	电脑技师	コンピューター技師
해킹	hacking	黑客侵入	ハッキング
워드 프로세서	word processor	文字编辑器	ワープロ
엑셀	Excel	电子表格	エクセル
파워포인트	Power Point	(电脑)图形软件	パワーポイント
하드디스크	hard disk	硬盘	ハードディスク
사용 설명서	manual	使用说明书	使用説明書
CD ROM	CD rom	CD光驱	CD ROM
DVD ROM	DVD rom	DVD光驱	DVD ROM
디스켓 함	diskette holder	磁盘盒	フロッピーケース
케이블 포트	cable port	电缆端口	ケーブルポート

Appendix p.164

Phrases & Expressions

- 컴퓨터를 켜다 / 끄다 to turn on / off computer
- 메일을 확인하다 / 체크하다 to check one's mail
- 마우스를 클릭하다 to click a mouse
- 문서를 작성하다 to write a document
- 디스켓을 넣다 / 빼다 to put diskette in / out
- 파일을 열다 / 닫다 to open / close file
- 파일을 불러오다 to open a file
- 파일을 복사하다 to copy a file
- 파일을 저장하다 to save a file
- 파일을 삭제하다 to delete a file
- 파일을 전송하다 to send a file
- 그림을 스캔하다 to scan a drawing
- 출력하다 / 프린트하다 to print
- 자료를 백업하다 to back up one's material
- 문서를 편집하다 to edit a document
- 자료를 다운받다 to download material
- 컴퓨터가 다운되다 to have a computer be down
- 바이러스 체크하다 to do a virus check

07 E-mail Email | 电子邮件 | E-mail

1. **아이디**
   ID, username
   登录名
   ID

2. **비밀번호**
   password
   密码
   パスワード

3. **받은편지함**
   inbox
   收件夹
   受信トレイ

4. **보낸편지함**
   outbox
   寄件夹
   送信トレイ

5. **지운편지함**
   trash
   回收站
   削除済みトレイ

6. **발신자 (보내는 사람)**
   From:, sender
   发送人
   発信者(送る人)

7. **수신자 (받는 사람)**
   To:, recipient
   收件人
   受信者(受け取る人)

8. **제목**
   subject
   题目
   題名

9. **편지쓰기**
   compose
   写邮件
   メールを書く

10. **편지읽기**
    open / read mail
    读邮件
    メールを読む

11. **수신 확인**
    confirmation of receipt
    回应
    受信確認

12. **주소록**
    contacts
    通讯录
    住所録

13. **메일 주소**
    mail address
    邮件地址
    メールアドレス

14. **스팸메일 차단**
    spam block
    邮件过滤
    スパムメール遮断

E-mail Email ¦ 电子邮件 ¦ E-mail

More Vocabulary

보낼편지함	drafts, unsent mail ¦ 草稿夹 ¦ 下書き
첨부파일	attachment ¦ 附件 ¦ 添付ファイル
로그인	login ¦ 登录 ¦ ログイン
로그아웃	logout ¦ 退出 ¦ ログアウト
도움말	Help ¦ 帮助 ¦ ヘルプ
완전 삭제	delete permanently ¦ 永久删除 ¦ 完全削除
취소	cancel ¦ 取消 ¦ 取り消し
다음 페이지	next page ¦ 下一页 ¦ 次のページ
이전 페이지	previous page ¦ 上一页 ¦ 前のページ
임시보관함	draft ¦ 临时保管箱 ¦ 臨時保管庫
공지 사항	alerts, notifications ¦ 公告 ¦ お知らせ
전체 메일 용량	total storage available ¦ 邮箱总容量 ¦ メールボックスの容量
사용 메일 용량	storage in use ¦ 已用空间 ¦ 使用メールの容量
환경 설정	settings, preferences ¦ 背景设置 ¦ 環境設定
편지 찾기	email search ¦ 查邮件 ¦ メール検索
편지함	mailbox ¦ 邮件夹 ¦ メールボックス
카드 메일	email greetings card ¦ 电子贺卡 ¦ カードメール
바이러스 감염	virus infection ¦ 病毒感染 ¦ ウイルス感染
채팅	chatting ¦ 网上聊天 ¦ チャット

Appendix p.164

Phrases & Expressions

- 로그인하다 to login
- 로그아웃하다 to logout
- 가입 신청하다 to apply for registration
- 아이디와 비밀번호를 넣다 (입력하다) to enter one's username and password
- 새 편지를 확인하다 to check for new mail
- 회신하다 to reply, answer
- 메일을 삭제하다 to delete mail
- 첨부파일을 보내다 / 받다 / 열다 to send / receive (open) attachment
- 저장하다 to save
- 편지를 읽다 / 쓰다 to read / write mail
- 주소록을 보다 to look at one's contacts (addresses)

07 공장 Factory | 工厂 | 工場

1. **창고**
 warehouse
 仓库
 倉庫

2. **지게차**
 forklift
 铲车
 フォークリフト

3. **타임클록 (시간기록시계)**
 time clock
 打卡机
 タイムクロック

4. **손수레**
 handcart
 手推车
 手押し車

5. **컨베이어 벨트**
 conveyer belt
 组装带
 ベルトコンベア

6. **근로자 (노동자)**
 worker (laborer)
 工人
 勤労者 (労働者)

More Vocabulary

부품	parts | 零部件 | 部品	제조하다	to manufacture | 制造 | 製造する
조립라인	assembly line | 组装线 | 組み立てライン	수송하다	to ship (freight) | 输送 | 輸送する
생산하다	to produce | 生产 | 生産する	운반하다	to transport (objects) | 搬运 | 運搬する
소비하다	to consume | 消费 | 消費する	주문하다	to order | 订购 | 注文する
디자인하다	to design | 设计 | デザインする	납품하다	to deliver goods | 供货 | 納品する

공장 Factory | 工厂 | 工場

7 안전모
safety helmet
安全帽
ヘルメット

8 보호안경
protective eyewear
保护眼镜
保護メガネ

9 안전마스크
safety mask
安全口罩
安全マスク

10 호흡마스크
mask with air filter function
呼吸口罩
呼吸マスク

11 귀마개
earplugs
耳塞
耳栓

12 고무장갑
rubber gloves
橡胶手套
ゴム手袋

13 안전장화
safety boots
安全靴子
安全長靴

14 안전조끼
safety vest
安全坎肩
安全チョッキ

15 소화기
fire extinguisher
消火器
消火器

More Vocabulary

안전 작업 기호	work safety signs	安全作业记号	安全作業のマーク
전기위험	Electric hazard	电危险	電気危険
인화물질	Flammable material	易燃物	引火物質
독성	Toxic	毒性	毒性
방사능	Radioactive	放射能	放射能

08 병원 | Hospital | 医院 | 病院

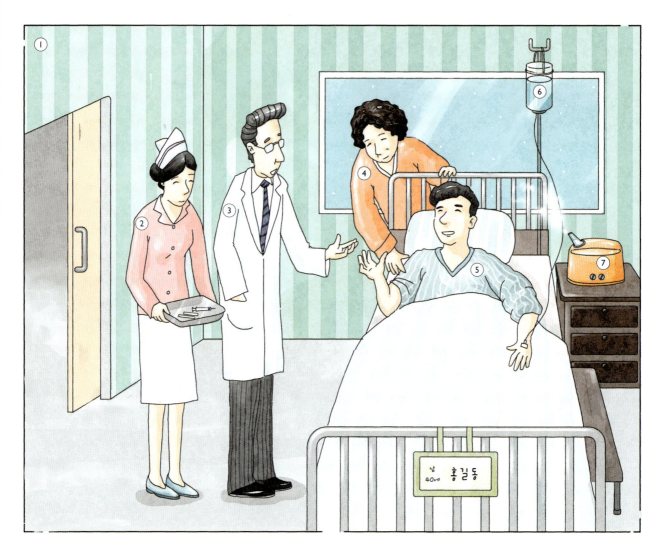

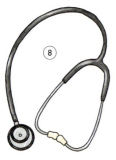
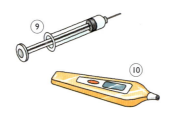

1 병실 (입원실)
hospital (room)
病房
病室 (入院部屋)

2 간호사
nurse
护士
看護士

3 의사
doctor
大夫
医者

4 간병인
person attending patient
护理人
看病人

5 환자
patient
病人
患者

6 링거
Ringer's solution
点滴
点滴

병원 Hospital | 医院 | 病院

7 가습기
humidifier
加湿器
加湿器

8 청진기
stethoscope
听诊器
聽診器

9 주사
injection
注射
注射

10 체온계
thermometer
体温表
体温計

11 붕대
bandage, dressing
绷带
包帯

12 혈압계
blood pressure gauge
血压计
血圧計

More Vocabulary

종합병원	general hospital	综合医院	総合病院
개인병원	private clinic	个人医院	個人病院
진찰실	examination room	门诊室	診察室
응급실	emergency room	急诊室	救急室
수술실	surgery room	手术室	手術室
산부인과	obstetrics and gynecology	妇产科	産婦人科
소아과	pediatrics	儿科	小児科
내과	internal medicine	内科	内科
외과	surgery	外科	外科
안과	ophthalmology	眼科	眼科
정형외과	orthopedics	正骨科	整形外科
이비인후과	ENT	耳鼻喉科	耳鼻咽喉科
정신과	psychiatry	神经科	精神科
비뇨기과	urology	泌尿科	泌尿器科
피부과	dermatology	皮肤科	皮膚科
성형외과	plastic surgery	整形外科	成形外科
치과	dentistry	口腔科	歯科
의료보험카드	medical insurance card	医疗保险卡	医療保険カード
한의원	Oriental medicine clinic	韩医院	漢方医院
진맥	pulse taking	号脉	診脈
침	acupuncture needle	唾液	針
한약	Oriental medicine	韩药	漢方薬

Appendix p.164

Phrases & Expressions

- 접수하다 to go through admittance / administrative procedures
- 예약하다 to make an appointment
- 진찰을 받다 to be examined
- X-ray를 찍다 to have an X-ray taken
- 검사를 받다 to be tested
- 링거를 맞다 to have a Ringer's injection
- 체온을 재다 to take a person's temperature
- 혈압을 재다 to take a person's blood pressure
- 연고를 바르다 to apply ointment
- 소독하다 to disinfect
- 입원하다 to admit, be admitted
- 수술하다 to operate
- 퇴원하다 to discharge, be discharged

증상 및 질병 Symptoms & Diseases | 症状及疾病 | 症状、疾病

1 **두통**
headache
头痛
頭痛

2 **치통**
toothache
牙痛
歯痛

3 **복통**
stomachache
腹痛
腹痛

4 **요통**
lumbago
腰痛
腰痛

5 **귀앓이**
earache
耳痛
耳痛

6 **목 아픔**
sore throat
咽喉痛
喉痛

증상 및 질병 Symptoms & Diseases | 症状及疾病 | 症状、疾病

7 코 막힘
stuffed nose
鼻塞
鼻づまり

8 오한
chills
恶寒
悪寒

9 구토
vomiting
呕吐
嘔吐

10 발진
skin rash
出疹子
発疹

11 고열
high fever
高烧
高熱

12 감기
a cold
感冒
風邪

13 빈혈
anemia
贫血
貧血

14 물집
blister
水泡
水脹れ

15 베인 상처
cut wound
刀伤
切り傷

16 여드름
pimple
粉刺
にきび

More Vocabulary

멍	bruise	淤血	あざ
암	cancer	癌症	癌
당뇨병	diabetes	糖尿病	糖尿病
뇌졸중	stroke	中风	脳卒中
알츠하이머병	Alzheimer's disease	老年性痴呆症	アルツハイマー病
고혈압	high blood pressure	高血压	高血圧
저혈압	low blood pressure	低血压	低血圧
생리통	menstrual pain	生理痛	生理痛
알레르기	allergy	过敏性反应	アレルギー
아토피	atopy	敏感性皮肤病	アトピー
디스크	disk	腰间盘突出	椎間板ヘルニア
비염	rhinitis	鼻炎	鼻炎
홍역	measles	麻疹	麻疹
수두	chicken pox	水痘	水ぼうそう
치매	dementia	痴呆	痴呆
땀띠	heat rashes	痱子	あせも
멀미	nausea	晕(车)	乗り物酔い
독감	influenza	重感冒	インフルエンザ
배탈	stomach upset	坏(拉)肚子	食あたり
설사	diarrhea	腹泻	下痢
변비	constipation	便秘	便秘
예방주사	inoculation	预防针	予防注射

08 약국 및 응급처치 Pharmacy and Emergency Care | 药店及应急措施 | 薬局、応急処置

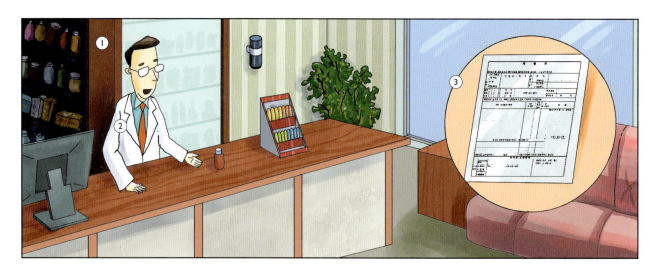

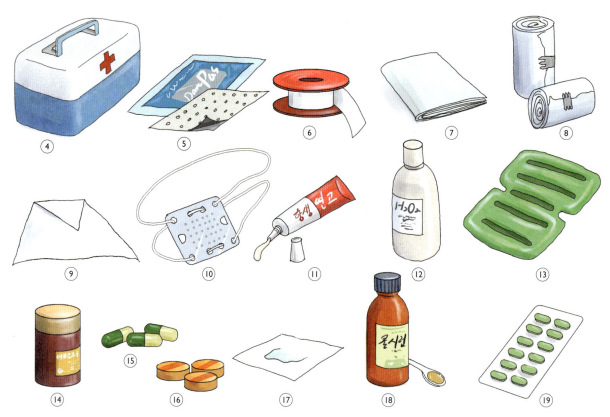

1 **약국** pharmacy 药店 薬局	3 **처방전** prescription 处方 処方箋	5 **파스** poultice 派司 貼り薬
2 **약사** pharmacist 药师 薬剤師	4 **응급치료상자** first aid kit 急救用箱子 救急箱	6 **반창고** Band-Aid, adhesive bandage 橡皮膏 絆創膏

104

약국 및 응급처치 Pharmacy and Emergency Care | 药店及应急措施 | 薬局、応急処置

7 **가제 (거즈)**
gauze
脱脂纱布
ガーゼ

8 **압박붕대 (탄력붕대)**
compress, elastic bandage
压力绷带
サポーター

9 **삼각붕대**
triangular bandage
三角绷带
三角巾

10 **안대**
eye patch
眼罩
眼帯

11 **항생연고제**
antibiotic ointment
抗生软膏
抗生物質軟膏

12 **소독약**
disinfectant
消毒药
消毒薬

13 **찜질팩**
massage pack
热敷带
温湿布

14 **머큐로크롬**
Mercurochrome
红药水
赤チン

15 **캡슐약**
capsule
胶囊
カプセル薬

16 **알약**
pill
药丸
錠剤

17 **가루약**
powdered medicine
药粉
粉薬

18 **시럽**
syrup
糖浆
シロップ

19 **소화제**
digestive solution
消化剂
消化剤

More Vocabulary

좌약	a suppository	栓剂	座薬
해열제	fever remedy	退烧药	解熱剤
비타민제	vitamin compound	维他命	ビタミン剤
진통제	pain killer	镇痛剂	鎮痛剤

연고	ointment	软膏	軟膏
밴드	band	邦迪	バンドエイド
보청기	hearing aid	助听器	補聴器
공기 정화기	air purifier	空气清新剂	空気浄化機

Phrases & Expressions

- 다치다 to injure (oneself)
- 의식을 잃다 to lose consciousness
- 쇼크 상태에 있다 to be in shock
- 심장마비를 일으키다 to have a heart attack
- 알레르기 반응을 보이다 to have an allergic reaction
- 화상을 입다 to get burned
- 물에 빠지다 to drown, sink in water
- 질식하다 to suffocate

- 출혈하다 to bleed, hemorrhage
- 숨을 못 쉬다 to be unable to breathe
- 뼈가 부러지다 to have a bone break
- 주사 맞다 to have an injection
- 약을 먹다 to take medicine (internally)
- 약을 과다 복용하다 to overdose
- 요양하다 to recuperate, convalesce

은행 Bank | 银行 | 銀行

1. **통장**
   bankbook
   存折
   通帳

2. **창구**
   teller window
   窗口
   窓口

3. **은행원**
   banker, bank employee
   银行职员
   銀行員

4. **대기자 번호표**
   que number, ticket with you number in line
   等候票
   待合番号

5. **전광판**
   electric billboard
   电光板
   電光掲示板

6. **경비원**
   guard
   警卫
   警備員

은행 Bank | 银行 | 銀行

7 감시용 카메라
security camera
监视用摄像头
監視用カメラ

8 통장 정리기
machine that updates bankbook
存折处理机
通帳記入機

9 자동 현금인출기
automated teller machine
自动取款机
自動現金引き出し機

10 돋보기안경
reading glasses, magnifying eyewear
花镜
老眼鏡

More Vocabulary

계좌번호	account number	账号	口座番号
신분증	personal identification	身份证	身分証
비밀번호	password	密码	暗証番号
서명, 사인	signature	签字	サイン
입금 신청 용지	deposit slip	存款申请表	入金申請用紙
출금 신청 용지	withdraw slip	取款申请表	引き出し申請用紙
인터넷 뱅킹	internet banking	网络银行	インターネットバンキング
폰뱅킹	phone banking	电话银行	テレバンク
수수료	fee	手续费	手数料

지로용지	giro form	储蓄存款凭证	振込用紙
당좌수표	check	现金支票	当座小切手
예금	deposit, savings	存款	預金
적금	installment savings	定期储蓄	積立金
대출	loan	贷款	貸し出し
이자	interest	利息	利子
자동이체	automated transfer (wire)	自动转账	自動振込
공과금	public imposts, duties	税金	公共料金
복권	lottery	彩票	宝くじ
고객 상담실	customer information	接洽室	顧客相談室

Appendix p.165

Phrases & Expressions

- 입금하다 (돈을 넣다) to deposit
- 출금하다 (돈을 찾다) to withdraw

- 자동 현금인출기 이용 방법 how to use an automated teller machine
  1. 현금 카드 또는 통장을 넣는다 put your cash card or bankbook in machine
  2. 해당 항목을 누른다 press the button for your transaction
  3. 비밀번호를 누른다 enter your password
  4. 출금 금액을 누른다 enter how much money you want to withdraw
     / 입금기에 입금액을 넣는다 place the money to be deposited in machine
  5. 돈을 확인한다 check the amount
  6. 명세서와 카드 또는 통장을 받는다 retrieve your statement and card or bankbook

우체국 Post Office 邮局 郵便局

1 **편지**
letter
信
手紙

2 **봉투**
envelope
信封
封筒

3 **우편번호**
postal code
邮编
郵便番号

4 **보내는 사람**
sender, From:
发件人
差出人

5 **우표**
stamp
邮票
切手

6 **우체국 소인**
postmark
邮局印章
郵便局の消印

우체국 Post Office | 邮局 | 郵便局

7 받는 사람
recipient, To:
收件人
受取人

8 엽서
postcard
明信片
はがき

9 카드
card
卡片
カード

10 소포
package
包裹
小包

11 저울
scale
秤
秤

12 우체통
mailbox
邮箱
郵便ポスト

13 우체부
letter carrier
邮递员
郵便配達人

14 우체국
post office
邮局
郵便局

More Vocabulary

빠른우편	express delivery	快速邮件	速達
보통우편	ordinary post	普通邮件	普通郵便
등기	registered mail	挂号邮件	書留
속달	special delivery	快邮	速達

국제우편	international post	国际邮件	国際郵便
규격상자	approved-size box	标准箱子	定形ダンボール
반송	returned mail	退回	返送

Appendix p.165

Phrases & Expressions

- 주소를 / 우편번호를 쓰다 to write the address / postal code
- 우표를 붙이다 to paste a stamp (on an envelope)
- 우체통에 넣다 to put in a mailbox
- 소포를 포장하다 to wrap a package
- 저울에 달다 to weigh on a scale
- 우체국 소인을 찍다 to cancel the stamp with post office postmark
- 축하카드 / 전보를 보내다 to send a congratulations card / telegram
- 편지 / 소포를 배달하다 to send a letter / package
- 우편 / 퀵서비스 / 택배로 보내다 to send by post / messenger / home delivery

미용실 / 이발소 Beauty Salon / Barbershop 美容店 / 理发店 美容室 / 理髪店

1. **거울**
   mirror
   镜子
   鏡

2. **젤**
   jell
   定型液
   ジェル

3. **스프레이**
   spray
   定型剂
   スプレー

4. **무스**
   mousse
   摩丝
   ムース

5. **가운 (숄)**
   gown
   工作服
   ガウン（ショール）

6. **미용사**
   beautician
   美容师
   容師

미용실 / 이발소 Beauty Salon / Barbershop 美容店 / 理发店 美容室 / 理髪店

7 빗
comb
梳子
櫛

8 드라이어
dryer
吹风机
ドライヤー

9 미용잡지
beauty magazine
美容杂志
美容雑誌

10 캡
cap
电热帽
キャップ

11 스팀기
steamer
蒸汽机
スチーム機

More Vocabulary

이발사	barber	理发员	理髪師
위생복	disinfected overgarment, gown	卫生服	生服
전기면도기	electric shaver	刮胡刀	かみそり
염색약	dying agent	染发剂	ヘアカラーリング剤
샘플	sample	样品	サンプル
컷	cut	剪	カット
롤	roll	卷发筒	ロール
퍼머넌트 (펌)	permanent (perm)	卷发	パーマ
집게	tongs	夹子	ヘアクリップ
핀	pin	发卡	ピン
할인	discount	优惠	割引
단골	regular customer	常客	得意先

Appendix p.165

Phrases & Expressions

- 머리를 자르다 to cut one's hair
- 컷을 하다 to get a (hair)cut
- 퍼머넌트를 하다 to get a permanent
- 머리를 말다 to set hair
- 캡을 쓰다 to wear a (shower) cap
- 염색하다 to dye (one's hair)
- 머리를 올리다 to put one's hair up
- 핀을 꽂다 to place a pin (in one's hair)
- 머리를 땋다 to put one's hair in braids
- 고무줄로 묶다 to tie with a rubber band
- 스프레이를 뿌리다 to spray (with spray)
- 손톱을 정리하다 (다듬다) to trim one's fingernails
- 매니큐어를 바르다 to apply nail polish

백화점 /쇼핑센터 Department Store / Shopping Center 百货商店 /购物中心 デパート / ショッピングセンター

1. **8층: 문화센터, 회원 서비스센터**
   Floor 8 : Cultural Center (Event Rooms), Member Service Center
   八层 : 文化活动中心, 会员服务中心
   8階 : 文化センター, 会員サービスセンター

2. **7층: 전문식당가**
   Floor 7 : Restaurants
   七层 : 餐厅
   7階 : 食堂街

3. **6층: 가전제품**
   Floor 6 : Electronics
   六层 : 家电
   6階 : 家電製品

4. **5층: 유아 / 아동복, 스포츠웨어**
   Floor 5 : Infant / Children's Wear, Sportswear
   五层 : 婴儿 /儿童, 运动服装
   5階 : 乳児/子供服, スポーツウエア

5. **4층: 신사복**
   Floor 4 : Men's Formalwear
   四层 : 男士服装
   4階 : 紳士服

6. **3층: 숙녀복**
   Floor 3 : Women's Formalwear
   三层 : 女士服装
   3階 : 婦人服

112

백화점 /쇼핑센터 Department Store / Shopping Center | 百货商店 / 购物中心 | デパート / ショッピングセンター

7 **2층 : 영캐주얼**
Floor 2 : Young People's Casual
二层：休闲装
2階：ヤングカジュアル

8 **1층 : 가방, 신발, 보석, 액세서리, 화장품**
Floor 1 : Baggage, Shoes, Jewelry, Accessories, and Makeup
一层：箱包, 鞋, 珠宝, 首饰, 化妆品
1階：鞄, 履物, 宝石, アクセサリー, 化粧品

9 **지하 B1층 : 식료품**
Basement / Underground Floor B1 : Grocery
地下一层：食品
地下B1階：食料品

10 **지하 B2〜6층 : 주차장**
Underground Floors B2 ~ B6 : Parking Lot
地下二〜六层：停车场
地下B2〜6階：駐車場

More Vocabulary

엘리베이터	elevator	电梯	エレベーター
에스컬레이터	escalator	自动扶梯	エスカレーター
안내데스크	information desk	接待处	案内カウンター
포장센터	gift wrapping	包装中心	包装センター
상품권	gift certificates	商品券	商品券
백화점 카드	department store (credit) card	百货店卡	デパートカード
할인쿠폰	discount coupon	优惠券	割引クーポン
주차권	parking ticket	停车卡	駐車券
주차 안내원	parking attendant	停车管理员	駐車案内員
엘리베이터 안내원	elevator operator	电梯服务员	エレベーターガール
직원 (판매원)	employee (salesperson)	销售员	職員 (販売員)
가격표	price tag	价码	価格表
정상가 (정가)	regular price	定价	標準価格 (定価)
세일가 (할인가)	sale price	打折价	セール価格 (割引価格)

Appendix p.165

Phrases & Expressions

- 사다 (구입하다) to buy, purchase
- 팔다 (판매하다) to sell
- 지불하다 to pay
- 반환하다 to return
- 교환하다 to exchange

09 버스와 택시 | Bus and Taxi | 公交车与出租车 | バス、タクシー

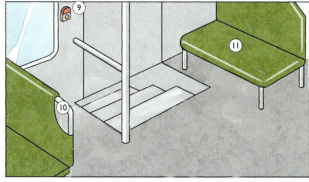

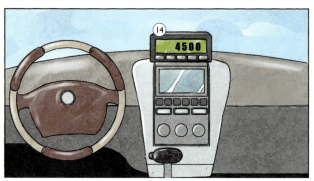

1 **버스 정류장(정거장)**
bus stop
公交车站
バス停 (停留所)

2 **노선번호**
(bus) line number
路线号码
路線番号

3 **버스**
bus
巴士
バス

4 **승객**
passenger
乘客
乗客

5 **교통카드**
"transportation card" used to pay for bus, subway
交通卡
(バス・地下鉄の)プリペイドカード

6 **운전기사 (운전사)**
driver
驾驶员
運転手

7 **카드단말기**
card reader
终端机
カード端末機

8 **요금함**
fare box
收费箱
料金箱

9 **벨**
bell
车门铃
ベル

버스와 택시 Bus and Taxi | 公交车与出租车 | バス、タクシー

10 손잡이
safety grip
手把
手すり

11 자리, 좌석
seat
座位
席、座席

12 택시 승차장
taxi stand
出租车站
タクシー乗り場

13 택시
taxi
出租车 (的士)
タクシー

14 요금 미터기
fare meter
标价器
料金メーター

More Vocabulary

경로석	seat reserved for elderly	敬老席	優先席
승차문	front door (for entering buss)	上车门	乗車扉
하차문	rear door (for exiting bus)	下车门	下車扉
차	automobile	汽车	車
대중교통	public transportation	公共交通	一般交通手段
마을버스	neighborhood bus	小区班车	近隣バス
고속버스	long distance bus	长途汽车	高速バス
시내버스	city route bus	城里公交车	市内バス
시외버스	inter-city bus	郊区公交车	都市間バス
관광버스	tour bus	旅游班车	観光バス
통근버스	commute bus	通勤班车	通勤バス
스쿨버스	school bus	学校班车	スクールバス
요금	fare	车费	料金
종점	last stop	终点站	終点
노선	line, route	路线	路線
노선도	route map	路线图	路線図
터미널	terminal	总站	ターミナル
경로 우대권	special ticket for the elderly	敬老优待券	お年寄り優待券
교통법규 위반	violation of traffic regulations	违反交通法	交通違反
범칙금	fine	罚款	罰金
심야할증	late-night charge	深夜加价	深夜割増し
합승	sharing a taxi	合乘	相乗り
모범택시	deluxe bus	模范出租车	高級タクシー
개인택시	driver-owned taxi	个人出租车	個人タクシー
콜택시	"call taxi"	呼叫出租车	呼び出しタクシー

Appendix p.165

Phrases & Expressions

- 버스가 오다 / 가다 to come / go by bus
- 버스에 타다 to take a bus
- 버스에서 내리다 to get off a bus
- 요금을 요금함에 넣다 to put fare in fare box
- 패스카드 / 교통카드를 대다 to swipe pass / "transportation card"
- 좌석에 앉다 to take a seat
- 좌석에서 일어나다 to get out of one's seat
- 자리를 양보하다 to give up one's seat
- 손잡이를 잡다 to grab a handle
- 안내방송을 듣다 to listen to announcement
- 벨을 누르다 to press the bell
- 버스를 잘못 타다 to get on the wrong bus
- 버스를 놓치다 to miss the bus
- 택시를 잡다 to grab a taxi
- 목적지를 말하다 to say one's destination

09 지하철 Subway | 地铁 | 地下鉄

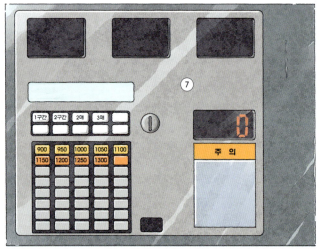

지하철 Subway | 地铁 | 地下鉄

1. **철로 / 선로**
tracks
铁路/线路
鉄路/線路

2. **안전선**
safety line
安全线
安全線

3. **플랫폼**
platform
站台
プラットホーム

4. **역무원**
station official
服务员
駅員

5. **개찰구**
ticket gate
检票口
改札口

6. **매표소**
ticket office
售票处
きっぷ売り場

7. **승차권 자동발매기**
automated ticket machine
自动售票机
乗車券自動発売機

8. **승차권**
passenger ticket
地铁票
乗車券

More Vocabulary

정기권	(period specific) prepaid ticket, commuter pass	定期票	定期券
환승역	transfer station	换乘站	乗り換え駅
지하철노선도	subway map	地铁路线图	地下鉄路線図
분실물 센터	lost and found center	失物招领处	紛失物センター
물품보관소	left luggage, baggage / article storage facility	存包处	物品保管所
지하도	underground passageway	地下通道	地下道
전철	subway	地铁	電車
출발역	station at end of line	出发站	始発駅
종착역	terminus	终点站	終着駅
환승역	transfer station	换乘站	乗り換え駅
지하철 출구	subway station exit	地铁出口	地下鉄出口
신문 판매대	newspaper stand	报刊销售亭	新聞販売台
노약자 보호석	seat reserved for feeble persons	老弱保护席	優先席
동전교환기	money changing machine	换铜钱机	コイン両替機

Appendix p.165

Phrases & Expressions

- 줄을 서다 to stand in line
- 표(정기권, 정액권)를 사다 to purchase a ticket (pre-set period, amount)
- 표를 넣다 / 빼다 to place ticket in / remove from
- 안전선 안쪽에서 기다리다 to wait inside of the safety (yellow) line
- 지하철이 만원이다 the subway is at full capacity
- 지하철을 타다 / 내리다 to get on / off the subway
- 환승역에서 갈아타다 to change at one's transfer station
- 에스컬레이터를 타다 to take an escalator
- 개찰구를 통과하다 to pass through the ticket gate
- 열차가 지연되다 to have one's train be delayed

09 교차로 Intersections 交叉路 交差点

1 **차도**
roadway
行车道
車道

2 **감시카메라**
traffic camera
监视摄像头
監視カメラ

3 **정지선**
stop line
停止线
停止線

4 **안전지대**
safety zone
安全地带
安全地帯

5 **가로등**
streetlight
路灯
街灯

6 **육교**
land bridge
天桥
陸橋

교차로 Intersections 交叉路 交差点

7 보도
pavement, sidewalk
人行道
歩道

8 가로수
tree lining a street
林荫树
街路樹

9 자전거
bicycle
自行车
自転車

10 오토바이
motorcycle
摩托车
オートバイ

11 횡단보도
crosswalk
人行横道
横断歩道

12 승용차
passenger car
轿车
乗用車

13 화물차
freight truck
货车
貨物車

14 신호등 (적색등, 청색등, 황색등)
traffic light (red, green, yellow)
信号灯(红灯, 绿灯, 黄灯)
信号 (赤、青、黄色)

15 승합차
passenger van
面包车
ワゴン車

16 모퉁이
corner
拐角
曲がり角

17 소형차
compact vehicle
小型车
小型車

18 교통경찰관
traffic cop
交通警察
交通警察官

More Vocabulary

차선 (1차선, 2차선, 3차선, 4차선)	lane (lane 1, lane 2, lane 3, lane 4) | 车道(一车道，二车道，三车道，四车道) | 車線(1車線、2車線、3車線、4車線)
블록	block ǀ 街区 ǀ ブロック
국도	national highway ǀ 国道 ǀ 国道
지방도	provincial highway ǀ 地方道 ǀ 県道
고속도로	expressway ǀ 高速公路 ǀ 高速道路
고속도로 통행카드	expressway tollgate ticket ǀ 高速通行卡 ǀ 高速道路通行カード
갓길	shoulder of the road ǀ 便路 ǀ 道路の両端
긴급전화	emergency telephone ǀ 应急电话 ǀ 緊急電話
통행권	road pass ǀ 通行卷 ǀ 通行券
통행료	road use fee ǀ 通行费 ǀ 通行料
속도측정기	speed measuring (detecting) device ǀ 测速器 ǀ 速度測定器
표지판	road sign ǀ 标志牌 ǀ 標識板
주차 단속원	parking enforcement officer ǀ 交通管理员 ǀ 駐車取り締まり員
주유소	petrol station ǀ 加油站 ǀ ガソリンスタンド
세차장	car wash ǀ 洗车场 ǀ 洗車場
카센터	auto supply shop ǀ 汽车服务中心 ǀ カーセンター
자동차 정비소	auto repair shop ǀ 汽车维修店 ǀ 自動車整備士
소화전	fire hydrant ǀ 消火栓 ǀ 消火栓

Appendix p.166

Phrases & Expressions

- 셀프주유 self-service refueling
- 자동세차 automatic car wash
- 셀프세차 self-service car wash
- 전면주차 park facing forward
- 후면주차 park facing backward

교통표지판 Traffic Signs | 交通标志 | 交通標識板

비보호
Left Turn without Signal
非保护
非保護

우회전 금지
No Right Turn
禁止右转
右折禁止

위험
Danger
注意危险
危険

유턴 금지
No U Turn
禁止掉头
転回禁止

일방통행
One Way
单行路
一方通行

직진 및 좌회전
Straight or Left Turn
直行和向左转弯
左折及び直進

직진 금지
Must Turn
禁止直行
直進禁止

터널
Tunnel
隧道
トンネル

최고속도제한
Speed Limit 50kph
最高限速标志
最高速度50(km/h)

주차 금지
No Parking
禁止停车
駐車禁止

화물차 통행 금지
No Large Trucks
禁货运汽车通行
貨物自動車等通行止め

최저속도제한
Minimum Speed 30kph
最低限速
最低速度

교통표지판 Traffic Signs | 交通标志 | 交通標識板

차중량제한
Mass at Most 5.5 Tons
限制质量
重量制限

차높이제한
Maximal Height 3.5 Meters
限制高度
高さ制限

T자형교차로
T-junction Ahead
T形交叉
T形道路交差点あり

우좌로 이중굽은도로
Winding Road
右(左)側绕行
右(左)つづら折りあり

도로폭이 좁아짐
Road Narrows
两侧变窄
幅員減少

오르막경사
Steep Ascend
上陡坡
上り急勾あり

좌측면통행
Pass Obstacle on the Left
靠左側道路行驶
指定方向外進行禁止

일시정지
Stop and Yield the Right of Way
停车让行
一時停止

양보
Yield the Right of Way
减速让行
先行優先

More Vocabulary

도로 공사중 Road Construction | 道路施工 | 道路工事中   버스 전용 Bus Lane | 公交专用车道 | 路線バス専用通行帯

121

09 자동차 운전 Driving Automobiles | 汽车驾驶 | 自動車運転

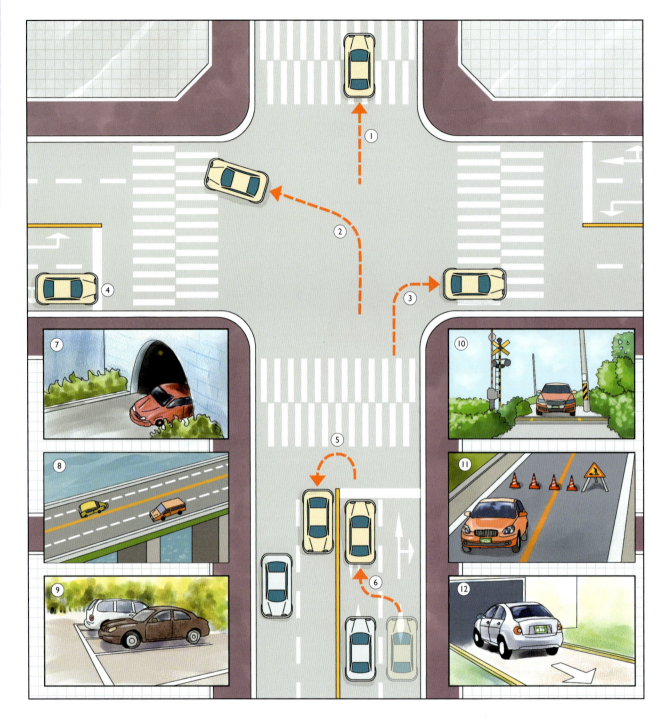

1 **직행하다**
to drive straight
直行
直進する

2 **좌회전하다**
to turn left
左转弯
左折する

3 **우회전하다**
to turn right
右转弯
右折する

4 **정지하다**
to stop
停止
停止する

5 **U턴하다**
to make a U-turn
掉头
ユーターンする

6 **끼어들다**
to squeeze into a line of vehicle
插进
割り込む

자동차 운전 Driving Automobiles | 汽车驾驶 | 自動車運転

7 터널을 통과하다
to pass through a tunnel
通过隧道
トンネルを通過する

8 다리를 건너다
to cross a bridge
过桥
橋を渡る

9 주차하다
to park
停车
駐車する

10 건널목을 통과하다
to pass through a (road/rail) crossing
通过路口
踏み切りを通過する

11 돌아가다
to go back
回去
戻る

12 후진하다
to go in reverse
倒车
後進する

More Vocabulary

전진하다	to move forward	前进	前進する
정차하다	to stop	停车	停車する
앞지르다	to pass (another vehicle)	超车	追い越す

Appendix p.166

Phrases & Expressions

- 안전벨트를 매다 / 풀다 to fasten / remove seatbelt
- 시동을 걸다 to start an engine
- 브레이크를 밟다 to apply the brakes
- 사이드 브레이크를 올리다 / 내리다 to put the parking brake on / off
- 핸들을 조절하다 to steer
- 기어를 넣다 to put (vehicle) in gear
- 액셀러레이터를 밟다 to push the accelerator
- 출발하다 / 도착하다 to depart / arrive
- 서행하다 to go slowly
- 경적을 울리다 to honk the horn
- 양보하다 to yield (to)
- 신호가 바뀌다 to have a traffic light change
- 급정거하다 to stop quickly

- 차선을 바꾸다 to change lanes
- 신호를 기다리다 to wait for signal
- 과속하다 to speed
- 추돌하다 to rear-end
- 신호를 위반하다 to violate / ignore the signal
- 중앙선을 침범하다 to cross the center line
- 차선을 위반하다 to violate lane lines
- 역주행하다 to go the wrong direction
- 감시카메라에 찍히다 to get picture taken by traffic camera
- 교통경찰관에게 걸리다 to get caught by traffic cop
- 딱지를 떼다 to get ticketed
- 음주운전을 하다 to drive drunk
- 교통사고를 내다 to cause a traffic accident
- 교통사고가 나다 to have a traffic accident happen

자동차 부품 Automobile Parts 汽车零部件 自動車部品

1. **앞 유리**
   windshield
   前挡风玻璃
   フロントガラス

2. **에어백**
   airbag
   安全气囊
   エアバック

3. **보닛**
   hood
   发动机盖
   ボンネット

4. **타이어**
   tire
   轮胎
   タイヤ

5. **휠캡**
   hubcap
   (车) 毂
   ホイールキャップ

6. **방향 지시등**
   turn signal
   转向灯
   方向指示器

7. **전조등**
   headlights
   前照灯
   ヘッドライト

8. **범퍼**
   bumper
   保险杠
   バンパー

9. **제동등**
   brakelights
   制动灯
   ブレーキライト

10. **미등**
    taillight
    尾灯
    テールライト

11. **트렁크**
    trunk
    后背箱
    トランク

12. **번호판**
    license plate
    车牌照
    ナンバープレート

자동차 부품 | Automobile Parts | 汽车零部件 | 自動車部品

13 **핸들**
steering wheel
方向盘
ハンドル

14 **와이퍼**
windshield wipers
雨刮器
ワイパー

15 **속도 계기판**
speedometer
速度表
速度計器盤

16 **주행거리 계기판**
odometer
里程表
走行距離計器盤

17 **연료 계기판**
gas gauge
燃料表
燃料計器盤

18 **네비게이션**
automobile navigation systems
汽车导航器
カーナビ

19 **경적**
horn
喇叭
クラクション

20 **클러치**
clutch
离合器
クラッチ

21 **브레이크**
brake
刹车
ブレーキ

22 **액셀러레이터**
accelerator
油门
アクセル

23 **기어**
gear
变速杆
ギア

24 **사물함**
glove compartment
手套箱
私物箱

25 **사이드 미러**
sideview mirror
后视镜
サイドミラー

More Vocabulary

수동변속	manual transmission	手动变速器	手動変速
레버	lever	杠杆	レバー
실내등	light	室内灯	室内灯
열선	heating wires	热线	熱線
스페어타이어	spare tire	备用轮胎	スペアタイヤ
배터리	battery	蓄电池	バッテリー
워셔액	washer fluid	洗涤液	ウォッシャー液
광택제 (왁스)	wax	蜡剂	光沢剤（ワックス）
도어록	door lock(s)	门锁	ドアロック
안테나	antenna	天线	アンテナ
차고	garage	车库	車庫
에어컨디셔너	air conditioner	空调设备	エアコン
히터	heater	加热器	ヒーター
잠금장치	lock	关闭装置	ロック装置
안전벨트	seat belt	安全带	安全ベルト
핸드 브레이크	parking brake	手闸	ハンドブレーキ
열쇠	key	钥匙	キー

Appendix p.166

Phrases & Expressions

- 배터리를 갈다 to change the battery
- 오일을 교환하다 to change the oil
- 타이어(바퀴)를 갈다 to change the tire(s)
- 세차를 하다 to wash a car
- 호스로 물을 뿌리다 to spray (a car) with water using a hose
- 스펀지로 닦다 to wipe / scrub with a sponge
- 마른걸레로 닦다 to wipe with a dry rag
- 광택제를 바르다 to apply auto wax
- 시트를 털다 to shake (off the dust from) a seat cover
- 엔진오일을 체크하다 to check the oil
- 냉각수를 채우다 to fill with coolant
- 보닛을 열다 / 닫다 to open / close the hood

09 공항 Airport | 机场 | 空港

1 **활주로**
runway
跑道
滑走路

2 **비행기**
airplane
飞机
飛行機

3 **캐리어**
luggage carrier
行李车
キャリア

4 **수하물 찾는 곳**
baggage claim area
取行李处
手荷物引渡場

5 **수하물**
baggage
行李
手荷物

6 **원형 컨베이어**
carousel
圆形输送机
円形コンベアー

7 **조종사**
pilot
驾驶员
操縦士

8 **승무원**
flight attendant
乘务员
乗務員

9 **승객**
passenger
乘客
乗客

10 **탑승**
boarding
搭乘
搭乗

공항 Airport | 机场 | 空港

More Vocabulary

공항 터미널	airport terminal	机场	空港ターミナル
공항 직원	airport employee	机场服务员	空港職員
관제탑	control tower	指挥塔	管制塔
국제선	international flight(s)	国际航线	国際線
국내선	domestic flight(s)	国内航线	国内線
출입국 신고서	exit and departure card	出入境填表	出入国申告書
입국심사	entrance inspection	入境检查	入国審査
출국심사	exist inspection	出境检查	出国審査
중량초과 요금	overweight charge	超重费	重量超過料金
검역	quarantine	检疫	検疫
세관	customs	海关	税関
기내식	inflight meals	机内便餐	機内食
공항버스	airport bus	机场班车	空港リムジンバス
체크인 카운터	check-in counter	登记手续窗口	チェックインカウンター
이착륙 모니터	arrival and departure monitor	航班消息显示板	離着陸モニター
세관 직원	customs employee	海关人员	税関職員
환전소	money change booth	换钱处	両替所
면세점	duty free shop	免税店	免税店

Appendix p.166

Phrases & Expressions

- 이륙하다 to take off
- 착륙하다 to land
- 경유하다 to have a stopover, go by way of
- 결항하다 to cancel a flight
- 연착하다 to be delayed
- 항공권을 사다 to purchase an airplane ticket
- 짐을 체크하다 to check baggage

- 보안 검사를 통과하다 to pass / go through security
- 게이트에서 체크인하다 to check in at the gate
- 비행기에 탑승하다 to board a plane
- 좌석을 찾다 to find one's seat
- 안전벨트를 하다 to put a seatbelt on
- 수하물을 찾다 to find one's baggag

10 취미와 놀이 Hobbies and Games | 爱好与游戏 | 趣味、遊び

1 **독서**
reading
读书
読書

2 **음악 감상**
listening to music
音乐欣赏
音楽鑑賞

3 **등산**
mountain climbing
登山
登山

4 **노래**
singing
唱歌
歌

5 **사진 찍기**
photography
拍照
写真を撮る

6 **인라인 스케이트**
inline skates
溜旱冰
インラインスケート

7 **영화 감상**
watching movies
电影欣赏
映画鑑賞

8 **낚시**
fishing
钓鱼
釣り

9 **댄스**
dance
跳舞
ダンス

취미와 놀이 Hobbies and Games | 爱好与游戏 | 趣味、遊び

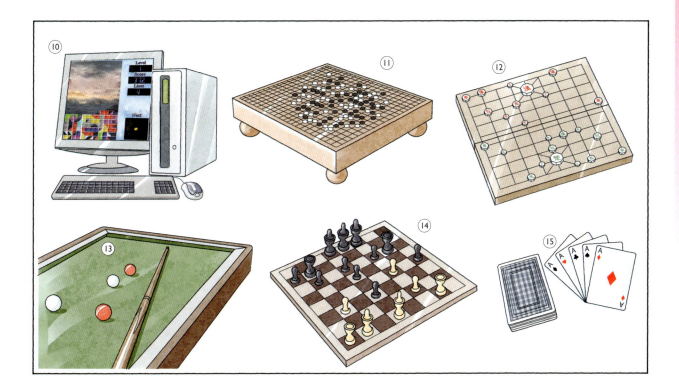

10 **컴퓨터 게임**
computer game
电脑游戏
コンピューターゲーム

11 **바둑**
baduk
围棋
囲碁

12 **장기**
janggi
象棋
将棋

13 **당구**
billiards
台球
ビリヤード

14 **체스**
chess
国际象棋
チェス

15 **카드놀이**
card game
玩牌
カード遊び

More Vocabulary

꽃꽂이	flower arranging	插花	生け花
뜨개질	knitting	编织	編み物
종이접기	origami	折纸	折り紙
퍼즐 맞추기	doing puzzles	拼图	ジグソーパズル
우표 수집	stamp collecting	集邮	切手収集
연날리기	kite flying	放风筝	凧揚げ
소꿉놀이	playing house	儿戏	ままごと
구슬치기	marbles	弹玻璃球	宝探し
숨바꼭질	hide-and-seek	捉迷藏	かくれんぼ

스포츠 Sports | 体育 | スポーツ

1 태권도
Taekwondo
跆拳道
テコンドー

2 축구
soccer
足球
サッカー

3 농구
basketball
篮球
バスケット

4 씨름
Ssireum, Korean wrestling
摔跤
シルム(韓国の相撲)

5 체조
gymnastics
体操
体操

6 스키
skiing
滑雪
スキー

스포츠 Sports | 体育 | スポーツ

7 수영
swimming
游泳
水泳

8 야구
baseball
棒球
野球

9 골프
golf
高尔夫球
ゴルフ

10 배구
volleyball
排球
バレーボール

11 테니스
tennis
网球
テニス

More Vocabulary

레슬링	wrestling	国际摔跤	レスリング
권투	boxing	拳击	ボクシング
유도	judo	柔道	柔道
핸드볼	handball	手球	ハンドボール
탁구	table tennis	乒乓球	卓球
배드민턴	badminton	羽毛球	バドミントン
스케이트	skating	滑冰	スケート
볼링	bolling	保龄球	ボーリング
펜싱	fencing	击剑	フェンシング
사격	shooting	射击	射撃
양궁	(Western-style) archery	射箭	アーチェリー
역도	weight lifting	举重	重量挙げ
조깅	jogging	慢跑	ジョギング
마라톤	marathon	马拉松	マラソン
수상스키	water skiing	滑水运动	水上スキー

대회	a match	大会	大会
아시안게임	Asian Games	亚运会	アジア大会
올림픽	Olympics	奥运会	オリンピック
월드컵	World Cup	世界杯	ワールドカップ
우승	victory	优胜	優勝
금메달 / 은메달 / 동메달	gold / silver / bronze medal	金牌 / 银牌 / 铜牌	金メダル / 銀メダル / 銅メダル
챔피언	champion	世界冠军	チャンピオン
예선전	preliminary match	预赛	予選
준준결승전 (8강전)	quarter final (final 8)	八强赛	準々決勝戦
준결승전 (4강전)	semifinal (final 4)	四强赛	準決勝戦
결승전	final (s)	决赛	決勝戦
선수	athlete	运动员	選手
감독	manager	总教练	監督
코치	coach	教练	コーチ

음악 Music | 音乐 | 音楽

1 가야금 gayageum 伽倻琴 カヤグム	**3 징** jing 锣 どら	**5 북** drum 鼓 太鼓	**7 아쟁** ajaeng 雅筝 7本の弦からなる弦楽器の一種
2 거문고 geomungo 玄鹤琴 韓国の琴	**4 장구** janggu 长鼓 チャング	**6 꽹과리** kkwaenggwari 小锣 鉦 (しょう)	**8 대금** daegeum 大琴 韓国固有の横笛

음악 Music | 音乐 | 音楽

9 **피아노**
piano
钢琴
ピアノ

10 **오르간**
organ
风琴
オルガン

11 **바이올린**
violin
小提琴
バイオリン

12 **첼로**
cello
大提琴
チェロ

13 **클라리넷**
clarinet
单簧管
クラリネット

14 **오보에**
oboe
双簧管
オーボエ

15 **색소폰**
saxophone
萨克斯管
サキソホン

16 **플루트**
flute
长笛
フルート

17 **트럼펫**
trumpet
小号
トランペット

18 **드럼**
drum
架子鼓
ドラム

19 **기타**
guitar
吉他
ギター

20 **캐스터네츠**
castanets
响板
カスタネット

21 **실로폰**
xylophone
木琴
木琴

22 **피리**
pipe
笛子
笛

23 **탬버린**
tambourine
铃鼓
タンバリン

More Vocabulary

타악기	percussion instrument	打击乐器	打楽器
현악기	stringed instrument	弦乐器	弦楽器
관악기	wind instrument	管乐器	管楽器
아코디언	accordion	手风琴	アコーディオン
트라이앵글	triangle	三角铁	トライアングル
트롬본	trombone	长号	トロンボーン
호른	horn	圆号	ホルン
지휘자	conductor	指挥	指揮者
악보	music score, sheet music	乐谱	楽譜
오케스트라	orchestra	管弦乐	オーケストラ
클래식	classic music	古典音乐	クラシック

성악	vocal music	声乐	声楽
재즈	jazz	爵士乐	ジャズ
팝송	(foreign) pop music	流行歌曲	ポップソング
록	rock	摇滚乐	ロック
발라드	ballads	叙事曲	バラード
댄스음악	dance music	舞曲	ダンス音楽
랩	rap	说唱	ラップ
레게	reggae	牙买加的传统音乐	レゲエ
트로트(뽕짝)	"trot"	快步舞曲	演歌
대중가요	popular music	大众歌曲	流行歌
디스코 음악	disco	迪斯科音乐	ディスコ音楽

미술, 영화와 공연 Art, Movies, Performances | 美术，电影与演出 | 美術、映画、公演

1 캔버스
canvas
帆布 (印花布)
キャンバス

2 붓
writing brush
毛笔
筆

3 물감
water paint
染料
絵の具

4 스케치북
sketch book
素描簿
スケッチブック

5 파스텔
pastels
彩色蜡笔
パステル

6 서예
(East Asian) calligraphy
书法
書道

미술, 영화와 공연 Art, Movies, Performances | 美术, 电影与演出 | 美術, 映画, 公演

7 조각
sculpture
雕刻
彫刻

8 배우
actor
演员
俳優

9 영사기
movie projector
放映机
映写機

10 필름
film
胶卷 / 影片
フィルム

11 포스터
poster
海报/宣传画
ポスター

More Vocabulary

크레파스	pastel crayon	蜡笔	クレパス
공예	industrial arts	工艺	工芸
판화	(a) print	版画	版画
유화	an oil painting	油画	油絵
영화배우	movie actor	电影演员	映画俳優
스크린	screen	银幕	スクリーン
자막	subtitles	字幕	字幕
연극	a play	戏剧 (话剧)	演劇
무대	stage	舞台	舞台
오페라	opera	歌剧	オペラ
발레	ballet	芭蕾舞	バレエ
무용	dance	舞蹈	舞踊
연주회	concert	演奏会	演奏会
뮤지컬	musical	歌舞剧	ミュージカル
주인공 (주연)	main character	主角	主人公 (主演)
조연	supporting actor	配角	助演
감독	director	导演	監督
촬영	filming, photography	摄影	撮影
연출	directing	编导	演出
조명	lighting	照明	照明
연기	acting	演技	演技
스타	a star	明星	スター
제작자	producer	制片人	製作者
세트장	a stage / movie set	布景	セット
영화제	film festival	电影节	映画祭
시사회	preview showing	首映式	試写会
시나리오(희곡)	drama script	剧本	シナリオ (戯曲)
비극	tragedy	悲剧	悲劇
희극	comedy	喜剧	喜劇
콘서트	concert	演唱会	コンサート
미술	art	美术	美術
화가	painter	画家	画家
미술관	art gallery / museum	美术馆	美術館
전시회	exhibition	展览会	展示会
회화	a painting	绘画	絵画
초상화	portrait	肖像画	肖像画
수묵화	traditional ink painting	水墨画	水墨画
수채화	watercolor painting	水彩画	水彩画
소묘	rough drawing	素描	デッサン
삽화	illustration	插图	挿絵
사진	photograph	照片	写真
디자인	design	设计	デザイン
컴퓨터 그래픽	computer graphics	电脑图表	コンピューターグラフィック
표(티켓)	ticket	票 (入场券)	券 (チケット)
매표소	ticket office	售票处	チケット売り場
예술	art	艺术	芸術
예술가	artist	艺术家	芸術家

TV와 오디오 Television and Audio | 电视与音响 | TV、オーディオ

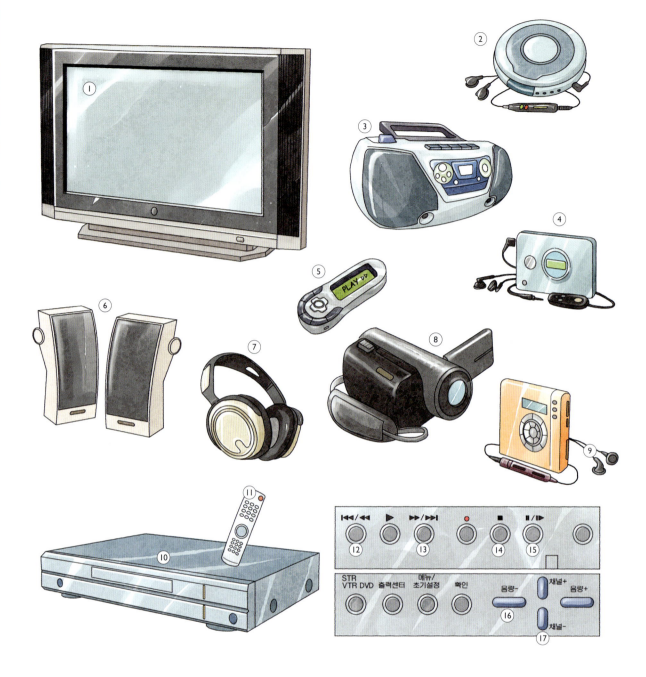

1. **TV**
television
电视
TV

2. **CD 플레이어**
CD player
CD 机
CDプレーヤー

3. **카세트 플레이어**
cassette player
磁带录音机
カセットプレーヤー

4. **워크맨**
Walkman
随身听
ウォークマン

5. **MP3 플레이어**
MP3 player
MP3
MP3プレーヤー

6. **스피커**
speaker
音箱
スピーカー

7. **헤드폰**
headphone
头戴式耳机
ヘッドホン

8. **비디오 카메라**
video camera
视频摄像机
ビデオカメラ

9. **이어폰**
earphone
耳机
イヤホン

10. **비디오 플레이어**
video player
录像机
ビデオプレーヤー

11. **리모컨**
remote control
遥控器
リモコン

12. **되감기**
rewind
快倒
巻戻し

TV와 오디오 Television and Audio | 电视与音响 | TV、オーディオ

13 빨리감기
fast forward
快进
早送り

14 정지
stop
停止
停止

15 일시정지
pause
暂停
一時停止

16 음량 (볼륨)
volume
音量
音量（ボリューム）

17 채널
channel
频道
チャンネル

More Vocabulary

DVD 플레이어	DVD player	DVD 播放机	DVD プレーヤー
라디오	radio	收音机	ラジオ
마이크	microphone	麦克风(话筒)	マイク
건전지	battery	电池	乾電池
카세트테이프	cassette tape	磁带	カセットテープ
비디오테이프	video tape	录像带	ビデオテープ
비디오대여점	video rental store	音像店	レンタルビデオ店
연체료	late fee	滞纳金	延滞料
방송국	broadcasting station	广播电台	放送局
케이블 TV	cable television	有线电视	ケーブルテレビ
생방송	live broadcast	现场直播	生放送
중계방송	relay, hook-up	转播	中継
녹화방송	filmed television broadcast	录播	録画放送
위성방송	satellite broadcast	卫星电视	衛星放送
뉴스	news	新闻	ニュース
드라마	drama	电视剧	ドラマ
다큐멘터리	documentary	纪录片	ドキュメンタリー
광고	advertisement	广告	CM
ARS 퀴즈	telephone quiz	ARS 智力竞赛	視聴者クイズ
시청자	television viewer	观众	視聴者
연예인	star, entertainment figure	演艺人	芸能人
탤런트	television star / performer	演员	タレント
가수	singer	歌手	歌手
아나운서	announcer	（电视, 广播的）广播员	アナウンサー

Appendix p.166

Phrases & Expressions

- 텔레비전(TV)을 켜다 / 보다 / 끄다 to turn on / watch / turn off a television
- 채널을 돌리다 to change channels
- 리모컨을 누르다 to press a remote control
- 볼륨을 높이다 / 낮추다 to turn up / down the volume
- 시청하다 / 청취하다 to watch / listen
- 프로그램을 녹화하다 to record a program
- 비디오를 켜다 / 끄다 to turn on / off a video
- 녹음하다 to record (a program)
- 비디오를 빌리다 to rent a video
- 비디오를 반납하다 to return a (borrowed) video
- 건전지를 갈아 끼우다 to change batteries
- 헤드폰(이어폰)을 끼다 to wear a headphone (earphone)
- 주파수를 맞추다 to find a frequency

여행 Travel 旅行 旅行

1. **텐트**
   tent
   帐篷
   テント

2. **캠프파이어**
   camp fire
   篝火
   キャンプファイヤー

3. **배낭**
   backpack
   背囊
   リュックサック

4. **침낭**
   sleeping bag
   睡袋
   寝袋

5. **지도**
   map
   地图
   地図

6. **나침반**
   compass
   指南针
   磁石

7. **손전등**
   flashlight
   手电筒
   懐中電灯

8. **우산**
   umbrella
   雨伞
   傘

9. **라이터**
   lighter
   打火机
   ライター

10. **사진기**
    camera
    照相机
    カメラ

11. **버너**
    (gas, oil) burner
    燃烧器
    バーナー

여행 Travel | 旅行 | 旅行

   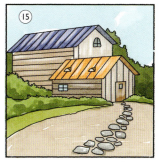

12 여관
yeogwan, Korean inn
旅馆
旅館

13 호텔
hotel
宾馆
ホテル

14 콘도미니엄
"condominium,"
time-share vacation
apartment units
度假村
コンドミニアム

15 펜션
pension
租赁木屋
ペンション

More Vocabulary

캠핑	camping	野营	キャンピング	
민박	home stay	农家院	民宿	
여행경비	travel expenses	旅行经费	旅行経費	
여행사	travel agency	旅行社	旅行社	
여권	passport	护照	旅券	
비자	visa	签证	ビザ	
안내책자	information pamphlet	旅行手册	ガイドブック	
가이드	guide	导游	ガイド	
성수기	high-demand season	旺季	旅行シーズン	
비수기	slack season	淡季	オフシーズン	
국립공원	national park	国立公园	国立公園	
관광객	tourist	旅客	観光客	
관광지	tourist region	旅游地	観光地	

특산물	products unique to a region	土特产	特産物
명소	famous spot, place of interest	名胜古迹	名所
해외여행	overseas travel	国外旅行	海外旅行
국내여행	domestic travel	国内旅行	国内旅行
배낭여행	backpack travel	背囊旅行	バックパッキング
가족여행	family travel	家庭旅行	家族旅行
효도관광	filial piety tourism, sending family elders on a tour	孝道旅行	両親に旅行をプレゼントすること
벚꽃놀이	cherry blossom viewing party, going to see cherry blossoms in bloom	赏樱花	花見
단풍놀이	an excursion to see autumn tree leaves	赏红叶	紅葉狩り

Appendix p.166

Phrases & Expressions

- 렌터카를 이용하다 to use a rental car
- (숙소를) 예약하다 to reserve (a place to stay)
- 사진을 찍다 to take a photograph
- 야영하다 to camp

나무 Trees 树木

1 뿌리 root(s) 树根 根	**4** 열매 fruit, nuts, berries 果实 果実	**7** 소나무 pine tree 松树 マツ	**10** 야자수 palm tree 椰子树 ヤシの木
2 줄기 trunk 树干 幹	**5** 잎 (잎사귀) leaf 树叶 (叶子) 葉	**8** 느티나무 zelkova tree 榉树 ケヤキ	**11** 은행나무 gingko tree 银杏树 イチョウ
3 가지 branch(es) 树枝 枝	**6** 아카시아 acacia 金合欢树 アカシア	**9** 대나무 bamboo 竹子 竹	**12** 선인장 cactus 仙人掌 サボテン

꽃 Flowers 花 花

1. **꽃잎** petal 花叶 花びら
2. **꽃봉오리** bud 花蕾 つぼみ
3. **튤립** tulip 郁金香 チューリップ
4. **해바라기** sunflower 向日葵 ヒマワリ
5. **장미** rose 玫瑰 バラ
6. **진달래** azalea 杜鵑花 カラムラサキツツジ
7. **개나리** forsythia 连翘 レンギョウ
8. **동백** camellia 山茶树 椿
9. **백합** lily 百合 ユリ
10. **코스모스** cosmos 大波斯菊 コスモス
11. **카네이션** carnation 康乃馨 カーネーション
12. **나팔꽃** morning glory 牵牛花 アサガオ

More Vocabulary

민들레	dandelion	蒲公英	タンポポ
무궁화	Rose of Sharon	无穷花	ムクゲ
벚꽃	cherry blossom	樱花	桜

목련	magnolia	木兰	木蓮
매화	Japanese apricot	梅花	梅

11 가축 Livestock, Domestic Animals | 牲畜 | 家畜

1 **개**	4 **소**	7 **염소**	10 **양**	13 **오리**
dog	cow	goat	lamb	duck
狗	牛	山羊	羊	鴨
犬	牛	ヤギ	羊	アヒル

2 **강아지**	5 **병아리**	8 **말**	11 **돼지**	14 **거위**
puppy	chick	horse	pig	goose
小狗	小鸡	马	猪	鹅
子犬	ひよこ	馬	豚	ガチョウ

3 **송아지**	6 **닭**	9 **망아지**	12 **고양이**	15 **토끼**
calf	chicken	foal	cat	rabbit
牛犊	鸡	马驹子	猫	兔
子牛	鶏	子馬	猫	ウサギ

142

야생동물 Wild Animals 野生动物 野生動物

1 **호랑이**
tiger
老虎
トラ

2 **사자**
lion
狮子
ライオン

3 **늑대**
wolf
狼
オオカミ

4 **여우**
fox
狐狸
キツネ

5 **곰**
bear
熊
クマ

6 **코알라**
koala
树袋熊
コアラ

7 **판다**
panda
熊猫
パンダ

8 **코뿔소**
rhinoceros
犀牛
サイ

9 **하마**
hippopotamus
河马
カバ

10 **코끼리**
elephant
大象
ゾウ

11 **고릴라**
gorilla
大猩猩
ゴリラ

12 **원숭이**
monkey
猴子
サル

13 **사슴**
deer
鹿
シカ

14 **캥거루**
kangaroo
袋鼠
カンガルー

15 **얼룩말**
zebra
斑马
シマウマ

16 **기린**
giraffe
麒麟
キリン

143

새 Birds | 鸟雀 | 鳥

1 부리 beak 喙 くちばし	**3 부엉이** owl 猫头鹰 コノハズク	**5 앵무새** parrot 鹦鹉 オウム	**7 백조** swan 天鹅 ハクチョウ	**9 독수리** eagle 秃鹫 クロハゲワシ	**11 펭귄** penguin 企鹅 ペンギン
2 날개 wings 翅膀 羽	**4 비둘기** pigeon, dove 鸽子 ハト	**6 참새** sparrow 麻雀 スズメ	**8 딱따구리** woodpecker 啄木鸟 キツツキ	**10 공작** peacock 孔雀 クジャク	

More Vocabulary

까치	magpie	喜鹊	カササギ	기러기	wild goose	雁	ガン
제비	swallow	燕子	ツバメ	꿩	pheasant	野鸡	キジ
까마귀	crow	乌鸦	カラス	타조	ostrich	鸵鸟	ダチョウ

144

파충류, 양서류, 곤충　Reptiles, Amphibia and Insects　爬虫类, 两栖类, 昆虫　爬虫類, 両生類, 昆虫

1. 악어
crocodile
鳄鱼
ワニ

2. 코브라
cobra
眼镜蛇
コブラ

3. 개구리
frog
蛙
カエル

4. 두꺼비
toad
癞蛤蟆
ヒキガエル

5. 도마뱀
lizard
蜥蜴
トカゲ

6. 뱀
snake
蛇
ヘビ

7. 달팽이
snail
蜗牛
カタツムリ

8. 나비
butterfly
蝴蝶
チョウ

9. 모기
mosquito
蚊子
カ

10. 파리
fly
苍蝇
ハエ

11. 벌
bee
蜜蜂
ハチ

12. 지렁이
worm
蚯蚓
ミミズ

13. 잠자리
dragonfly
蜻蜓
トンボ

14. 거미
spider
蜘蛛
クモ

15. 개미
ant
蚂蚁
アリ

More Vocabulary

메뚜기　grasshopper　蚱蜢　トノサマバッタ　　　매미　cicada　蝉　セミ

145

12 우주 Cosmos | 宇宙 | 宇宙

1 **지구** earth 地球 地球	3 **수성** Mercury 水星 水星	5 **화성** Mars 火星 火星	7 **토성** Saturn 土星 土星	9 **해왕성** Neptune 海王星 海王星
2 **태양** sun 太阳 太陽	4 **금성** Venus 金星 金星	6 **목성** Jupiter 木星 木星	8 **천왕성** Uranus 天王星 天王星	10 **명왕성** Pluto 冥王星 冥王星

More Vocabulary

태양계	solar system	太阳系	太陽系
은하계	galactic system	银河系	銀河系
혜성	comet	彗星	彗星
달	moon	月亮	月

보름달	full moon	圓月	滿月
초승달	new moon	新月	三日月
반달	half moon	半月	半月

자연 Nature | 自然 | 自然

1	**바다**	3	**동굴**	5	**강**	7	**하늘**
	sea		cave		river		sky
	海洋		洞		江		天空
	海		洞窟		川		空

2	**육지 (땅)**	4	**호수**	6	**산**		
	land		lake		mountain		
	陆地		湖		山		
	陸地（土地）		湖		山		

More Vocabulary

계곡	gorge	峡谷	渓谷
화산	volcano	火山	火山
지진	earthquake	地震	地震

| 해일 | tidal wave | 海啸 | 津波 |
| 대륙 | continent | 大陆 | 大陸 |

세계 World | 世界 | 世界

중국
China
中国
中国

대만
Taiwan
台湾
台湾

일본
Japan
日本
日本

몽골
Mongolia
蒙古
モンゴル

베트남
Vietnam
越南
ベトナム

방글라데시
Bangladesh
孟加拉国
バングラディシュ

파키스탄
Pakistan
巴基斯坦
パキスタン

타이
Thailand
泰国
タイ

필리핀
the Philippines
菲律宾
フィリピン

인도
India
印度
インド

인도네시아
Indonesia
印度尼西亚
インドネシア

이라크
Iraq
伊拉克
イラク

이스라엘
Israel
以色列
イスラエル

사우디아라비아
Saudi Arabia
沙特阿拉伯
サウジアラビア

터키
Turkey
土耳其
トルコ

말레이시아
Malaysia
马来西亚
マレーシア

네덜란드
the Netherlands
荷兰
オランダ

노르웨이
Norway
挪威
ノルウェー

벨기에
Belgium
比利时
ベルギー

덴마크
Denmark
丹麦
デンマーク

독일
Germany
德国
ドイツ

러시아
Russia
俄罗斯
ロシア

영국
Britain
英国
イギリス

아일랜드
Ireland
爱尔兰
アイルランド

이탈리아
Italy
意大利
イタリア

세계 | World | 世界 | 世界

프랑스
France
法国
フランス

에스파냐/스페인
Spain
西班牙
スペイン

포르투갈
Portugal
葡萄牙
ポルトガル

미국
United States
美国
アメリカ

캐나다
Canada
加拿大
カナダ

뉴질랜드
New Zealand
新西兰
ニュージーランド

멕시코
Mexico
墨西哥
メキシコ

오스트레일리아/호주
Australia
澳大利亚
オーストラリア

남아프리카공화국
Republic of South Africa
南非共和国
南アフリカ共和国

케냐
Kenya
肯尼亚
ケニア

이집트
Egypt
埃及
エジプト

브라질
Brazil
巴西
ブラジル

아르헨티나
Argentina
阿根廷
アルゼンチン

페루
Peru
秘鲁
ペルー

More Vocabulary

태평양	Pacific Ocean	太平洋	太平洋
대서양	Atlantic Ocean	大西洋	大西洋
인도양	Indian Ocean	印度洋	インド洋
지중해	Mediterranean	地中海	地中海
북극	North Pole	北极	北極
남극	South Pole	南极	南極
국가, 나라	state, country	国家	国家, 国
인류	humanity	人类	人類
인종	race	人种	人種
국민	citizenry	国民	国民
국적	citizenship	国籍	国籍
외국	foreign country	外国	外国
해외	overseas	海外	海外
국내	domestic	国内	国内
교포	permanent overseas Korean	侨胞	海外同胞
동포	Korean brethren	同胞	同胞
이민	immigration and emigration	移民	移民
망명	defection	亡命	亡命
수교	establish diplomatic relations	建交	修交
외교	diplomacy	外交	外交
대사관	embassy	大使馆	大使館
외교관	diplomat	外交官	外交官
UN 안전보장이사회	United Nations Security Council	联合国安理会	UN安全保障理事会
WTO	World Trade Organisation	WTO	WTO
정상회담	summit talks	首脑会谈	首脳会談

13 행정구역과 지리 Administrative Districts and Geography | 行政区域与地理 | 行政区域、地理

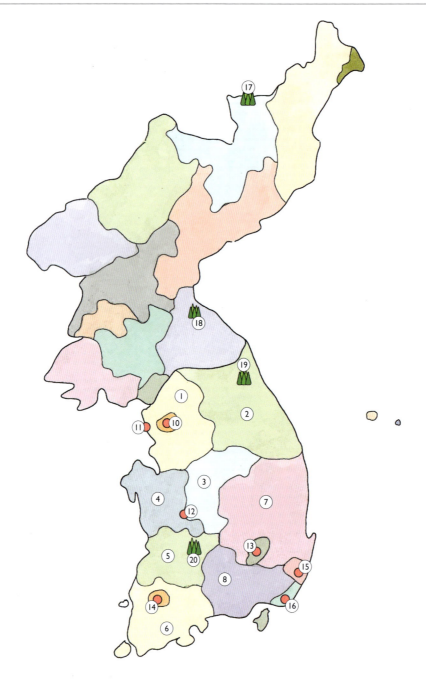

1 경기도 Gyeonggi Province 京畿道 京畿道	**3 충청북도** Chungcheongbuk-do 忠清北道 忠清北道	**5 전라북도** Jeollabuk-do 全罗北道 全羅北道	**7 경상북도** Gyeongsangbuk-do 庆尚北道 慶尚北道
2 강원도 Gangwon Province 江原道 江原道	**4 충청남도** Chungcheongnam-do 忠清南道 忠清南道	**6 전라남도** Jeollanam-do 全罗南道 全羅南道	**8 경상남도** Gyeongsangnam-do 庆尚南道 慶尚南道

행정구역과 지리 Administrative Districts and Geography | 行政区域与地理 | 行政区域、地理

9 **제주도**
Jeju Province
济州道
済州道

10 **서울특별시**
Seoul Metropolis
首尔特别市
ソウル特別市

11 **인천광역시**
Incheon Metropolitan City
仁川广域市
インチョン広域市

12 **대전광역시**
Daejeon Metropolitan City
大田广域市
テジョン広域市

13 **대구광역시**
Daegu Metropolitan City
大丘广域市
テグ広域市

14 **광주광역시**
Gwangju Metropolitan City
光州广域市
クァンジュ広域市

15 **울산광역시**
Ulsan Metropolitan City
蔚山广域市
ウルサン広域市

16 **부산광역시**
Busan Metropolitan City
釜山广域市
プサン広域市

17 **백두산**
Mount Baekdu
白头山
白頭山

18 **금강산**
Mount Geumgang
金刚山
金剛山

19 **설악산**
Mount Seorak
雪岳山
雪岳山

20 **지리산**
Mount Jiri
智异山
智異山

21 **한라산**
Mount Halla
汉拿山
漢拏山

More Vocabulary

수도	capital	首都	首都
수도권	greater capital region	首都圈	首都圏
도심	city center	市中心	都心
강남	Gangnam, Seoul's "South of the River" neighborhoods	江南	江南
강북	Gangbuk, Seoul's "North of the River" neighborhoods	江北	江北
근교	suburbs	近郊	近郊
전국	the whole country	全国	全国
영남	Yeongnam region	岭南	嶺南
호남	Honam region	湖南	湖南
지방	region, provinces, district	地方	地方
도시	city	都市	都市
대도시	major city	大都市	大都市
마을	village, hamlet, neighborhood	村庄	村
농촌	farm village, farming region	农村	農村
어촌	fishing village	渔村	漁村
시골	country, countryside	乡下	田舎

시내	downtown	城内	市内
시외	outskirts, outside the city	城外	市外
특별시	metropolis, special city	特别市	特別市
광역시	metropolitan city	广域市	広域市
도	province	道	道
시	city	市	市
구	gu, ward, district	区	区
군	gun, county, district	郡	郡
면	myeon, township, subdivision of a gun	面	面
리	ri, subdivision of a myeon	里	里
태백산맥	Taebaek Mountains	太白山脉	太白山脈
소백산맥	Sobaek Mountains	小白山脉	小白山脈
노령산맥	Noryeong Mountains	芦岭山脉	蘆嶺山脈
한강	Han River	汉江	漢江
낙동강	Nakdong River	洛东江	洛東江
섬진강	Seomjin River	蟾津江	蟾津江

13 역사와 문화 History and Culture | 历史与文化 | 歴史、文化

국가의 성립과 발전 emergence and development of states | 国家的成立与发展 | 国家の成立と発展

B.C.
- 2333년 단군, **고조선** 건국 ①
- 108년 고조선 멸망, 한(漢)사군 설치
- 57년 박혁거세, **신라** 건국 ⑤
- 37년 주몽, **고구려** 건국 (~A.D. 608) ③ ②
- 18년 온조, **백제** 건국 (~A.D. 660) ④

A. D.
- 676년 신라, 삼국통일 (**통일신라**) ⑦
- 698년 대조영, **발해** 건국 ⑥
- 918년 왕건, **고려** 건국 (~1392) ⑧
- 1392년 고려 멸망, **조선** 건국 ⑨
- 1443년 훈민정음 창제
- 1910년 **국권 피탈** (**일제강점기**) ⑩
- 1919년 3.1 운동 ⑫
- 1945년 8.15 해방(광복) ⑬
- 1948년 대한민국 정부수립 ⑪
- 1950년 6.25 전쟁 ⑭
- 1960년 4.19 혁명 ⑮
- 1970년 새마을운동 시작 ⑯
- 1980년 5.18 광주민주화운동 ⑰
- 1986년 제10회 서울 아시안게임 개최 ⑱
- 1988년 제24회 서울 올림픽 개최 ⑲
- 2002년 한일 월드컵 개최 ⑳

1 **고조선**
Gojoseon
古朝鲜
古朝鮮

2 **삼국시대**
Three Kingdoms Period
三国时代
三国時代

3 **고구려**
Goguryeo
高句丽
高句麗

4 **백제**
Baekje
百剂
百済

5 **신라**
Silla
新罗
新羅

6 **발해**
Balhae
渤海
渤海

7 **통일신라**
Unified Silla
统一新罗
統一新羅

8 **고려**
Goryeo
高丽
高麗

9 **조선**
Joseon
朝鲜
朝鮮

10 **일제강점기**
Japanese colonial period
日本殖民地
日帝植民地期

11 **대한민국**
Republic of Korea
大韩民国
大韓民国

역사적 사건 historical incidents | 历史事件 | 歴史的事件

12 **3.1 운동**
"March 1st Movement"
3.1 运动
3.1 運動

13 **8.15 해방**
Liberation, "August 15 Liberation"
8.15 解放
8.15 解放

14 **6.25 전쟁**
Korean War, "June 25 War"
6.25 战争
6.25 戦争

15 **4.19 혁명**
"March 19 Revolution"
4.19 革命
4.19 革命

16 **새마을운동**
Saemaeul Movement
新农村运动
セマウル運動

17 **광주민주화운동**
Gwangju Democratic Campaign
光州民主化运动
光州民主化運動

18 **아시안게임**
Asian Games
亚运会
アジア大会

19 **서울 올림픽**
Seoul Olympics
首尔奥运会
ソウルオリンピック

20 **2002 월드컵**
2002 World Cup
2002 世界杯
2002 ワールドカップ

역사와 문화 History and Culture | 历史与文化 | 歴史、文化

문화재 cultural assets / properties | 文化遗产 | 文化財

불국사
Bulguk Temple
佛国寺
仏国寺

석굴암
Seokguram
石窟庵
石窟庵

남대문
Namdaemun
南大门
南大門

동대문
Dongdaemun
东大门
東大門

경복궁
Gyeongbok Palace
景福宫
景福宮

팔만대장경
Palman Daejang Gyeong
八万大藏经
八萬大蔵経

훈민정음
Hunmin Jeongeum
训民正音
訓民正音

태극기
Taegeukgi
太极旗
太極旗

무궁화
Rose of Sharon
无穷花
ムクゲ

More Vocabulary

대동여지도 Daedongyeojido | 大东舆地图 | 大東輿地図
애국가 national anthem | 爱国歌 | 愛国歌

명절 traditional holidays | 节日 | 祝祭日

설날(음력 1월 1일)
  Seollal (1st day of the 1st month on the lunar calendar)
  | 春节(阴历一月一日) | 元旦(陰暦1月1日)

정월 대보름(음력 1월 15일)
  Jeongwol Daeboreum (15th day of the 1st month on the lunar calendar)
  | 元宵节(阴历一月十五日) | 正月15日(陰暦1月15日)

추석(음력 8월15일)
  Chuseok (15th day of the 8th month on the lunar calendar)
  | 中秋节(阴历八月十五日) | お盆(陰暦8月15日)

국경일 state holidays | 国庆日 | 国慶日(国家の慶事を記念する日)

3.1절(양력 3월 1일)
  March 1st (Independence Movement) Day (March 1)
  | 三.一节 | 三一節(3月1日の独立運動記念日)

광복절(양력 8월 15일)
  Liberation Day (August 15)
  | 光复节 | 光復節(日本の植民統治からの解放を記念する日)

개천절(양력 10월 3일)
  "The Day Heaven Opened" (National Foundation Day) (October 3) | 开天节 | 開天節(建国記念日)

공휴일 legal holidays | 公休日 | 公休日

어린이날(양력 5월 5일) Children's Day (May 5)
  | 儿童节 | 子供の日(陽暦5月5日)

현충일(양력 6월 6일) Memorial Day (June 6)
  | 显忠日 | 顕忠日(国家の防衛に命を捧げた人々の忠誠を記念する日)

성탄절(양력 12월 25일)
  Christmas (December 25) | 圣诞节 | クリスマス

13 정치와 법률 Politics and Law | 政治与法律 | 政治、法律

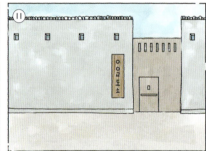

1 **국회**
National Assembly
国会
国会

2 **법정**
court, courtroom
法庭
法廷

3 **판사**
judge
审判官
判事

4 **검사**
prosecution
检察官
検事

5 **변호사**
lawyer
律师
弁護士

6 **피고**
defendant, accused
被告
被告

7 **원고**
plaintiff
原告
原告

8 **증인**
witness
证人
証人

정치와 법률 Politics and Law | 政治与法律 | 政治、法律

9 경찰관
police officer
警察官
警察官

10 경찰서
police station
警察署
警察署

11 감옥 (교도소)
prison
监狱
監獄（刑務所）

12 죄수
prisoner
犯人
罪人

More Vocabulary

청와대	Cheong Wa Dae	青瓦台	青瓦台
투표	voting	投票	投票
후보자	candidate	候选人	候補者
정부	government	政府	政府
대통령	president	总统	大統領
행정부	executive branch	行政部	行政府
사법부	judicial branch	司法部	司法府
입법부	legislative branch	立法部	立法府
헌법재판소	Constitutional Court	宪法裁判所	憲法裁判所
대법원	Supreme Court	大法院	大法院(最高裁)
대법원장	chief justice of the Supreme Court	大法院长	大法院長
법원	court	法院	裁判所
국회의원	member of the National Assembly	国会议员	国会議員
국회의장	speaker of the National Assembly	国会议长	国会議長
선거	election	选举	選挙
당선	election victory	当选	當選
총리	prime minister	总理	総理
장관	minister	长官(部长)	長官(大臣)
정치권	the political world, members of the National Assembly	政治圈	政界
정치인	politician	从政人	政治家
민주주의	democracy	民主主义	民主主義
지방자치제	regional autonomy	地方自治制	地方自治体
정당	political party	政党	政党
법, 법률	law	法律	法, 法律
재판	trial	裁判	裁判
심문	examination	审问	審問
판결	judgment	判决	判決
불법	illegality	违法	不法
범죄	crime	犯罪	犯罪
무죄	innocent	无罪	無罪
유죄	guilty	有罪	有罪
범인	criminal	犯人	犯人
피해자	victim	被害者	被害者
체포	detain	逮捕	逮捕
구속	arrest	拘留	拘束
수사	investigation	搜查	捜査
처벌	punishment	处罚	処罰
용의자	suspect	嫌疑犯	容疑者
증거	evidence	证据	証拠
살인	murder	杀人	殺人
사기	fraud	欺诈	詐欺
납치	kidnapping	绑架	拉致
강도	burglar	强盗	強盗
절도	larcenist	盗窃	窃盗
유괴	abduction (usually a child)	诱拐	誘拐
명예훼손	defamation of character	损害名誉	名誉毀損

13 산업과 경제 Industry and Economy | 产业与经济 | 産業、経済

1 **농업**
agriculture
农业
農業

2 **임업**
forestry
林业
林業

3 **어업**
fishery
渔业
漁業

4 **광업**
mining
矿业
鉱業

5 **제조업**
manufacturing
制造行业
製造業

6 **서비스업**
service industry
服务行业
サービス業

7 **건설업**
construction industry
建设行业
建設業

8 **전기통신**
telecommunications
电子通讯
電気通信

9 **주가**
stock prices
股价
株価

More Vocabulary

증권거래소	securities exchange	证券交易所	証券取引所	
주식	shares, stocks	股票	株式	
펀드	a fund	基金	ファンド	
부동산	real estate	房地产	不動産	

투기	speculation	投机	投機
경매	auction	拍卖	競売
환율	exchange rate	汇率	為替相場

종교 Religion | 宗教 | 宗教

불교 Buddhism | 佛教 | 仏教

부처	절	스님	염주	목탁
Buddha	temple	monk	string of beads	wooden gong
佛像	寺庙	和尚	佛珠	木铎
仏	寺	お坊さん	数珠	木魚

기독교 Christianity (Protestantism) | 基督教 | キリスト教

예수	교회	목사	성경	십자가
Jesus	church	minister	Bible	cross
耶稣	教堂	牧师	圣经	十字架
イエス	教会	牧師	聖書	十字架

천주교 Catholicism | 天主教 | カトリック教

마리아	미사	교황	신부	수녀	묵주
Mary	mass	pope	priest	nun	rosary
玛丽亚	弥撒	教皇	神父	修女	圣珠
マリア	ミサ	教皇	神父	修道女	ロザリオ

More Vocabulary

유교	Confucianism	儒教	儒教
불공	mass	佛供	供養
불경	scripture	佛经	お経
예배	worship service	礼拜	礼拝

찬송가	hymn	赞颂歌	讃美歌
성가대	choir	圣歌队	聖歌隊
성당	cathedral	教堂	聖堂

13 군사와 무기 Military and Weaponry 军事与武器 軍事、武器

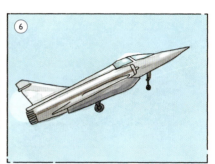
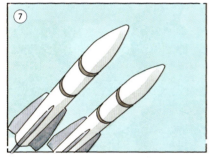
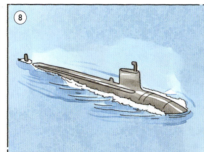

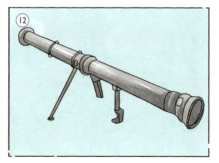

군사와 무기 Military and Weaponry | 军事与武器 | 軍事、武器

1. **군인**
soldier
军人
軍人

2. **육군**
army
陆军
陸軍

3. **해군**
navy
海军
海軍

4. **여군**
female soldier
女兵
女性軍人

5. **탱크**
tank
坦克
タンク

6. **전투기**
jet fighter
战斗机
戦闘機

7. **미사일**
missile
导弹
ミサイル

8. **잠수함**
submarine
潜水艇
潜水艦

9. **총**
gun
枪
銃

10. **헬기**
helicopter
直升机
ヘリコプター

11. **수류탄**
grenade
手榴弹
手榴弾

12. **대포**
cannon
大炮
大砲

More Vocabulary

장갑차	armored vehicle	装甲车	裝甲車
공군	air force	空军	空軍
군대	troops, military	军队	軍隊
적군	the enemy	敌军	敵軍
아군	our forces, friendly forces	我军	我が軍
계급	rank	军衔	階級
장군	general	将军	将軍
대령	colonel	上校	大佐
중령	lieutenant colonel	中校	中佐
소령	major	少校	少佐

대위	captain	大尉	大尉
중위	first lieutenant	中尉	中尉
소위	second lieutenant	少尉	少尉
하사관	noncommissioned officer	下士	下士官
병사	private	士兵	兵士
전쟁	war	战争	戦争
전투	combat, battle	战斗	戦闘
전술	tactics	战术	戦術
공격	attack	攻击	攻撃
훈련	training	训练	訓練

Appendix

Phrases & Expressions ○
Practical Vocabulary ○
Verbs & Adjectives ○
Index ○

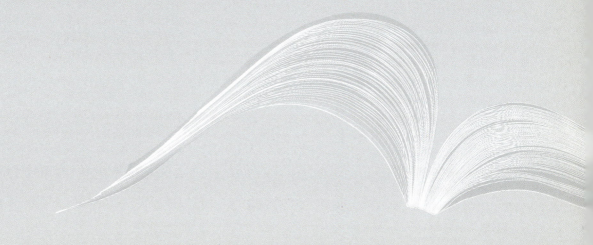

Phrases & Expressions

화폐(돈) Currency │ 货币 │ 貨幣(お金)　　p.23
- 한턱 내다　　请客 │ おごる
- 수표 뒷면에 이서하다　　在支票背面上签字 │ 小切手の裏にサインする
- 카드 영수증에 사인하다 (서명하다)　　刷卡单上签字 │ カードの領収書にサインする（署名する）
- 카드를 제시하다　　出示卡 │ カードを提示する
- 신분증을 제시하다　　出示身份证 │ 身分証を提示する
- 돈을 주다 (지불하다)　　付款 │ お金を払う（支払う）
- 돈을 세다　　数钱 │ お金を数える
- 잔돈을 받다　　收零钱 │ おつりを受け取る
- 영수증을 받다　　拿发票 │ 領収書を受け取る
- 팁을 주다　　给小费 │ チップをあげる

얼굴 Face │ 脸 │ 顔　　p.25
- 얼굴을 씻다 (세수하다)　　洗脸 │ 顔を洗う
- 손을 닦다 (손을 씻다)　　擦手 (洗手) │ 手を洗う
- 이를 닦다 (양치질하다)　　刷牙 │ 歯を磨く
- 입안을 헹구다　　漱口 │ 口の中をすすぐ
- 머리를 감다　　洗头 │ 髪を洗う
- 머리를 헹구다　　冲洗头发 │ 髪をすすぐ
- 머리를 말리다　　吹干头发 │ 髪を乾かす
- 코를 풀다　　擤鼻子 │ 鼻をかむ
- 눈을 뜨다 / 감다　　睁眼睛 / 闭眼睛 │ 目を開ける / 閉じる
- 입을 벌리다 / 다물다　　张嘴 / 闭嘴 (合上嘴) │ 口を開ける / 閉じる
- 고개를 숙이다/들다　　低头 / 抬头 │ 頭を下げる / 上げる
- 머리를 빗다　　梳头 │ 髪をとかす
- 머리를 묶다　　扎头 │ 髪を束ねる

나이(연령) Age │ 年龄 │ 年齢　　p.29
- 나이가 많다　　年纪大 │ 年を取っている
- 연세가 많다　　年老 │ お年を召している
- 나이가 적다　　年纪小 │ 年が若い
- 연세가 적다　　年少 │ お年が若い
- 젊어 보이다　　显年轻 │ 若く見える
- 늙어 보이다　　显老 │ 老けて見える
- 나이 들어 보이다　　显大 │ 年を取って見える

가족 Family │ 家族 │ 家族　　p.31
- 약혼하다　　订婚 │ 婚約する
- 결혼하다　　结婚 │ 結婚する
- 장가가다　　娶媳妇 │ (男が) 結婚する
- 시집가다　　出嫁 │ 嫁に行く
- 이혼하다　　离婚 │ 離婚する
- 재혼하다　　再婚 │ 再婚する

세탁 Laundry │ 洗涤 │ 洗濯　　p.49
- 탈수를 하다, 옷을 짜다　　脱水, 拧干 │ 脱水をする、服を絞る
- 옷을 털다　　抖衣服 │ 服をはたく
- 옷을 널다　　晾衣服 │ 服を干す
- 옷을 말리다　　晒衣 │ 服を乾かす
- 옷을 개다　　叠衣 │ 服をたたむ
- 옷걸이에 걸다　　挂在衣挂上 │ ハンガーにかける
- 빨래를 삶다　　煮衣物 │ 洗濯を煮洗いする
- 비누칠하다　　抹肥皂 │ せっけんをつける
- 옷을 비비다　　搓洗衣服 │ 服をもみ洗いする
- 옷을 헹구다　　漂洗衣服 │ 服をゆすぐ
- 다리다　　熨衣 │ アイロンをかける
- 얼룩을 제거하다　　清除斑点 │ しみを取る
- 물이 빠지다 (탈색되다)　　退色 │ 色落ちする
- 옷이 줄어들다　　缩水 │ 服が縮まる

식료품 Foodstuff │ 食品 │ 食料品　　p.63
- 짜다　　咸 │ 塩辛い
- 맵다　　辣 │ 辛い
- 달다　　甜 │ 甘い
- 쓰다　　苦 │ 苦い
- 시다　　酸 │ 酸っぱい
- 싱겁다　　淡 │ (味が) 薄い
- 칼칼하다　　渴 │ 少し辛い
- 텁텁하다　　涩 │ さっぱりしない
- 매콤하다　　微辣 │ やや辛い
- 얼큰하다　　又辣又爽 │ ひりひりする
- 시원하다　　爽口 │ さっぱりしている
- 느끼하다　　油腻 │ 脂っこい

패스트푸드 Fast Food │ 快餐 │ ファーストフード　　p.65
- 메뉴를 고르다 / 결정하다　　点菜 / 选菜 │ メニューを選ぶ / 決める
- 세트메뉴를 주문하다　　订套餐 │ セットメニューを注文する
- 회원카드를 제시하다　　出示会员卡 │ 会員カードを示す
- 햄버거를 먹다　　吃汉堡 │ ハンバーガーを食べる
- 소스를 뿌리다　　撒沙司 │ ソースをかける
- 음료수를 마시다　　喝饮料 │ 飲み物を飲む
- 음료수를 리필하다　　添加饮料 │ 飲み物をおかわりする
- 음식을 흘리다　　掉食物 │ 食べ物をこぼす
- 휴지로 닦다　　用手纸擦 │ ティッシュで拭く
- 테이블을 치우다　　收拾餐桌 │ テーブルの上を片付ける
- 테이블이 더럽다 / 깨끗하다　　餐桌脏 / 干净 │ テーブルが汚い / 綺麗だ
- 음식을 포장하다　　打包 │ 食べ物を包装する

식당 (음식점) Restaurant │ 餐厅 │ 食堂（飲食店）　　p.69
- 주문을 받다　　接受点菜 │ 注文を受ける
- 음식을 주문하다 / 시키다　　点菜 │ 食事を注文する
- 반찬을 더 주문하다　　加点菜 │ おかずをさらに注文する
- 개인접시에 음식을 덜다　　分菜给个人用碟子上 │ 銘々皿に食べ物を分ける

- 냅킨으로 입을 닦다　用餐巾纸擦嘴｜ナプキンで口を拭く
- 계산하다, 돈을 내다　结账｜計算をする、お金を払う
- (돈을) 각자 내다　各付各的｜(お金を)各自で出す
- 예약하다　预定｜予約する
- 예약을 취소하다　取消预定｜予約を取り消す
- 친절하다 / 불친절하다　亲切 / 不亲切｜親切だ / 不親切だ
- 자리가 없다　没有座位｜席が無い
- 배달하다　外卖｜配達する

주거 형태　Forms of Domicile｜居住形态｜住居の形態　p.71

- 엘리베이터를 타다　坐电梯｜エレベーターにのる
- 계단을 올라가다 / 내려가다　上楼梯 / 下｜階段を上がる/下りる
- 주차장에 차를 주차시키다 (주차하다)　把车停在停车场
  駐車場に車を駐車させる (駐車する)

주방　Kitchen｜厨房｜キッチン　p.73

- (야채를) 볶다　炒菜｜(野菜を) 炒める
- (시금치를) 데치다　汤(菠菜)｜(ほうれん草を) ゆがく
- (나물을) 무치다　凉拌野菜｜(ナムルを) あえる
- (콩나물을) 삶다　煮豆芽｜(豆もやしを) 茹でる
- (호박전을) 부치다　煎南瓜饼｜(カボチャチョンを) 焼く
- (오징어를) 튀기다　炸鱿鱼｜(イカを) 揚げる
- (국 / 찌개를) 끓이다　烧汤(汁 / チゲを) 温める
- (콩을) 졸이다　炖(豆)｜(豆を) 煮詰める
- 밥상을 펴다 / 접다　打开桌腿 / 折叠桌腿｜膳を広げる / 畳む
- 밥을 푸다　盛饭｜ご飯をよそう
- 국을 뜨다　盛汤｜汁をよそう
- 숟가락질을 / 젓가락질을 하다　用勺子 / 用筷子
  (口に) スプーンを / 箸を運ぶ
- 생선 가시를 바르다　挑出鱼刺｜魚のとげをこそげ取る
- 간장에 찍다　粘酱｜醤油につける
- 숭늉을 마시다　喝锅巴汤｜おこげ湯を飲む
- 빈 그릇을 치우다　收拾空碗｜空いた皿を片付ける
- 그릇을 씻다　洗碗｜食器を洗う
- 그릇을 말리다　烘干碗筷｜食器を乾かす
- 설거지를 하다　洗碗｜後片付けをする

욕실　Bathroom｜浴室｜浴室　p.77

- 용변을 보다　上厕所｜用便を足す
- 물을 내리다　放水｜水を流す
- 물을 틀다 / 잠그다　放水 / 关水｜蛇口をひねる / しめる
- 비누를 칠하다　抹香皂｜石鹸をつける
- 세수를 하다　洗脸｜顔を洗う
- 수건으로 닦다　用毛巾擦头｜タオルで拭く
- 수건을 걸다　挂毛巾｜タオルを掛ける
- 치약을 짜다　挤牙膏｜歯磨き粉を絞る
- 면도하다　刮胡子｜髭を剃る
- 샤워를 하다　洗澡｜シャワーをする
- 욕조에 물을 받다　往浴缸放水｜浴槽に水をはる
- 목욕을 하다　洗澡｜入浴する
- 체중을 달다　称体重｜体重を量る
- 렌즈를 끼다 / 빼다　戴隐形眼镜 / 取｜レンズをはめる / 外す

청소용구　Cleaning Devices｜清扫工具｜掃除用具　p.79

- 침대를 정돈하다　整理床｜ベッドを整える
- 시트를 갈다　换床单｜シーツを替える
- 이불을 개다 / 펴다　叠被子 / 铺｜布団を畳む / ひく
- 환기시키다　换空气｜換気する
- 장난감을 치우다　收拾玩具｜おもちゃを片付ける
- (카펫을) 진공청소하다　吸地毯｜(カーペットに) 真空掃除機をかける
- 마룻바닥을 쓸다 / 닦다　扫地板 / 擦｜床を掃く / 磨く
- 걸레질하다　拖地｜ふき掃除をする
- 책장을 정리하다　整理书柜｜本棚を整理する
- 가구의 먼지를 털다　掸家具｜家具のほこりをはたく
- 창문을 닦다　擦窗户｜窓を磨く
- 쓰레기통을 비우다　倒垃圾桶｜ゴミ箱を空にする
- 쓰레기를 버리다　倒垃圾｜ゴミを捨てる
- 화분에 물주다　给花盆浇水｜植木鉢に水をやる
- 정원을 가꾸다　整理院子｜庭を手入れする

공구　Tools｜工具｜工具　p.81

- 고장 나다　出故障｜故障する
- 전원이 나가다　停电｜電気が切れる
- 지붕이 새다　屋顶漏水｜雨漏りがする
- 벽에 금이 가다　墙上出裂纹｜壁にひびが入る
- 유리창이 깨지다　玻璃碎了｜窓ガラスが割れる
- 자물쇠가 부러지다　锁断了｜錠が折れる
- 계단이 부서지다　阶梯破碎｜階段が壊れる
- 보일러가 고장 나다　锅炉出故障｜ボイラーが故障する
- 수도꼭지가 새다　水龙头漏水｜蛇口から水が漏れる
- 싱크대 물이 새다　水槽漏｜シンク台から水が漏れる
- 배수구가 / 변기가 막히다　排水口 / 马桶堵住｜排水口が / 便器がつまる
- 파이프가 얼다　钢管被冻了｜パイプが凍る

교실　Classroom｜教室｜教室　p.83

- 앉으세요　请坐｜座ってください
- 일어나세요　请起来｜立ってください
- 다시 한 번 설명해 주세요　请再讲一次｜もう一度説明してください
- 읽어보세요　请读｜読んでください
- 써보세요　请写｜書いてください
- 따라 하세요　跟读｜では、一緒に
- 잘 들으세요　请听好｜よく聞いてください
- 숙제가 있습니다　有作业｜宿題があります
- 토론하다　讨论｜討論する
- 발표하다　发言｜発表する
- 공책에 쓰다　写在笔记本上｜ノートに書く
- 지우개로 지우다　用橡皮擦｜消しゴムで消す
- 질문하다　提问题｜質問する
- 학생들이 떠들다　学生喧嚷｜学生が騒ぐ

163

- 수업이 시작되다 / 끝나다　　上课 / 下课｜授業が始まる / 終わる
- 교실로 / 교실에 들어오다　　进教室｜教室に入ってくる
- 출석을 부르다　　点名｜出席をとる
- 대답하다　　喊到｜答える
- 사전을 빌려주다　　借词典｜辞典を貸す
- 단어를 찾다　　查单词｜単語を探す
- 단어를 암기하다　　背单词｜単語を暗記する
- 숙제를 제출하다　　提交作业｜宿題を提出する

도서관　Library｜图书馆｜図書館　　p.87
- 책을 신청하다　　申请书｜本を申請する
- 도서를 예약하다　　预订图书｜図書を予約する
- 목차를 보다　　查目录｜目次を見る
- 컴퓨터로 (도서를 / 책을) 검색하다　　用电脑检索 (图书 / 书)｜コンピューターで (図書 / 本を) 検索する
- 책을 찾다　　找书｜本を探す
- 대출 중이다　　出借中｜貸し出し中である
- 연체료를 지불하다　　付延期费｜延滞料を払う
- 복사하다　　复印｜コピーする
- 책을 빌리다 / 반납하다　　借书 / 还书｜本を借りる / 返す

사무실 1　Office 1｜办公室 1｜事務室 1　　p.91
- 인사하다　　问候｜挨拶する
- 명함을 주고받다　　交换名片｜名刺を交換する
- 악수하다　　握手｜握手する
- 자신을 소개하다　　自我介绍｜自分を紹介する
- 사무실을 안내하다　　介绍办公室｜事務室に案内する
- 업무를 설명하다　　介绍业务｜業務を説明する
- 회의하다　　开会｜会議する
- 협상하다　　协商｜協議する
- 접대하다　　招待｜接待する

사무실 2　Office 2｜办公室 2｜事務室 2　　p.92
- 출근하다　　上班｜出勤する
- 퇴근하다　　下班｜退勤する
- 전화하다　　打电话｜電話する
- 서류에 사인하다　　在文件上签字｜書類にサインする
- 보고서를 작성하다　　写报告｜報告書を作成する
- 결재를 올리다　　提交报告｜(上司に) 決裁をあげる
- 도장을 찍다　　盖章｜印を押す

전화　Telephone｜电话｜電話　　p.93
- 전화를 걸다 / 끊다　　打电话 / 挂｜電話を掛ける / 切る
- 전화를 잘못 걸다　　打错电话｜電話を掛けまちがう
- 응답기를 확인하다　　接听留言｜留守電を確認する
- 전화번호부를 찾다　　找电话簿｜電話帳で探す
- 114에 문의하다　　问114｜114に問い合わせる

컴퓨터　Computer｜电脑｜コンピューター　　p.95
- 컴퓨터를 켜다 / 끄다　　开电脑 / 关｜パソコンをつける / 消す
- 메일을 확인하다 / 체크하다　　打开｜メールを確認する / チェックする
- 마우스를 클릭하다　　点击鼠标｜マウスをクリックする
- 문서를 작성하다　　写文件｜文書を作成する
- 디스켓을 넣다 / 빼다　　放软盘 / 拔｜ディスクを入れる / 抜く
- 파일을 열다 / 닫다　　打开文件 / 关｜ファイルを開く / 閉じる
- 파일을 불러오다　　打开文件｜ファイルを呼びだす
- 파일을 복사하다　　复印文件｜ファイルをコピーする
- 파일을 저장하다　　保存文件｜ファイルを保存する
- 파일을 삭제하다　　删除文件｜ファイルを削除する
- 파일을 전송하다　　发送文件｜ファイルを転送する
- 그림을 스캔하다　　扫描图片｜絵をスキャンする
- 출력하다 / 프린트하다　　打印｜出力する / プリントする
- 자료를 백업하다　　备份资料｜資料をバックアップする
- 문서를 편집하다　　编辑文件｜文書を編集する
- 자료를 다운받다　　下载资料｜資料をダウンロードする
- 컴퓨터가 다운되다　　死机｜コンピューターがダウンする
- 바이러스 체크하다　　检查病毒｜ウイルスチェックをする

E-mail　Email｜电子邮件｜E-mail　　p.97
- 로그인하다　　登陆｜ログインする
- 로그아웃하다　　退出｜ログアウトする
- 가입 신청하다　　申请会员｜加入申請する
- 아이디와 비밀번호를 넣다 (입력하다)　　输入登陆名与密码｜IDとパスワードを入れる (入力する)
- 새 편지를 확인하다　　打开收件箱｜新しいメールを確認する
- 회신하다　　回复｜返信する
- 메일을 삭제하다　　删除电子邮件｜メールを削除する
- 첨부파일을 보내다 / 받다 / 열다　　发送附件 / 收 / 打开｜添付ファイルを送る / 受け取る / 開く
- 저장하다　　储存｜保存する
- 편지를 읽다 / 쓰다　　读邮件 / 写邮件｜メールを読む / 書く
- 주소록을 보다　　打开通讯录｜住所録を見る

병원　Hospital｜医院｜病院　　p.101
- 접수하다　　挂号｜受付する
- 예약하다　　预约｜予約する
- 진찰을 받다　　做检查｜診察を受ける
- X-ray를 찍다　　拍X片｜レントゲンを撮る
- 검사를 받다　　医诊｜検査を受ける
- 링거를 맞다　　打点滴｜点滴を打つ
- 체온을 재다　　量体温｜体温を測る
- 혈압을 재다　　量血压｜血圧を測る
- 연고를 바르다　　抹软膏｜軟膏を塗る
- 소독하다　　消毒｜消毒する
- 입원하다　　住院｜入院する
- 수술하다　　动手术｜手術する
- 퇴원하다　　出院｜退院する

약국 및 응급처치 Pharmacy and Emergency Care
药店及应急措施 | 薬局、応急処置　p.105

- 다치다　受伤　けがをする
- 의식을 잃다　昏迷　意識を失う
- 쇼크 상태에 있다　休克状态　ショック状態にある
- 심장마비를 일으키다　心脏麻痹　心臓麻痺を起こす
- 알레르기 반응을 보이다　过敏反应　アレルギー反応を見せる
- 화상을 입다　烧伤　やけどをする
- 물에 빠지다　掉水里　水におぼれる
- 질식하다　窒息　窒息する
- 출혈하다　出血　出血する
- 숨을 못 쉬다　不能喘气　息が吸えない
- 뼈가 부러지다　骨折　骨が折れる
- 주사 맞다　打针　注射を受ける
- 약을 먹다　吃药　薬を飲む
- 약을 과다 복용하다　用药过度　薬を過多に服用する
- 요양하다　疗养　療養する

은행 Bank | 银行 | 銀行　p.107

- 입금하다 (돈을 넣다)　存款　入金する(=お金を入れる)
- 출금하다 (돈을 찾다)　取款　お金を引き出す
- 자동현금인출기 이용 방법　使用自动取入款机说明　自動現金引き出し機の利用方法
  1. 현금 카드 또는 통장을 넣는다　放进卡或存折　キャッシュカードまたは、通帳を入れる
  2. 해당 항목을 누른다　按相关键　該当項目を押す
  3. 비밀번호를 누른다　输入密码　暗証番号を押す
  4. 출금 금액을 누른다　输入取款金额　引出金額を押す /입금기에 입금액을 넣는다　把存款金额放进存款机上　入金機に入金額を入れる
  5. 돈을 확인한다　把存款金额放进存款机上　お金を確認する
  6. 명세서와 카드 또는 통장을 받는다　取出清单和卡或存折　明細書とカード、通帳を受け取る

우체국 Post Office | 邮局 | 郵便局　p.109

- 주소를 / 우편번호를 쓰다　写地址 / 邮编　住所を / 郵便番号を書く
- 우표를 붙이다　贴邮票　切手を貼る
- 우체통에 넣다　放进邮箱里　郵便ポストに入れる
- 소포를 포장하다　包装包裹　小包を包装する
- 저울에 달다　称量　秤につるす
- 우체국 소인을 찍다　盖邮局注销印章　郵便局の消印を押す
- 축하카드 / 전보를 보내다　打贺卡 / 电报　お祝いカード / 電報を送る
- 편지 / 소포를 배달하다　送信 / 包裹　手紙 / 小包を配達する
- 우편 / 퀵서비스 / 택배로 보내다　发邮件 / 特快传递 / 宅配送　郵便 / クイックサービス / 宅配便で送る

미용실 / 이발소 Beauty Salon / Barbershop
美容店 / 理发店 | 美容室 / 理髪店　p.111

- 머리를 자르다　剪头　髪を切る
- 컷을 하다　剪短发　カットをする
- 퍼머넌트를 하다　烫发　パーマをする
- 머리를 말다　卷头发　髪を巻く
- 캡을 쓰다　戴热帽　キャップを被る
- 염색하다　染发　髪を染める
- 머리를 올리다　盘头　髪を上げる
- 핀을 꽂다　插发卡　ピンを挿す
- 머리를 땋다　扎辫子　髪を編む
- 고무줄로 묶다　用橡皮筋扎　ゴムで束ねる
- 스프레이를 뿌리다　喷定型剂　スプレーをかける
- 손톱을 정리하다 (다듬다)　修指甲　爪を整える
- 매니큐어를 바르다　抹指甲油　マニキュアを塗る

백화점 / 쇼핑센터 Department Store / Shopping Center
百货商店 / 购物中心 | デパート / ショッピングセンター　p.113

- 사다 (구입하다)　买　買う(購入する)
- 팔다 (판매하다)　卖　売る(販売する)
- 지불하다　支付　支払う
- 반환하다　退货　返品する
- 교환하다　交换　交換する

버스와 택시 Bus and Taxi
公交车与出租车 | バス、タクシー　p.115

- 버스가 오다/가다　公交车到 / 开　バスが来る / 行く
- 버스에 타다　上(公交)车　バスに乗る
- 버스에서 내리다　下(公交)车　バスから降りる
- 요금을 요금함에 넣다　把车费放进收费箱　料金を料金箱に入れる
- 패스카드 / 교통카드를 대다　过交通卡　プリペイドカードをかざす
- 좌석에 앉다　坐上座位　座席に座る
- 좌석에서 일어나다　从座位起来　座席から立つ
- 자리를 양보하다　让座　席を譲る
- 손잡이를 잡다　把手把　手すりにつかまる
- 안내방송을 듣다　听报站广播　案内放送を聞く
- 벨을 누르다　摁车门铃　(降車の) ベルを押す
- 버스를 잘못 타다　坐错车　バスに間違って乗る
- 버스를 놓치다　没赶上(公交)车　バスに乗りそこなう
- 택시를 잡다　叫出租车　タクシーを拾う
- 목적지를 말하다　告诉目的地　目的地を言う

지하철 Subway | 地铁 | 地下鉄　p.117

- 줄을 서다　排队　列に並ぶ
- 표 (정기권, 정액권)를 사다　买票 (定期票, 定额票)　切符 (定期券、定額乗車券) を買う
- 표를 넣다 / 빼다　插卡 / 取卡　切符を入れる / 取る
- 안전선 안쪽에서 기다리다　在安全线以里等候　安全線の内側で待つ
- 지하철이 만원이다　地铁坐满　地下鉄が満員だ

- 지하철을 타다 / 내리다　坐地铁 / 下地铁｜地下鉄に乗る / 降りる
- 환승역에서 갈아타다　在换乘站换车｜乗換駅で乗り換える
- 에스컬레이터를 타다　上自动扶梯｜エスカレーターに乗る
- 개찰구를 통과하다　通过检票口｜改札口を通過する
- 열차가 지연되다　火车延误｜列車が遅れる

교차로　Intersections｜交叉路｜交差点　p.119
- 셀프주유　自己加油｜セルフスタンド
- 자동세차　电动洗车｜自動洗車
- 셀프세차　自己洗车｜セルフ洗車
- 전면주차　正面停车｜前面駐車
- 후면주차　朝后停车｜後方駐車

자동차 운전　Driving Automobiles｜汽车驾驶｜自動車運転　p.123
- 안전벨트를 매다 / 풀다　带安全带 / 解开安全带｜安全ベルトをしめる / はずす
- 시동을 걸다　发动｜エンジンをかける
- 브레이크를 밟다　踩刹车｜ブレーキを踏む
- 사이드 브레이크를 올리다 / 내리다　向上拉手闸 / 向下推｜サイドブレーキを上げる / 下ろす
- 핸들을 조절하다　操纵方向盘｜ハンドルを調節する
- 기어를 넣다　挂挡｜ギアを入れる
- 액셀러레이터를 밟다　踩油门｜アクセルを踏む
- 출발하다 / 도착하다　出发 / 到达｜出発する / 到着する
- 서행하다　慢行｜徐行する
- 경적을 울리다　摁喇叭｜警笛を鳴らす
- 양보하다　让行｜譲る
- 신호가 바뀌다　信号灯变更｜信号が変わる
- 급정거하다　急刹车｜急停止する
- 차선을 바꾸다　变换车道｜車線を変える
- 신호를 기다리다　等信号｜信号を待つ
- 과속하다　超速｜スピードを出しすぎる
- 추돌하다　剐蹭｜追突する
- 신호를 위반하다　违反交通信号｜信号違反をする
- 중앙선을 침범하다　侵犯中央线｜中央線を越える
- 차선을 위반하다　违反行车线｜車線違反をする
- 역주행하다　逆行｜逆走する
- 감시카메라에 찍히다　被摄像机拍照｜監視カメラに撮られる
- 교통경찰관에게 걸리다　被交警发现｜交通警察官にひっかかる
- 딱지를 떼다　开罚单｜切符を切られる
- 음주운전을 하다　酒后驾驶｜飲酒運転する
- 교통사고를 내다　出交通事故｜交通事故を起こす
- 교통사고가 나다　发生交通事故｜交通事故が起こる

자동차 부품　Automobile Parts｜汽车零部件｜自動車部品　p.125
- 배터리를 갈다　换蓄电池｜バッテリーを取り替える
- 오일을 교환하다　换机油｜オイルを交換する
- 타이어(바퀴)를 갈다　换轮胎｜タイヤを取り替える
- 세차를 하다　洗车｜洗車する
- 호스로 물을 뿌리다　用水管喷水｜ホースで水をまく
- 스펀지로 닦다　用海绵擦｜スポンジで磨く
- 마른걸레로 닦다　用干布擦｜空布巾で磨く
- 광택제를 바르다　打蜡｜ワックスを塗る
- 시트를 털다　抖脚踏垫｜シートをはたく
- 엔진오일을 체크하다　检查发动机油｜エンジンオイルをチェックする
- 냉각수를 채우다　加冷却液｜冷却水を満たす
- 보닛을 열다 / 닫다　打开发动机盖 / 关｜ボンネットを開ける / 閉じる

공항　Airport｜机场｜空港　p.127
- 이륙하다　起飞｜離陸する
- 착륙하다　降落｜着陸する
- 경유하다　路径｜経由する
- 결항하다　停航｜欠航する
- 연착하다　晚点｜延着する
- 항공권을 사다　买机票｜航空券を買う
- 짐을 체크하다　检查行李｜荷物をチェックする
- 보안 검사를 통과하다　通过检查｜保安検査を通過する
- 게이트에서 체크인하다　搭乘口检查｜ゲートでチェックインする
- 비행기에 탑승하다　搭乘飞机｜飛行機に搭乗する
- 좌석을 찾다　找座位｜座席を探す
- 안전벨트를 하다　带安全带｜安全ベルトをする
- 수하물을 찾다　取行李｜手荷物を探す

TV와 오디오　Television and Audio｜电视与音响｜TV, オーディオ　p.137
- 텔레비전(TV)을 켜다 / 보다 / 끄다　打开电视 / 看/关｜テレビをつける / 見る / 消す
- 채널을 돌리다　换频道｜チャンネルを回す
- 리모컨을 누르다　按遥控器｜リモコンを押す
- 볼륨을 높이다 / 낮추다　调高音量 / 调低音量｜ボリュームを上げる / 下げる
- 시청하다 / 청취하다　收看 / 收听｜視聴する / 聴取する
- 프로그램을 녹화하다　拍摄节目 / 策划节目｜番組を録画する / 予約する
- 비디오를 켜다 / 끄다　开录像 / 关｜ビデオをつける / 消す
- 녹음하다　录音｜録音する
- 비디오를 빌리다　借录像带｜ビデオを借りる
- 비디오를 반납하다　还录像带｜ビデオを返す
- 건전지를 갈아 끼우다　换电池｜乾電池を取り替える
- 헤드폰(이어폰)을 끼다　戴耳机｜ヘッドホン (イヤホン) をつける
- 주파수를 맞추다　调频｜周波数を合わせる

여행　Travel｜旅行｜旅行　p.139
- 렌터카를 이용하다　用租赁汽车｜レンタカーを利用する
- (숙소를) 예약하다　预订房间｜(宿を) 予約する
- 사진을 찍다　拍照｜写真を撮る
- 야영하다　野营｜野営する

Practical Vocabulary

ㄱ

가게	store	店铺	店
가격	price	价格	価格
가구	furniture	家具	家具
가까이	near	近	近く
가능성	possibility	可能性	可能性
가로	width	横	横
가루	powder	粉	粉
가슴속	in one's mind / heart	心里	心中(しんちゅう)
가요	ballad	歌谣	歌謡
가죽	leather	皮	革
가짜	fake	假	偽物
각각	each	各	それぞれ
각국	each nation	各国	各国
각자	each person	各自	各自
각종	various kinds	各种	各種
간식	snack	零食	間食
감동	strong impression	感动	感動
감사	thanks	感谢	感謝
감상	appreciation (art, etc)	欣赏	感想
감정	emotion	感情	感情
값	price	价	値段
강물	river water	河水	川の水
강제	force	强制	強制
개인	an individual	个人	個人
거리	street	距离	街
거짓	false	虚假	嘘
거짓말	lie	谎言	嘘
걱정	anxiety	担心	心配
건강	health	健康	健康
건너편	the other side	对面	向かい側
건물	building	建筑物	建物
건축	building construction	建筑	建築
걸음	walking	走步	歩み
검사	examination	检查	検査
겁	fear	胆	恐れ
겉	surface	表面	表(おもて)
게임	game	游戏	ゲーム
결과	result	结果	結果
결국	after all	结果	結局
결정	decision	决定	決定
결혼	marriage	结婚	結婚
경기	match	比赛	競技
경기장	sports venue	体育场	競技場
경영	business management	经营	経営
경우	situation	情况	場合
경제적	economic	经济性(的)	経済的
경찰관	police officer	警官	警察官
경치	scenery	景色	景色
경험	experience	经验	経験
곁	side	旁(边)	側(そば)
계란	(hen's) egg	鸡蛋	鶏卵
계산	calculation	计算	計算
계약	contract	合同	契約
계획	plan	计划	計画
고개	the nape	头	うなじ
고개	the pass	山岭	峠
고객	customer	顾客	顧客
고교	high school (abbreviation)	高中	高校
고급	high rank	高级	高級
고기	meat	肉	肉
고등학생	high school student	高中生	高校生
고민	agony	苦恼	悩み
고생	suffering	吃苦	苦労
고속	high-speed	高速	高速
고전	classic(s)	古典	古典
고통	pain	痛苦	苦痛
고향	hometown	故乡	故郷
골목	side street	小巷	路地
골목길	side street	胡同	小路
골프장	golf course	高尔夫球场	ゴルフ場
곳	place	地方	場所
곳곳	here and there	处处	あちこち
공	ball	球	ボール
공간	space	空间	空間
공동	joint	共同	共同
공무원	civil servant	公务员	公務員
공부	study	学习	勉強
공짜	free	免费	無料
과	lesson	课	課
과	department	科	課
과거	the past	过去	過去
과목	subject	课目	科目

과장	an exaggeration	夸张	誇張
과장	department head	科长	課長
과제	task	课题	課題
과학	science	科学	科学
과학자	scientist	科学家	科学者
관계	relationship	关系	関係
관련	relation	相关	関連
관리	management	管理	管理
관습	custom	习惯	慣習
관심	interest	关心	関心
교류	exchange	交流	交流
교문	school gate	校门	校門
교수	professor	教授	教授
교육	education	教育	教育
교통	transportation	交通	交通
교환	change	交换	交換
구경	sightseeing	观看	見物
구멍	hole	洞	穴
구체적	concrete	具体的	具体的
국립	national	国立	国立
국어	national language	国语	国語
국제적	international	国际的	国際的
귀국	return to (one's) country	回国	帰国
규칙	rule(s)	规则	規則
규칙적	regular	规则性	規則的
그날	that (very) day	那天	その日
그늘	shade	荫凉	日陰
그다음	the next	然后	その次
그동안	during that time	这段时间	その間
그때	at that time	那时	その時
그룹	group	集团	グループ
그림	drawing	图画	絵
그림자	shadow	影子	影
그중	among them / those	其中	その中
근무	duty, work	上班	勤務
근처	vicinity, close-by	附近	近所
글	writing	文章	文
글쓰기	composition	写文章	作文
글씨	handwriting	字	(書かれた) 文字
글자	letter	文字	字
금	gold	(黄)金	金
금년	this year	今年	今年
금연	smoking prohibited	禁烟	禁煙
금지	prohibition	禁止	禁止
긍정적	positive	肯定的	肯定的
기간	period	期间	期間
기계	machine	机械	機械
기대	expectation	期待	期待
기도	prayer	祈祷	お祈り
기본	basis, foundation	基本	基本
기분	mood	心情	気分
기쁨	joy	喜悦	喜び
기사 (신문기사)	newspaper article	消息	記事 (新聞記事)
기술	technology, skill	技术	技術
기억	memory	记忆	記憶
기온	(atmospheric) temperature	气温	気温
기운	(personal) energy	力气	気
기자	journalist	记者	記者
기준	standard	标准	基準
기초	basis, foundation	基础	基礎
기침	cough(ing)	咳嗽	咳
기회	chance	机会	機会
긴장	(nervous) tension	紧张	緊張
길	road	路	道
길가	roadside	路边	道端
길거리	street, road	街头	街頭
까닭	reason, cause	原因	原因
까만색	the color black	黑色	黒
꼭대기	summit, peak	顶	頂上
꿈	dream	梦	夢
끝	end	端	先

ㄴ

나머지	the rest	剩余	残り
나물	herbs, wild vegetables	野菜	ナムル
나뭇가지	tree branch	树枝	枝
나뭇잎	tree / bush leaf	树叶	木の葉
나중	the last	以后	あと
나흘	four days	四天	4日間
낙엽	fallen leaf / leaves	落叶	落ち葉
날	day	天	日
남녀	man and woman	男女	男女
남성	the male sex	男性	男性
남쪽	the south	南边	南
남학생	a male student	男学生	男子学生
낱말	word	单词	単語

내년	next year	明年	来年
내용	contents	内容	内容
냄새	smell	气味	におい
노랫소리	the sound of a song	歌声	歌声
노력	effort	努力	努力
노트	note	笔记本	ノート
녹색	green	绿色	緑色
논문	academic paper	论文	論文
농사	farming	农活儿	農業
눈물	tear(s)	眼泪	涙
눈빛	the look / mood of one's eyes	眼神	目つき
눈앞	before one's face	眼前	目の前
느낌	feeling	感觉	感じ
능력	ability	能力	能力

ㄷ

다	all, everything	都	皆
다리(교량)	bridge	桥	橋
다수	a large number	多数	多数
다음	next	下次	次
단맛	sweet (taste)	甜味	甘み
단어	word, vocabulary	单词	単語
단점	shortcoming	短处	短所
단체	group, organization	团体	団体
단편	a short story / film	短篇	短編
달러	dollar	美元	ドル
달빛	moonlight	月光	月光
담배	cigarette, tobacco	香烟	タバコ
담임	homeroom teacher (a teacher in charge)	班主任	担任
답장	reply (to a letter, email)	回信	返書
닷새	five days	五天	5日間
당장	immediately	马上	その場
대답	response (to question)	回答	答え
대부분	most	大部分	大部分
대신	instead of	代替	代わり
대중	the general public	大众	大衆
대중문화	pop culture	大众文化	大衆文化
대표	representative, a delegate	代表	代表
대학교수	university professor	大学教授	大学教授
대학생	university student	大学生	大学生
대화	conversation, dialogue	对话	対話
덕분	indebtedness, favor, thanks	福庇	おかげ
도구	tool, utensil	工具	道具
도둑	thief	小偷	泥棒
도로	road	道路	道路
도움	help, support	帮助	助け
도자기	chinaware, pottery	陶瓷	陶磁器
도중	on the way, en route	途中	途中
도착	arrival	到达	到着
독일어	German	德语	ドイツ語
돌	stone, rock	石头	石
동네	neighborhood, village	小区	町
동물원	zoo	动物园	動物園
동시	the same time	同时	同時
동안 (시간의 길이)	space of time	期间	期間
동양	the Orient, the East	东方	東洋
동쪽	the east	东边	東
동화	children's story	童话	童話
동화책	children's storybook	童话书	童話の本
뒤쪽	the rear, backside	后边	後ろ側
등록	registration	注册	登録
등록금	registration fee	注册费	登録金
디자이너	designer	设计师	デザイナー
땀	sweat	汗	汗
땅	land, earth	地	土地
땅콩	peanut	花生	ピーナッツ
때 (시간)	(point in) time, occasion	时候	時間
뚜껑	cap, lid	盖儿	蓋
뜻	meaning, intent	意思	意味

ㄹ

레스토랑	restaurant	餐厅	レストラン
리듬	rhythm	节奏	リズム

ㅁ

마루	(wooden) floor	地板	板の間
마사지	massage	按摩	マッサージ
마음	mind, heart	心	心
마음속	bottom of one's heart	心里	心中 (しんちゅう)
마중	receiving / welcoming someone	迎接	出迎え
마지막	the last, final	最后	最後
마찬가지	sameness	同样	同じこと
만남	meeting	相逢	出会い
만두	dumpling	饺子	ギョーザ
만약	if, in case	如果	もし
만일	if, by chance	假如	万一
말	word, language	话	言葉

말씀	word(s), language (honorific form)	话(敬语) お言葉
맛	taste	味道 味
맞은편	the other / opposite side	对面 向かい側
매력	attraction, fascination	魅力 魅力
매일	every day	每天 毎日
머릿속	in one's head	脑子里 頭の中
먼지	dust	灰尘 ほこり
멋	smartness, stylishness	风度 おしゃれ
메모	memo	记录 メモ
며칠	a few days, how many days	几天, 几号 何日
명령	an order	命令 命令
모델	model	模特 モデル
모두	all	都 すべて
모습	looks, appearances	样子 姿
모양	shape, form	模样 形
모임	gathering, meeting	聚会 集まり
목소리	voice	声音 声
목욕탕	bathhouse, public bath	澡堂 銭湯
목적	purpose, object	目的 目的
목표	target, goal	目标 目標
몸	body	身体 体
몸무게	body weight	体重 体重
몸살	illness caused by fatigue	四肢酸痛 過労による体調不良
무게	weight	重量 重さ
무더위	hot and humid	酷暑 蒸し暑さ
무역	trade	贸易 貿易
문자	letters, character	文字 文字
문장	writing, a sentence	文章 文章
문제점	the point at issue	问题 問題点
문학	literature	文学 文学
문화	culture	文化 文化
물건	thing, an object	东西 物
물고기, 생선	fish	鱼, 鲜鱼 魚
물론	of course	当然 もちろん
물음	question	疑问 問い
미디어	media	媒体 メディア
미래	future	未来 未来
미소	smile	微笑 微笑
미인	beautiful woman	美人 美人
미팅	"meeting" (type of date)	会议 ミーティング
민족	nation, ethnic group	民族 民族
믿음	trust, faith	信任 信頼

ㅂ

바늘	needle	针 針
바닷가	seashore	海边 海辺
바닷물	seawater	海水 海水
바람	wind	风 風
바보	fool	傻瓜 ばか
박물관	museum (not for art)	博物馆 博物館
박사	doctor, Ph.D.	博士 博士
박수	applause	鼓掌 拍手
반 (절반)	half	一半 半分
반대	opposition	反对 反対
반말	banmal (familiar speech form)	非敬语 ため口
반찬	side dishes	小菜 おかず
받침	a support, prop	韵尾 支え
발견	discovery	发现 発見
발달	development	发达 発達
발생	occurrence	发生 発生
발음	pronunciation	发音 発音
발전	development, growth	发展 発展
발표	announcement	发表 発表
밤낮	night and day	日夜 昼夜
밤중	middle of the night	半夜 夜更け
밥맛	appetite	胃口 ご飯の味
밥솥	rice-cooker	饭锅 ご飯釜
방	a room	房间 部屋
방문 (방문하다)	visit (to call on)	访问 訪問 (訪問する)
방법	method, way	方法 方法
방송	broadcasting	广播 放送
방학	school vacation	放假 (学校の) 休み
밭	field, garden	旱田 畑
배	ship	船 船
배	double, times	倍 倍
배경	background	背景 背景
버릇	habit	习惯 癖
번역	translation	翻译 翻訳
번호	number (in a sequence)	号码 番号
벌레	insect	虫子 虫
변화	change	变化 変化
별	star	星 星
보고	report, information	报告 報告
보고서	written / published report	报告书 報告書
보람	worth	意义 やりがい
보통	normally	普通 普通

보험	insurance	保险	保險
보호	protection	保护	保護
복습	review (study)	复习	復習
볶음밥	stir-fried rice	炒饭	炒めご飯
본래	originally	本来	本来
볼일	errand	事务	用事
부근	neighborhood, vicinity	附近	付近
부분	part, portion	部分	部分
부엌	kitchen	厨房	台所
부자	rich person	富翁	金持ち
부작용	side effect, reaction	副作用	副作用
부잣집	rich person's house	富家	金持ちの家
부장	head of a department	部长	部長
부족	lack, shortage	不足	不足
부족	tribe	部落	部族
부탁	a request, a favor	请求	依頼
북쪽	the north	北边	北
분위기	atmosphere	气氛	雰囲気
불	fire, light	火, 灯	火
불꽃	flame	火花	花火
불만	discontent	不满	不満
불빛	light (from fire, bulb)	火光, 灯光	明かり
불안	anxiety, unrest	不安	不安
비교	comparison	比较	比較
비닐	vinyl	塑料	ビニール
비닐봉지	plastic bag	塑料袋	ビニール袋
비밀	secret	秘密	秘密
비용	cost	费用	費用
비타민	vitamin	维生素	ビタミン
빌딩	building	高楼	ビル
빛	light	光	光
빨래	laundry	洗衣服	洗濯

ㅅ

사고	an accident	事故	事故
사람	person	人	人
사랑	love	爱	愛
사모님	wife of man in respected position	师母	奥様
사무	business, official matters	办公	事務
사물	objects, things	事物	事物
사실	fact, reality	事实	事実
사업	project, enterprise	事业	事業
사용	use, consumption	使用	使用
사용자	user	使用者	使用者
사원	company employee	职员	社員
사장	president (of company)	经理	社長
사투리	dialect	方言	方言
사회	society	社会	社会
사회적	social	社会性(的)	社会的
사흘	three days	三天	3日間
산소	grave, tomb	墓所	墓
살	skin, flesh	肉	肉
상	prize, award	奖	賞
상대	counterpart, opponent	对手	相手
상대방	counterpart, partner	对方	相手方
상상	imagination	想象	想像
상자	box	箱子	箱
상처	wound, cut	伤口	傷
상품	product, goods	商品	商品
새끼	young animal	崽	動物の子
새해	a new year	新年	新年
색	color	色	色
생각	thought, idea	思绪	考え
생신	birthday (honorific form)	生辰	誕生日の尊敬語
생활	(act of) living	生活	生活
생활환경	living environment	生活环境	生活環境
샤워	shower	淋浴	シャワー
서로	mutually, one another	互相	互いに
서류	document	文件	書類
서비스	service	服务	サービス
서양	the West, the Occident	西方	西洋
서쪽	the west	西边	西
석유	oil	石油	石油
선물	gift	礼物	贈り物
선배	predecessor, one with seniority	前辈	先輩
선택	choice	选择	選択
선풍기	electric fan	电风扇	扇風機
설거지	dishwashing	洗碗	皿洗い
설명	explanation	说明	説明
섭씨	centigrade	摄氏	摂氏
성	surname	姓	姓
성격	character, personality	性格	性格
성공	success	成功	成功
성별	sex, gender	性别	性別
성적	grade, result	成绩	成績
세계적	global, worldwide	世界性(的)	世界的

세금	tax	税金	税金
세기	century	世纪	世紀
세로	length, height	竖	縦
세상	the world, society	世上	世の中
세수	face washing	洗脸	洗顔
세탁소	laundromat	洗衣店	洗濯屋
소개	introduction	介绍	紹介
소나기	a passing rain shower	阵雨	夕立
소리	sound	声音	音
소문	rumor	传闻	うわさ
소비자	consumer	消费者	消費者
소설	novel	小说	小説
소설가	novelist	小说家	小説家
소식	tidings, news	消息	消息
속	the inside, the interior	内	中
속담	proverb	俗话	ことわざ
속도	speed	速度	速度
손님	guest, customer	客人	お客
손발	hand and feet	手脚	手足
손뼉	palm of one's hand	掌	手のひら
손수건	handkerchief	手绢	ハンカチ
송이	bunch, cluster (of fruit, flowers)	朵	〜房
쇼	show	表演	ショー
쇼핑	shopping	购物	ショッピング
수돗물	tap / running water	自来水	水道水
수업	teaching, lessons	课	授業
수염	beard, mustache, whiskers	胡子	ひげ
수입	income, revenue	收入	収入
수입	importation	进口	輸入
수출	exportation	出口	輸出
수필	essay, miscellany	随笔	随筆
수학	mathematics	数学	数学
숙소	place where one is staying, lodging	住所	宿泊場所
숙제	homework, task	作业	宿題
순간	moment, an instant	瞬间	瞬間
순서	order, sequence	顺序	順序
술병	liquor bottle	酒瓶	酒瓶
술자리	gathering for a drink	酒席	酒席
술잔	glass (for alcoholic beverage)	酒杯	杯
술집	a drinking establishment	酒吧	飲み屋
숨	breath, respiration	呼吸	息
슈퍼마켓	supermarket	超市	スーパーマーケット
스스로	oneself, by oneself	自己	自ら
스케줄	schedule	日程	スケジュール
스키장	skiing area	滑雪场	スキー場
스타일	style	样式	スタイル
슬픔	sadness	悲哀	悲しみ
습관	habit	习惯	習慣
시대	era	时代	時代
시리즈	series	系列	シリーズ
시민	citizen	市民	市民
시설	facilities, equipment	设施	施設
시인	poet	诗人	詩人
시작	beginning	开始	始め
시장	a market	市场	市場
시절	season, the times	时光	時
시청	city hall	市政府	市庁
식구	members of a family	家人	家族
식빵	sliced bread	主食面包	食パン
식사	a meal	吃饭	食事
식품	food articles	食品	食品
신고	a statement, declaration	申报	申告
신문사	a newspaper company	报社	新聞社
신문지	a newspaper printed on	报纸	新聞紙
신용	confidence, credit	信用	信用
신입생	new student, freshman	新生	新入生
신청	application, petition	申请	申請
신호	signal, gesture	信号	信号
실내	indoors	室内	室内
실력	one's ability, talent	实力	実力
실례	rudeness	失礼	失礼
실수	mistake	过错	失敗
실제	actuality	实际	実際
실패	a failure	失败	失敗
심리	mental state, psychology	心理	心理
심부름	errand	跑腿儿	お使い
싸움	fight, struggle	吵架 / 打架	喧嘩
아까	a moment ago, just now	刚才	さっき
아래쪽	below, lower area	下边	下の方
아래층	downstairs, lower floors	下层	下の階
아무것	anything, something, nothing	什么	何 (も〜ない)
아버님	father (honorific form)	父亲	お父様
아픔	pain, ache	痛	痛み
악수	handshake	握手	握手

안방	inner room, master bedroom	里屋	居間
안전	safety	安全	安全
앞길	the road ahead	前面的路	前の通り
앞뒤	before and behind	前后	前後
앞쪽	the front	前面	前
애인	lover, sweetheart	情人	恋人
야외	in the open, outskirts	野外	野外
약간	some, a little	略微	若干
약속	promise, engagement	约会	約束
어둠	darkness	黑暗	暗がり
어른	adult, grown-up	大人	大人
어머님	mother (honorific form)	母亲	お母様
어젯밤	last night	昨夜	昨夜
언어	language	语言	言語
얼마	how much / many	多少	いくら
업무	business affairs, office work	业务	業務
에너지	energy	能源	エネルギー
여고생	female high school student	女高中生	女子高生
여기저기	here and there	到处	あちこち
여대생	female university student	女大学生	女子大生
여성	woman, women (kind)	女性	女性
여유	room, mental space	余裕	余裕
여직원	female employee	女职员	女子職員
여학생	female student	女学生	女学生
역사가	historian	历史家	歴史家
역사적	historical	历史性	歴史的
역할	role	作用	役割
연구	research	研究	研究
연구소	(research) institute, laboratory	研究所	研究所
연구자	researcher	研究员	研究者
연기	smoke	烟	煙
연락처	contact information	联络处	連絡先
연말	year-end	年底	年末
연세	age (honorific form)	岁数	お年
연습	practice, an exercise	练习	練習
연휴	consecutive holidays	连休	連休
열	heat	热	熱
영상	above zero (temperature)	零上	(気温が)零度以上
영어	the English language	英语	英語
영하	below zero (temperature)	零下	零下
옆방	the adjoining room	隔壁屋	隣の部屋
옆집	the house next door / nearby	隔壁	隣の家
예	an example	例子	例
예상	forecast, expectation	预料	予想
예전	formerly, the old days	以前	昔
예절	etiquette	礼节	礼節
예정	expectation, plan	预定 / 打算	予定
옛날	ancient times, the past	古时	昔
옛날이야기	an old story	昔日故事	昔話
오늘날	these days, nowadays	如今	今日
오래간만, 오랜만	after a long interval	隔了好久	久しぶり
오래전	a long time ago	很久以前	ずっと以前
오랫동안	for a long period of time	好久	長い間
오른발	right foot	右脚	右足
오른손	right hand	右手	右手
온도	temperature	温度	温度
온몸	the whole body	全身	全身
올해	this year	今年	今年
옷	clothing	衣服	衣服
와인	wine	葡萄酒	ワイン
왕	king	国王	王
외국어	a foreign language	外国语	外国語
외국인	a foreigner	外国人	外国人
외출	going out	外出	外出
왼발	left foot	左脚	左足
왼손	left hand	左手	左手
요리	cooking	菜	料理
요즈음, 요즘	these days, nowadays	最近	近頃
요청	request, demand	邀请	要請
욕심	greed	贪心	欲
용돈	pocket money, an allowance	零花钱	小遣い
우리나라	my country	我们国家	わが国
우리말	my national language	我国语	私たちの言葉
운	luck, fortune	运气	運
운전	driving	驾驶	運転
울음	crying	哭	泣くこと
웃어른	one's elders	长辈	目上の人
웃음	laugh(ter), smile	笑	笑い
원래	originally, primarily	原来	元来
웨이터	waiter	男服务员	ウェイター
웬일	what matter, what reason	怎么回事	何ごと
위반	violation	违反	違反
위아래	up and down	上下	上下
위쪽	the upper direction	上边	上の方
위층	the upper floor, upstairs	楼上	上の階
위험	danger, risk	危险	危険

유리	glass	玻璃	ガラス
유리창	(glass) window	玻璃窗	ガラス窓
유명	fame, well known	有名	有名
유학	studying abroad	留学	留学
유학생	student studying abroad	留学生	留学生
유행	fashion	流行	流行
음료수	beverage	饮料	飲み物
음악가	musician	音乐家	音楽家
의견	opinion, view(s)	意见	意見
의미	meaning, significance	意思	意味
이것저것	this and / or that	这个那个	あれこれ
이곳저곳	here and there	到处	あちこち
이날	this day	这天	この日
이동	movement, transfer	移动	移動
이때	at this / that time	这时	この時
이미지	an image	印象	イメージ
이번	this time	这次	この度
이사	moving (one's residence, office)	搬家	引越し
이상	above, beyond	以上	以上
이상	an ideal, goal	理想	理想
이상	oddity	异常	異常
이성	reason, rationality	理性	理性
이야기 (얘기)	conversation, talk	(谈)话	話
이외	except, besides	以外	以外
이용	use, utilize	利用	利用
이웃	the neighborhood	街坊	隣
이웃집	neighbor's house, a house nearby	邻居	隣の家
이유	reason, cause	理由	理由
이익	profit, gain	利益	利益
이전	before said period	以前	以前
이제	now, at this point	现在	今
이튿날	the next / following day	第二天	次の日
이틀	two days	两天	2日間
이하	less than, below	以下	以下
이해	understanding	理解	理解
이후	after this, henceforth	以后	以後
인간	humanity, a human being	人间	人間
인구	population	人口	人口
인기	popularity	人气	人気
인사말	greetings, an introduction	问候语	あいさつの言葉
인삼	ginseng	人参	高麗人参
인상	impression, imprint	印象	印象
인생	life, human existence	人生	人生
인원	the number of persons	人员	人員
인터뷰	interview	采访	インタビュー
인형	a doll	绒布玩具	人形
일기	a diary, journal	日记	日記
일등	first place / rank, first class	一等	一等
일반	general, the whole	一般	一般
일반적	generally	一般的	一般的
일본어	the Japanese language	日语	日本語
일부	a part, section, portion	一部分	一部
일상	every day, daily	日常	日常
일상생활	everyday life	日常生活	日常生活
일정	itinerary, schedule	日程	日程
일주일	one week	一个星期	一週間
일회용	disposable, throwaway	一次性	一回用
일회용품	disposable product	一次性产品	使い捨て用品
임금	pay, wages	租金	賃金
임시	temporary	临时	臨時
임신	pregnancy	怀孕	妊娠
입구	entryway	入口	入り口
입원	hospitalization	住院	入院

ㅈ

자가용	private car	私家车	自家用車
자격	qualification, competence	资格	資格
자기	oneself, self	自己	自己
자동	automation	自动	自動
자료	material, data	资料	資料
자리	a seat, place	位子	席
자신	oneself	自己	自身
자신	self-confidence	自信	自信
자유	freedom	自由	自由
자체	oneself, of itself	本身	自体
작가	an author, writer	作家	作家
작년	last year	去年	昨年
잔	cup, glass	杯子	杯
잔치	feast, party	喜宴	宴
잘못	a fault, mistake	错	過ち
잠	sleep	觉	眠り
잠깐	for a little while	一会儿	しばらくの間
잠시	a short while	暂时	しばらくの間
장난감	a toy	玩具	おもちゃ
장래	the future, the time to come	将来	将来
장르	genre	体裁	ジャンル

장사	business, trade	生意	商売
장소	a place, location	场所	場所
장점	merit, a strong point	长处	長所
재료	ingredients, material	材料	材料
재미	interest, amusement	趣味	面白さ
재산	property, assets	财产	財産
재작년	the year before last	前年	おととし
재채기	sneezing, a sneeze	喷嚏	くしゃみ
저자	an author, writer	著者	著者
저축	saving(s)	储蓄	貯蓄
적	enemy	敌	敵
적극적	positively, actively	积极的	積極的
전	before, previous, former	前	以前
전개	development, expansion	展开	展開
전공	one's specialty, major	专业	専攻
전기	electricity	电(气)	電気
전날	the other day, before	前一天	前日
전문	specialty, expertise	专门	専門
전문가	specialist, expert	专家	専門家
전부	all, the whole	全部	全部
전자	an electron	电子	電子
전체	the whole, totally	全体	全体
전통	tradition	传统	伝統
전화번호	telephone number	电话号码	電話番号
절반	half	一半	半分
젊은이	a young person	年轻人	若者
점수	points	分数	点数
점심	lunch	午饭	昼食
점심때	lunchtime, noontime	中午	昼食時
점심시간	lunch hour	午间	昼食時間
점원	store employee	店员	店員
정	affection	情	情
정거장	train / space station	车站	停留所
정답	the correct answer	正确答案	正答
정도	grade, degree	程度	程度
정리	arrangement	整理	整理
정말	truth, really	真的	本当に
정보	information, data	信息	情報
정상	normalcy	正常	正常
정식	formality, official	正式	正式
정신	mind, spirit, mentality	精神	精神
정신적	mental, emotionally	精神上	精神的
제일	number one, the first	第一	第一
제품	a (manufactured) product	产品	製品
제한	a limit, restriction	限制	制限
조건	a condition, qualification	条件	条件
조금	a little, small quantity	一点儿	少し
조사	an inquiry, examination	调查	調査
조상	ancestor(s)	祖先	先祖
존댓말	honorific language	敬语	尊敬語
졸업생	a graduate	毕业生	卒業生
종류	a kind, sort, type	种类	種類
종이	paper	纸	紙
종이컵	paper cup	纸杯	紙コップ
종일	all day, daylong	整日	終日
종합	synthesis	综合	総合
좌우	left and right	左右	左右
주머니	pocket, mini purse	衣兜	ポケット
주먹	a fist	拳头	こぶし
주변	nearby, surroundings	周边	周辺
주부	housewife	主妇	主婦
주소	one's address	地址	住所
주요	the important, the essential	主要	主要
주위	surroundings	周围	周囲
주제	the theme, subject	主题	テーマ
주택	a residence, dwelling	住宅	住宅
죽	gruel, porridge	粥	粥
죽음	death	死亡	死
준비	preparation	准备	準備
준비물	items one must be brought	备用品	準備する物
줄거리	plot	梗概	あらすじ
중간	the middle, halfway	中间	中間
중국어	the Chinese language	汉语	中国語
중국집	Chinese restaurant	中餐	中国料理屋
중심	center	中心	中心
중요성	importance	重要性	重要性
중학생	middle school student	初中生	中学生
즉시	immediately, at once	马上	即時
즐거움	pleasure, delight	喜悦	楽しみ
증세	symptoms	症状	症状
지금	the present, now	现在	今
지난달	last month	上个月	先月
지난번	last time	上次	先ごろ
지난해	last year	去年	昨年
지붕	a roof	屋顶	屋根
지역	area, region	地区	地域

지점	a spot, point	地点	地点
지하	underground	地下	地下
직업	an occupation, job	职业	職業
직장	one's place of work	工作单位	職場
직접	immediateness, direct	亲自	直接
진짜	the genuine article, really	真的	本物
진출	advance, penetration	打入 / 走进	進出
질	quality	品质	質
질문	question	疑问	質問
질서	order, system	秩序	秩序
짐	load, luggage	行李	荷物
집안	family, household	家里	身内
집중	concentration, centralization	集中	集中
짓	an act, behavior	行为	ふるまい
짜증	temper, irritability	烦躁	嫌気
쪽	page	页	ページ
찌개	stew	汤	チゲ

ㅊ

차남	a second son	次子	次男
차례	order, sequence	顺序	順序
차이	difference, disparity	区别	違い
찬물	cold water	凉水	冷水
찻잔	a teacup	茶杯	湯飲み茶碗
창밖	beyond the window	窗外	窓の外
책임	responsibility	责任	責任
책임자	person responsibility	负责人	責任者
처음	the first time, the beginning	第一次	最初
첫날	first day	第一天	初日
청소	cleaning	清扫	清掃
체육	physical exercise	体育	体育
체중	body weight	体重	体重
초대	invitation	招待	招待
초보	first step, beginner	初步	初歩
초보자	a beginner	新手	初心者
초청장	invitation card	请柬	招請状
최고	the best, highest	最高	最高
최근	the latest, recently	最近	最近
최대	the biggest	最大	最大
최선	the best (choice), one's best	全力	最善
최소한	a minimum	至少	最小限
최초	the first	最初	最初
추억	memory, retrospection	回忆	追憶
축구공	a football	足球	サッカーボール
축제	a festival	狂欢节	祭り
축하	congratulations, celebration	贺喜	お祝い
출구	exit, the way out	出口	出口
출근	going to work	上班	出勤
출발	departure	出发	出発
출입	entering and leaving, admission	出入	出入り
출입문	(first/outer) door	出入口	出入りの門
충격	impact, shock	冲击	衝撃
취직	finding a job, being hired	就业	就職
치료	medical treatment	治疗	治療
친구	friend	朋友	友達
친절	kindness, goodwill	亲切	親切
칭찬	praise, admiration	称赞	賞賛

ㅋ

카페	café	咖啡馆	カフェ
코피	nosebleeding, nose blood	鼻血	鼻血
콤플렉스	a complex	自卑感	コンプレックス
크기	size	大小	大きさ
크리스마스	Christmas	圣诞节	クリスマス
큰길	a main road	马路	大通り
큰소리	a loud voice, shouting	大声	大声
큰일	an important affair	大事	重大なこと
키	height	个子	背丈

ㅌ

탑	a tower, pagoda	塔	塔
태도	attitude, approach	态度	態度
태풍	typhoon	台风	台風
터널	tunnel	隧道	トンネル
테스트	test	考试	テスト
텍스트	text	文章	テキスト
토론	debate	讨论	討論
통	bucket, can	桶	桶
통신	communications, correspondence	通讯	通信
통일	reunification	统一	統一
퇴근	to leave work, be off duty	下班	退勤
특별	special	特别	特別
특징	characteristic	特点	特徴
팀	team	team (团)队	チーム

ㅍ

파도	wave, surf	海浪	波

파일	file	文件	ファイル
파티	party	宴会	パーティー
판단	a judgment, decision	判断	判断
판매	sales, merchandizing	销售	販売
패션	fashion	时装	ファッション
평생	one's whole life, lifelong	一辈子	一生
평소	ordinary times, normally	平时	平素
평화	peace	和平	平和
포스터	poster	海报	ポスター
폭	width, range	幅度	幅
표정	facial expression	表情	表情
표현	an expression	表达	表現
풍경	a landscape, a scene	风景	風景
프로	professional	职业的	プロ
프로, 프로그램	program	程序	プログラム
플라스틱	plastic	塑料	プラスチック
피 (~를 흘리다)	blood	(出)血	血(血を流す)
피로	fatigue	疲惫	疲労
필요	necessity, requirement	必要	必要

ㅎ

하루	a day	一天	一日
하품	a yawn	哈欠	あくび
학기	semester	学期	学期
학년	year, grade	学年	学年
학습	studying (specific material)	学习	学習
학원	private educational institute	补习班	塾, 予備校
한국말	the Korean language	韩国语	韓国語
한국어	the Korean language	韩国语	韓国語
한글	Hangeul, the Korean script	韩文	ハングル
한동안	for quite some time	一阵	しばらく
한번	once	一次	一度
한숨	a breath, relief	叹气	一息
한자	Chinese characters	汉字	漢字
한쪽	one side, one way	一边	一方
한참	for some time, for a time	一阵 / 半天	しばらく
한편	on the other hand	一方面	一方
합격	passing an examination	合格	合格
해결	resolution, solution	解决	解決
해석	interpretation	解释	解釈
햇볕	sunlight	日光	日光
햇빛, 햇살	sunbeam	阳光	日差し
행동	action, movement	行动	行動
행복	happiness, good fortune	幸福	幸福
행사	an event, function	活动	行事
향기	fragrance	香气	香り
현관	the porch, the entrance	门口	玄関
현대	the present day, modern times	现代	現代
현재	the present, now, currently	现在	現在
형님	elder brother (honorific form)	哥哥	お兄さん
혼자	one person, alone	独自	一人で
혼잣말	talking to oneself	自言自语	独り言
홈페이지	homepage	网页	ホームページ
화 (~를 내다)	anger	(发)脾气	怒り(腹を立てる)
확인	confirmation, verification	确认	確認
환경	the environment	环境	環境
환영	welcome, reception	欢迎	歓迎
활동	activity, action	活动	活動
회사	a company	公司	会社
회원	member	会员	会員
회의	a meeting, conference	会议	会議
회장	chairman	会长	会長
효과	effect	效果	効果
후	after (wards)	(之)后	あと
후배	one's junior (s)	晚辈	後輩
휴일	holiday, a day off	假日	休日
흥미	interest, amusement	兴趣	興味
희곡	drama, a play	戏曲	戯曲
희망	hope, aspiration	希望	希望
힘	strength, power	力气	力

Verbs & Adjectives

가

가꾸다	to cultivate	培植	(植物を)育てる
가늘다	to be thin	细	細い
가라앉다	to sink	沉淀 / 沉没	沈む
가리다	to hide	遮掩	遮る
가리다	to pick	分辨	選ぶ
가리키다	to point	指	示す
가지다	to take (with)	具有	持つ
간직하다	to keep, cherish	珍藏	大切にしまっておく
갇히다	to be confined	被关	閉じ込められる
갈다	to change	换	替える
갈다	to be sharpen	磨	研ぐ
갈다	to cultivate	耕 (田)	耕す
갈아입다	to change clothing	换 (衣服)	着替える
감다	to wind round	缠 (绷带)	(糸を) 巻く
감사하다	to audit	监查	監査する
감싸다	to wrap	裹	くるむ
감추다	to hide	藏	隠す
강조하다	to stress	强调	強調する
강하다	to be strong	强	強い
갖추다	to prepare	具备	整える
개다	to clear up	转晴	晴れる
거두다	to gather	收 / 获得	取り入れる
거르다	to skip	隔 / 滤	抜かす
거만하다	to be arrogant	傲慢	傲慢だ
거세다	to be rough	强烈	荒くて強い
거스르다	to oppose	逆	逆らう
거스르다	to give change	找钱	釣り銭をもらう
거절하다	to refuse	拒绝	拒絶する
건네다	to hand over	递给	渡す
건드리다	to touch	招惹 / 触动	触れる
건지다	to pick up	捞	取り出す
걷다	to walk	走 (路)	歩く
걸다	to hang	挂	掛ける
걸다	to initiate a conversation	搭 (话)	(ことばを) かける
걸다	to dial a telephone	打 (电话)	(電話を) かける
걸리다	to hang	被挂上	かかる
걸치다	to extend over	搭 / 披	かかる
검다	to be black	黑	黒い
게으르다	to be lazy	懒	怠惰だ
겪다	to undergo	经历	経験する
견디다	to bear	忍耐	我慢する
결심하다	to resolve (to do something)	决心	決心する
결정하다	to decide	决定	決定する
경쟁하다	to compete	竞争	競争する
경험하다	to experience	经验	経験する
계산하다	to calculate	计算	計算する
계시다	to be (honorific form)	在 (敬语)	いらっしゃる
고르다	to choose	挑选	選ぶ
고백하다	to confess	告白	告白する
고생하다	to suffer	吃苦	苦労する
고장나다	to break (down)	出故障	故障する
구별하다	to distinguish	区别	区別する
구하다	to purchase, ask for	求	求める
구하다	to rescue	救	求める
굵다	to be thick	粗	太い
굽다	to roast, toast, grill	烤	焼く
굽다	to be bent	弯曲	曲がっている
굽히다	to bend	屈服	曲げる
귀국하다	to return to (one's) country	回国	帰国する
그리다	to draw (a sketch, drawing)	画(画儿)	(絵を)描く
그리워하다	to miss	怀念	恋しがる
그립다	to be missed	想念	恋しい
그만하다	to be enough	充分	まあまあだ
근무하다	to be at work	上班	勤務する
긁다	to scratch	搔	搔く
기대다	to lean	靠	寄りかかる
기대하다	to expect	期待	期待する
기도하다	to pray	祈祷	祈る
기록하다	to record	记录	記録する
기르다	to raise	养育	育てる
기억하다	to remember	记忆	記憶する
긴장하다	to be tense	紧张	緊張する
길다	to be long	长	長い
깊다	to be deep	深	深い
깎다	to shave off	削 (果皮)	削る
깔다	to spread	铺	敷く
깨끗하다	to be clean	干净	清潔だ
깨다	to break (a dish)	打碎	(食器を) 割る
깨다	to wake (from sleep)	(睡)醒	(眠りから) 覚める
깨닫다	to realize	领悟	悟る
깨물다	to crunch	咬	噛む
깨우다	to wake up	叫醒	覚ます

178

깨지다	to break	被打碎	壊れる
꺼내다	to pick out (of pocket)	拿出来	取り出す
꺾다	to break	掐 (花)	折る
껴안다	to embrace	搂抱	抱きしめる
꽂다	to stick into	插	差し込む
꾸다	to borrow	借 (钱)	(お金を) 借りる
꾸미다	to decorate	装饰	飾る
꿈꾸다	to dream	做梦	夢を見る
끄다	to extinguish	关 (灯) / 灭 (火)	消す
끊다	to cut off	断 / 戒 (烟, 酒)	切る
끌다	to pull	拖	引きずる
끌리다	to be drawn	被拉	引かれる
끓다	to boil	沸	沸く
끓이다	to make boil	烧 (使动)	沸かす
끝나다	to come to an end	结束	終わる
끼다	to join	夹	加わる
끼다	to wear (eyewear)	戴 (眼镜)	(眼鏡を) かける
끼우다	to insert	夹	挟む

나

나가다	to go out	出去	出る
나누다	to divide	分 / 分成	分ける
나뉘다	to be divided into	被分成	分けられる
나쁘다	to be bad	不好 / 坏	悪い
나오다	to come out of	出来	出てくる
나타나다	to appear	出现	現れる
날다	to fly	飞	飛ぶ
날씬하다	to be thin	苗条	すらっとしている
날아가다	to fly away	飞走	飛んでいく
날아오다	to fly over	飞来	飛んでくる
남기다	to leave	剩下 / 留下	残す
남다	to remain	剩余 / 留下	余る
낫다	to be better	比…更好	優れている
낭비하다	to waste	浪费	浪費する
낮다	to be low	低	低い
낮추다	to lower	降低	低くする
낯설다	to be unfamiliar	陌生	見慣れない
낳다	to bear (children)	生 / 下 (蛋)	生む
내다보다	to look out over	向外看	外を見る
내던지다	to throw (away from)	扔出去	勢いよく投げる
내려가다	to descend	下去	下りてゆく
내려오다	to come down	下来	下りてくる
내리다	to come down of	下 (车)	下りる
내리다	to fall (snow, rain)	下 (雨 / 雪)	降る
내밀다	to protrude	伸出	突き出る
내뱉다	to spit out	吐出	吐き出す
내버리다	to throw away	扔掉	捨てる
냉정하다	to be cold	冷静	薄情で冷たい
넉넉하다	to be plentiful	充足	十分だ
넓다	to be wide	宽	広い
넘다	to exceed	超过	あふれる
넘어가다	to cross over (border)	越过	越える
넘어지다	to fall	跌倒	倒れる
넘치다	to overflow	溢出 / 充满	あふれる
넣다	to put in	放进	入れる
노랗다	to be yellow	黄	黄色い
노래하다	to sing	唱歌	歌う
노력하다	to endeavor	努力	努力する
녹다	to melt	溶化 / 融化	溶ける
녹이다	to make melt	销熔	溶かす
놀다	to play	玩儿	遊ぶ
놀라다	to be surprised	吃惊	驚く
놀리다	to tease	玩弄	からかう
높다	to be high	高	高い
높이다	to elevate	提高	高める
놓다	to set (down)	放	置く
누르다	to press	按	押す
눈치채다	to sense	察觉	気づく
눕다	to lie down	躺	横になる
느끼다	to feel	感觉	感じる
느리다	to be slow	慢	のろい
늘다	to increase	增长	増える
늘리다	to make increase	增长 (使动)	伸ばす
늙다	to grow old	老	年を取る
늦다	to be late	晚	遅い

다

다가가다	to approach	靠近	近寄る
다녀오다	to be back, to go and see	去回来	行って来る
다니다	to go to and from	来往	通う
다듬다	to trim	修整	整える
다르다	to be different	不同	異なっている
다물다	to close (one's lips)	闭 (嘴 / 口)	つぐむ
다짐하다	to pledge	决心	誓う
다치다	to get hurt	受伤	けがをする
다투다	to quarrel	吵架	けんかする
닦다	to polish	擦	磨く
단순하다	to be simple	单纯	単純だ

닫다	to close	关	閉める
달다	to hang	带	(名札を) ぶら下げる
달다	to weigh	称	(重さを) 量る
달래다	to calm (down)	哄	慰める
달려가다	to run to	跑去	走って行く
달려오다	to come running	跑来	走って来る
달리다	to run	跑	走る
달아나다	to run off, to escape	逃跑	逃げる
닮다	to look like	像	似る
담그다	to soak (in liquid)	泡	漬ける
담다	to put into	盛	盛る
대접하다	to entertain	接待	もてなす
더럽다	to be dirty	脏	汚い
던지다	to throw	扔	投げる
덜다	to deduct	减轻	減らす
덮다	to cover	覆盖	覆う
덮이다	to be covered	被覆	覆われる
데려가다	to take (a person somewhere)	带走	連れて行く
도망가다	to escape	逃跑	逃げる
(운동장을)돌다	to go round	转 (操场)	(運動場を) 回る
돌아다니다	to wander about	游	歩き回る
돌아보다	to look back	回头看 / 回顾	振り返って見る
돕다	to help	帮助	手伝う
되다	to become	成	なる
두껍다	to be thick	厚	厚い
뒤지다	to fall behind	落后	立ち後れる
뒤지다	to search	翻	くまなく探す
드리다	to give (honorific form)	赠 (敬语)	差し上げる
듣다	to listen	听	聞く
들다	to hold	拿	持つ
들리다	to hear	听见	聞こえる
때다	to make a fire	烧(火)	(火を) たく
떨다	to tremble	发抖	震える
떨리다	to be trembling	发抖 (被动)	震える
떨어뜨리다	to drop	掉	落とす
떼다	to take off	撕下	はがす
똑똑하다	to be smart	聪明	明瞭だ
뚫다	to bore	穿孔 / 钻(墙)	貫通する
뚱뚱하다	to be fat	胖	太っている
뛰어가다	to run (to)	跑去	走って行く
뜨겁다	to be hot	热	熱い
뜨다	to float (on water)	漂	浮く
뜨다	to fly (into sky)	飞	浮く
뜯다	to tear down	拆	取る
띠다	to assume duty, to be charged with	带	帯びる

마

마르다	to dry up	干	乾く
막다	to block	堵	ふさぐ
만족하다	to be satisfied	满足	満足する
말다	to roll	卷	巻く
말리다	to dry	晾干	乾かす
맛보다	to taste	品尝	味わう
망설이다	to hesitate	犹豫	ためらう
망하다	to go to ruin	破产	滅びる
맞다	to be right	对, 合适	当たる
맞다	to receive (a guest)	迎接	迎える
맞다	to be hit	挨打	殴られる
맡다	to be entrusted with	担任	受け持つ
매다	to tie	系	結ぶ
머물다	to stay	停留	止まる
먹다	to eat (food)	吃	食べる
멀다	to go blind	失明	目が見えなくなる
멀다	to be far	远	(距離が) 遠い
멋지다	to be gorgeous	精彩	すてきだ
메다	to shoulder (a bag)	扛	担ぐ
명령하다	to command	命令	命令する
모자라다	to be insufficient	不够	足りない
무겁다	to be heavy	重	重い
무덥다	to be sultry	闷热	蒸し暑い
무시하다	to disregard	无视	無視する
묵다	to stay (in a hotel)	住	泊まる
묶다	to bind	捆绑	くくる
묻다	to ask	问	聞く
묻다	to bury	埋	埋める
묻다	to be stained	粘	付く
묻히다	to get buried	被埋	埋もれる
물다	to bite on	咬	噛む
미끄러지다	to slide	滑	滑る
미루다	to put off	推迟	延ばす
미치다	to be crazy	疯	狂う
밀다	to push	推	押す

바

바르다	to paint	抹 / 涂	塗る
바르다	to be straight	正直	正しい
반성하다	to reflect	反省	反省する

반짝이다	to shine	闪烁	きらめく
반하다	to fall in love with	迷恋	惚れる
받다	to receive	接受	受け取る
발견하다	to discover	发现	発見する
발달하다	to grow	发达	発達する
밟다	to step	踩	踏む
방해하다	to obstruct	妨碍	妨害する
배고프다	to be hungry	饿	空腹だ
뱉다	to spit (out)	吐	吐く
버리다	to discard	扔掉 / 抛弃	捨てる
벌리다	to spread open	张开/展开	あける
벗기다	to remove (clothes)	脱 (使动)	脱がせる
베다	to cut (off)	割	刈る
병들다	to become diseased	生病	病気にかかる
보관하다	to maintain custody of (object)	保管	保管する
보내다	to send (object, person)	派 / 送	送る
보다	to see	看	見る
보살피다	to take care of	照顾	面倒を見る
보이다	to show	看见	見える
복잡하다	to be complicated	复杂	複雑だ
볶다	to roast	炒	炒る
뵙다	to meet (honorific form)	见 (敬语)	お目にかかる
부끄러워하다	to feel shame	害羞	恥らう
부드럽다	to be soft	柔和	柔らかい
부딪히다	to hit	碰撞	ぶつかる
부르다	to call out to	叫	呼ぶ
부서지다	to break	破碎	砕ける
부지런하다	to be diligent	勤快	勤勉だ
부치다	to send (a letter)	寄	送る
불다	to blow	吹 (口哨) / 刮 (风)	吹く
불쌍하다	to be poor	可怜	気の毒だ
붉다	to be red	红	赤い
붓다	to have a bloated face	发肿	(顔が)腫れる
붓다	to pour (liquid)	倒 (水)	(水を)注ぐ
붙잡다	to seize	抓住	つかむ
비교하다	to compare	比较	比較する
비비다	to rub (one's eyes)	揉 (眼睛)	こする
비비다	to mix (food)	拌 (饭)	混ぜ合わせる
비슷하다	to be similar	相似	似ている
비싸다	to be expensive	贵	高い
비웃다	to laugh at	嘲笑	あざ笑う
비참하다	to be pitiable	悲惨	悲惨だ
비틀거리다	to totter	踉跄	ふらふら歩く
빌다	to pray	祈求	祈る
빌리다	to lend	借	借りる
빠르다	to be fast	快	速い
빨갛다	to be red	红	赤い
빨다	to do laundry	洗 (衣服)	(洗濯を) 洗う
빨다	to suck (on candy)	吸 / 咂	(飴を)なめる
빼다	to pull out	拔 / 扣除	取り除く
빼앗다	to snatch	抢	奪い取る
뺏다	to take away	抢	奪う
뻗다	to stretch out	伸展	伸びる
뽑다	to pull out	拔	引き抜く
뽑다	to select	抽	選ぶ
뿌리다	to sprinkle	撒	まく

사

사과하다	to apologize	道歉	わびる
사귀다	to make friends	结交	付き合う
사납다	to be fierce	凶	荒々しい
산책하다	to take a walk	散步	散歩する
살다	to live	活	生きる
삶다	to boil	煮	茹でる
삼키다	to swallow (food)	吞下	飲み込む
상관없다	to have nothing to do with	无关	関係がない
상하다	to become damaged	伤害 (身体/ 自尊心)	傷む
생각하다	to think	想	考える
생겨나다	to have something new appear	长出来	生じる
생기다	to get	出现 (皱纹) / 发生 (事故)	できる
생활하다	to live, to subsist	生活	生活する
서다	to stand	站立	立つ
서럽다	to be sad	委屈	悲しい
서운하다	to be sorry	舍不得	名残惜しい
서투르다	to be unrefined	不熟练	下手だ
섞다	to mix	混合	混ぜる
설명하다	to explain	说明	説明する
성공하다	to succeed	成功	成功する
세다	to count	数	数える
세다	to be strong	强	強い
세우다	to make stand	立	立てる
소개하다	to introduce	介绍	紹介する
소리치다	to shout	喊	大声を上げる
소중하다	to be precious	珍贵	大事だ
속다	to be cheated	上当	だまされる
속이다	to deceive	欺骗	だます
숨다	to hide	隐藏	隠れる

쉬다	to rest	休息	休む
슬퍼하다	to feel sad	伤心	悲しむ
식사하다	to have a meal	吃饭	食事する
싣다	to load onto	载	載せる
실례하다	to be rude	失礼	失礼する
심다	to plant	种植	植える
싸다	to be inexpensive	便宜	(値段が) 安い
싸다	to wrap	包裹	(包装紙で) 包む
쌓다	to pile	堆积	積む
썩다	to spoil	腐烂	腐る
쏘다	to shoot (gun, arrow)	射(箭)	射る
쓰다	to wear on head (hat, glasses, etc)	戴(帽子)	(帽子を)かぶる
쓰다듬다	to stroke	抚摸	なでる
쓸다	to sweep	扫	掃く
씹다	to chew	嚼	かむ

아

아깝다	to be regrettable	可惜	もったいない
아끼다	to be sparing of	节省	節約する
아끼다	to value	珍惜	大切にする
아쉽다	to feel the lack of	惋惜	物足りない
안기다	to be hugged by	抱(被动)	抱かれる
안내하다	to guide	向导	案内する
안다	to hold (in one's arms)	抱	抱く
안타깝다	to be heartbreaking	心焦	気の毒だ
앓다	to be ill	生病	病む
약속하다	to promise	约	約束する
약하다	to be weak	弱	弱い
얇다	to be thin	薄	薄い
얘기하다	to tell	谈话	話す
어둡다	to be dark	黑暗	暗い
어리석다	to be foolish	愚蠢	愚かだ
어색하다	to be awkward	不自然／尴尬	ぎこちない
엎드리다	to lie prostrate	趴	うつ伏せになる
연습하다	to practice	练习	練習する
오다	to come	来	来る
오래되다	to have been for a long time	很久	古い
올라가다	to go up	上去	登る
옳다	to be right	对	正しい
외우다	to memorize	背	覚える
외출하다	to go out	出门	外出する
용서하다	to forgive	宽恕	許す
운전하다	to drive	驾驶	運転する
움직이다	to move	动	動く
원하다	to want	愿意	願う
위로하다	to comfort	安慰	慰労する
위험하다	to be dangerous	危险	危険だ
유명하다	to be famous	有名	有名だ
유행하다	to be in fashion	流行	流行する
의심하다	to doubt	怀疑	疑う
이기다	to win	赢	勝つ
이다	to be, to become	是	だ
이야기하다	to tell	谈话	話す
이해하다	to understand	理解	理解する
익다	to be ripe	熟	実る
일어서다	to stand up	站起来	立ち上がる
일하다	to work	工作	仕事する
읽다	to read	读	読む
잃어버리다	to lose	丢掉	なくす
입다	to put on	穿	着る
입학하다	to be admitted to school	入学	入学する
있다	to be, to exist	在／有	ある
잊어버리다	to completely forget	忘掉	忘れる

자

자다	to sleep	睡	寝る
자라다	to grow (up)	生长	育つ
자랑하다	to be proud	炫耀	自慢する
자르다	to cut	切断	切る
자연스럽다	to be natural	自然	自然だ
자유롭다	to be free	自由	自由だ
잘못하다	to make a mistake	做错	間違う
잘하다	to do well	擅长	上手だ
잠그다	to lock	锁	しめる
잠들다	to fall asleep	入睡	寝付く
잠자다	to sleep	睡觉	寝る
잡다	to hold on to	抓	つかむ
잡수시다	to eat (honorific form)	吃(敬语)	召し上がる
잡히다	to get caught	被抓(被动)	捕まる
재다	to measure	量	量る
적다	to write	记	(字を) 記す
적다	to be few	少	(量が) 少ない
절약하다	to economize	节约	節約する
점잖다	to be dignified	文雅／稳重	おとなしい
접다	to fold	折	畳む
정답다	to be friendly	亲切	仲がよい
정직하다	to be honest	正直	正直だ

정하다	to decide (on)	定	決める
정확하다	to be accurate	准确	正確だ
조르다	to press (someone to do something)	纠缠	締める
조르다	to tighten	捆紧	せがむ
조심하다	to be careful	小心	用心する
조용하다	to be quiet	安静	静かだ
존경하다	to respect	尊敬	尊敬する
졸다	to doze off	瞌睡	居眠りする
좁다	to be narrow	窄	狭い
죄송하다	to be sorry	抱歉	申し訳ない
주다	to give	给	与える
주무시다	to sleep (honorific form)	安寝 (敬语)	お休みになる
죽이다	to kill	杀	殺す
줄다	to decrease	减少	減る
줍다	to pick up	捡拾	拾う
지내다	to spend time	过 (日子)	過ごす
지다	to be defeated	输	負ける
지우다	to erase	删除	消す
지치다	to be exhausted	疲惫	疲れる
진하다	to be dark (coffee)	浓	濃い
짐작하다	to guess	估计	推測する
집다	to pick up (with thongs, fingers)	夹	握る
짙다	to be dark	浓	濃い
짜다	to wring out	拧 (洗濯を)	絞る
짧다	to be short	短	短い
쫓기다	to be chased	追赶 (被动)	追われる
쫓다	to drive away	追 (赶)	追う
찌다	to steam	蒸	蒸す
찍다	to stamp	盖 (图章)	撮る
찡그리다	to frown	皱眉	しかめる
찢다	to tear	撕开	破る

차

차다	to become filled	满	(水がいっぱいに) 満ちる
차다	to kick	踢	(ボールを) 蹴る
차다	to be cold	凉	(気候が) 肌寒い
차분하다	to be calm	文静	もの静かだ
착하다	to be good	善良	善良だ
참다	to bear	忍耐	我慢する
체하다	to suffer from indigestion	积食	食もたれする
초대하다	to invite	招待	招待する
축하하다	to congratulate	祝贺	祝う
춥다	to be cold	冷	寒い

취직하다	to find a job	就业	就職する
취하다	to become intoxicated	醉	酔う
치다	to strike	打 (球)	打つ
칭찬하다	to praise	称赞	賞賛する

카

켜다	to turn on	点 (灯) / 打 (火)	つける
크다	to be big (in size)	大	(ゾウが) 大きい
크다	to grow (up)	长大	(子供が) 育つ

타

타다	to burn	烧	(火が) 燃える
타다	to get on (a bus)	乘 (车)	(バスに) 乗る
타다	to put in, mix	冲 (水)	(コーヒーを) 入れる
타다	to play (gayageum)	弹 (琴)	(伽耶琴を) 弾く
태우다	to give (someone) a ride	上	焼く
털다	to shake off (dust)	抖	はたく
토하다	to vomit	呕吐	吐く
튼튼하다	to be strong	结实	丈夫だ

파

파다	to dig	挖	掘る
파랗다	to be blue	蓝	青い
팔다	to sell	卖	売る
팔리다	to be sold	卖 (被动)	売れる
편리하다	to be convenient	方便	便利だ
표현하다	to express	表达	表現する
피다	to bloom	开 (花)	咲く
피우다	to set fire to	抽 (烟)	吸う
피하다	to avoid	躲避	避ける

하

하다	to do	做	する
헤매다	to wander	徘徊	さまよう
혼나다	to be scolded	被教训	ひどい目にあう
화내다	to get angry	发火	腹を立てる
후회하다	to regret	后悔	後悔する
훌륭하다	to be excellent	优秀	立派だ
훔치다	to steal	偷	盗む
흉내내다	to imitate	模仿	まねる
흐르다	to flow	流	流れる
흐리다	to be cloudy	阴沉	曇っている
흔들다	to shake	摇	揺する
흘러가다	to flow along	流	流れていく
흥분하다	to be excited	激动	興奮する

Index

ㄱ

한국어	English	中文	日本語	Page
가격표	price list, price tag	价格(表)	価格表	69, 113
가구 광택제	furniture brightener	家具亮洁剂	家具光沢剤	79
가글	gargle	漱口水	うがい薬	77
가득한	full	满满的	いっぱいの	13
가래떡	garaetteok	条糕	カレトック	57
가로등	streetlight	路灯	街灯	118
가로수	tree lining a street	林荫树	街路樹	119
가루약	powdered medicine	药粉	粉薬	105
가방	bag	箱包	鞄	44
가벼운	light	轻轻的	軽い	13
가수	singer	歌手	歌手	137
가스	gas	煤气	ガス	81
가스레인지	gas stove, gas oven	煤气炉	ガスレンジ	73
가스밸브	gas valve	煤气阀门	ガスバルブ	73
가슴	chest	胸脯	胸	26
가습기	humidifier	加湿器	加湿器	101
가야금	gayageum	伽倻琴	カヤグム	132
가옥	house	房屋	家屋	71
가운, 숄	gown, robe	睡袍, 工作服	ガウン、ショール	40, 110
가운데	middle	中间	真ん中	15
가위	scissors	剪刀	はさみ	92
가을	fall	秋	秋	11
가이드	guide	导游	ガイド	139
가정	family, home	家庭	家庭	28
가정부	maid	帮佣手	家政婦	79
가제 (거즈)	gauze	脱脂纱布	ガーゼ	105
가족	family	家族	家族	30
가족여행	family travel	家庭旅行	家族旅行	139
가죽코트	leather coat	皮大衣	レザーコート	40
가지	branch(es)	树枝	枝	140
각도기	protractor	半圆规	分度器	88
간	liver	肝	肝	27
간병인	person attending patient	护理人	看病人	100
간장	soy sauce	酱油	醤油	63
간호사	nurse	护士	看護士	100
갈비	ribs, galbi	牛排, 排骨	カルビ	53, 56
갈비탕	galbitang	排骨汤	カルビタン	56
갈색	brown	棕色(褐色)	茶色	14
갈치	hairtail	带鱼	タチウオ	52
감	persimmon	柿子	柿	51
감기	a cold	感冒	風邪	103
감독	manager, director	总教练,导演	監督	131, 135
감사하다	to thank	感谢	感謝する	35
감시용 카메라	security camera	监视用摄像头	監視用カメラ	107
감시카메라	traffic camera	监视摄像头	監視カメラ	118
감옥 (교도소)	prison	监狱	監獄(刑務所)	155
감자	potato	土豆	ジャガイモ	50
갓길	shoulder of the road	便路	道路の両端	119
강	river	江	川	147
강남	Gangnam	江南	江南	151
강당	lecture hall	礼堂	講堂	85
강도	burglar	强盗	強盗	155
강북	Gangbuk	江北	江北	151
강아지	puppy	小狗	子犬	142
강원도	Gangwon Province	江原道	江原道	150
강의실	classroom	教室	講義室	84
개	dog	狗	犬	142

184

개구리	frog	蛙	カエル	145
개나리	forsythia	连翘	レンギョウ	141
개미	ant	蚂蚁	アリ	145
개인병원	private clinic	个人医院	個人病院	101
개인접시	dish	个人用碟子	銘々皿	68
개인택시	driver-owned taxi	个人出租车	個人タクシー	115
개찰구	ticket gate	检票口	改札口	117
개천절	National Foundation Day	开天节	開天節	153
거들	girdle	腹带	ガードル	42
거래처	client, customer	客户	取引先	91
거문고	geomungo	玄鹤琴	韓国の琴	132
거미	spider	蜘蛛	クモ	145
거실	livingroom	大厅	居間	74
거울	mirror	镜子	鏡	75, 110
거위	goose	鹅	ガチョウ	142
거품	bubbles, foam	泡沫	泡	77
거품기	eggbeater	泡沫机	泡だて器	73
건설업	construction industry	建设行业	建設業	156
건전지	battery	电池	乾電池	137
건조대	clothes rack	晾衣架	物干し台	49
검사	prosecution	检察官	検事	154
검색어	search word	搜索词	検索語	87
검역	quarantine	检疫	検疫	127
검은색	black	黑色	黒	14
검지	index finger	食指	人差し指	27
게	crab	螃蟹	カニ	52
게시판	bulletin board	公告栏	掲示板	83
겨드랑이	armpit	腋窝	わき	27
겨울	winter	冬	冬	11
겨울 방학	winter vacation	寒假	冬休み	89
견	silk	绢	絹	41
결석	absence	缺席	欠席	83
결승전	final(s)	决赛	決勝戦	131
결재파일	file to be approved	批准文件	決裁ファイル	91
결재함	to be approved box	批准文件架	決裁箱	91
결제	payment	结算	決済	23
결혼식	marriage ceremony	婚礼	結婚式	32
경기도	Gyeonggi Province	京畿道	京畿道	150
경력사원	employee with previous experience	资深职员	中途採用社員	91
경로 우대권	special ticket for the elderly	敬老优待券	お年寄り優待券	115
경로석	seat reserved for elderly	敬老席	優先席	115
경매	auction	拍卖	競売	156
경복궁	Gyeongbuk Palace	景福宫	景福宮	153
경비원	guard	警卫	警備員	106
경상남도	Gyeongsangnam-do	庆尚南道	慶尚南道	150
경상북도	Gyeongsangbuk-do	庆尚北道	慶尚北道	150
경적	horn	喇叭	クラクション	125
경찰관	police officer	警察官	警察官	155
경찰서	police station	警察署	警察署	155
계곡	gorge	峡谷	渓谷	147
계급	rank	军衔	階級	159
계단	stairs	楼梯	階段	70
계량기	gauge	计量器	計量器	81
계산(서)	bill, check	清单	計算(書)	23
계산기	calculator	计算器	計算機	92
계산서	check, bill	清单	計算書	69
계절	season	季节	季節	11
계좌번호	account number	账号	口座番号	107
고객 상담실	customer information	接洽室	顧客相談室	107
고구려	Goguryeo	高句丽	高句麗	152
고구마	sweet potato	地瓜	さつまいも	50

고드름	icicle	冰柱	つらら	12
고등어	mackerel	青鱼	サバ	52
고등학교	high school	高中	高校	89
고려	Goryeo	高丽	高麗	152
고릴라	gorilla	大猩猩	ゴリラ	143
고맙다	to be thankful	谢谢	ありがたい	37
고모	(paternal) aunt	姑姑	父の姉妹	31
고모부	husband of one's (paternal) aunt	姑父	父の姉妹の夫	31
고무신	rubber shoes	胶皮鞋	ゴム靴	43
고무장갑	rubber gloves	橡皮手套	ゴム手袋	78, 99
고속도로	expressway	高速公路	高速道路	119
고속도로 통행카드	expressway tollgate ticket	高速通行卡	高速道路通行カード	119
고속버스	long distance bus	长途汽车	高速バス	115
고양이	cat	猫	猫	142
고열	high fever	高烧	高熱	103
고조선	Gojoseon	古朝鲜	古朝鮮	152
고추	red (hot) pepper	辣椒	唐辛子	50
고추잡채	chilli chop suey	辣椒杂菜	コチュチャプチェ	58
고추장	gochujang	辣椒酱	唐辛子みそ	63
고춧가루	chilli powder	辣椒粉	唐辛子粉	63
고혈압	high blood pressure	高血压	高血圧	103
골프	golf	高尔夫球	ゴルフ	131
곰	bear	熊	クマ	143
곰팡이 제거제	mold removal solution	防蛀剂	カビ取り(剤)	79
공개채용	open hiring	公开录用	公開採用	91
공격	attack	攻击	攻撃	159
공과금	public imposts, duties	税金	公共料金	107
공구	tool	工具	工具	80
공군	air force	空军	空軍	159
공기 정화기	air purifier	空气清新剂	空気浄化機	105
공연	performance	演出	公演	134
공예	industrial arts	工艺	工芸	135
공작	peacock	孔雀	クジャク	144
공장	factory	工厂	工場	98
공중전화(기)	public phone	公用电话	公衆電話	85
공지 사항	alerts, notifications	公告	お知らせ	97
공책	notebook	笔记本	ノート	83
공항	airport	机场	空港	126
공항 직원	airport employee	机场服务员	空港職員	127
공항 터미널	airport terminal	机场	空港ターミナル	127
공항버스	airport bus	机场班车	空港リムジンバス	127
공휴일	legal holidays	公休日	公休日	153
과식	overeating	过食	食べ過ぎ	63
과음	overdrinking	酗酒	飲み過ぎ	63
과일	fruit	水果	果物	51
과일주	fruit wine	果子酒	果実酒	55
과자	confectionary	饼干	菓子	61
관광객	tourist	旅客	観光客	139
관광버스	tour bus	旅游班车	観光バス	115
관광지	tourist region	旅游地	観光地	139
관리실 (경비실)	guard box	门卫	管理室 (警備室)	70
관악기	wind instrument	管乐器	管楽器	133
관제탑	control tower	指挥塔	管制塔	127
광고	advertisement	广告	CM	137
광복절	Liberation Day	光复节	光復節	153
광업	mining	矿业	鉱業	156
광역시	metropolitan city	广域市	広域市	151
광주광역시	Gwangju Metropolitan City	光州广域市	クァンジュ広域市	151
광주민주화운동	Gwangju Democratic Campaign	光州民主化运动	光州民主化運動	152
광택제 (왁스)	wax	蜡剂	光沢剤 (ワックス)	125
교과서	textbook	教科书	教科書	83

교복	school uniform	校服	(学校の)制服	41
교수 연구실	professor's office	教授研究室	教授研究室	85
교실	classroom	教室	教室	82
교차로	intersection	交叉路	交差点	118
교통경찰관	traffic cop	交通警察	交通警察官	119
교통법규 위반	violation of traffic regulations	违反交通法	交通違反	115
교통카드	transportation card	交通卡	プリペイドカード	114
교통표지판	traffic sign	交通标志	交通標識板	120
교포	permanent overseas Korean	侨胞	海外同胞	149
교황	pope	教皇	教皇	157
교회	church	教堂	教会	157
구	gu, ward, district	区	区	151
구두	(usually) leather shoes	皮鞋	靴	43
구둣주걱	shoehorn	鞋拔	靴べら	43
구름	cloud	云彩	雲	12
구속	arrest	拘留	拘束	155
구슬치기	marbles	弹玻璃球	宝探し	129
구입 신청	request for purchase	申请购买	購入申請	87
구토	vomiting	呕吐	嘔吐	103
국	soup, broth	汤	汁	67
국가, 나라	state, country	国家	国家、国	149
국경일	state holidays	国庆日	国慶日	153
국그릇	soup/broth bowl	汤碗	吸い物椀	67
국기	national flag	国旗	国旗	83
국내	domestic	国内	国内	149
국내선	domestic flight(s)	国内航线	国内線	127
국내여행	domestic travel	国内旅行	国内旅行	139
국도	national highway	国道	国道	119
국립공원	national park	国立公园	国立公園	139
국민	citizenry	国民	国民	149
국수	noodles	面条	麺類	56, 62
국자	lade, dipper	汤勺	しゃくし	67
국적	citizenship	国籍	国籍	149
국제선	international flight(s)	国际航线	国際線	127
국제우편	international post	国际邮件	国際郵便	109
국회	National Assembly	国会	国会	154
국회의원	member of the National Assembly	国会议员	国会議員	155
국회의장	speaker of the National Assembly	国会议长	国会議長	155
군	gun, county, district	郡	郡	151
군것질	snacking between meals	零食	間食	63
군대	troops, military	军队	軍隊	159
군만두	toasted dumplings	煎饺子	焼きギョーザ	58
군인	soldier	军人	軍人	159
굴	oyster	牡蛎	カキ	52
굽	heel	鞋跟	かかと	43
권투	boxing	拳击	ボクシング	131
귀	ear	耳朵	耳	25
귀걸이	earring	耳环	イヤリング	45
귀마개	earplugs	耳盖, 耳塞	耳あて、耳栓	45, 99
귀앓이	earache	耳痛	耳痛	102
귓불	earlobe	耳垂儿	耳たぶ	25
규격상자	approved-size box	标准箱子	定形ダンボール	109
귤	mandarin orange	橘子	みかん	51
그릇	vessel, container, bowl, dish	餐具	食器	72
그제 (그저께)	the day before yesterday	前天	おととい	11
근교	suburbs	近郊	近郊	151
근로자 (노동자)	worker (laborer)	工人	勤労者 (労働者)	98
글피	two days after tomorrow	大后天	しあさって	11
금강산	Mount Geumgang	金刚山	金剛山	151
금메달	gold medal	金牌	金メダル	131
금성	Venus	金星	金星	146

금식	fasting	禁食	断食	63
금연석	no smoking seat	禁烟席	禁煙席	69
금요일	Friday	星期五	金曜日	10
기내식	inflight meals	机内便餐	機内食	127
기독교	Christianity (Protestantism)	基督教	キリスト教	157
기러기	wild goose	雁	ガン	144
기린	giraffe	麒麟	キリン	143
기분 나쁘다	to be in a bad mood	心情坏	不愉快だ	35
기분 좋다	to be in a good mood	心情好	気持ちが良い	35
기쁘다	to be happy	高兴	嬉しい	35
기숙사	dormitory	宿舍	学生寮	84
기어	gear	变速杆	ギア	125
기타	guitar	吉他	ギター	133
긴 머리	long hair	长发	ロングヘアー	25
긴급전화	emergency telephone	应急电话	緊急電話	119
길이	length	长度	長さ	19
김	dry laver	海苔	海苔	62
김밥	gimbap	紫菜卷饭	のり巻き	57
김초밥	nori maki	紫菜饭卷	のり巻き	59
김치	kimchi	泡菜	キムチ	67
김치냉장고	kimchi refrigerator	泡菜冰箱	キムチ冷蔵庫	73
김치찌개	kimchi jjigae	泡菜汤	キムチチゲ	56
깊이	depth	深度	深さ	19
까마귀	crow	乌鸦	カラス	144
까치	magpie	喜鹊	カササギ	144
깍두기	kkakdugi	萝卜块儿泡菜	カクテギ	66
깐풍기	fried chicken in garlic sauce	干烹鸡	乾烹鶏	58
깨	sesame	芝麻	ゴマ	63
껌	gum	口香糖	ガム	61
꼬리	oxtail	牛尾	尾	53
꼬막	ark shell	泥蚶	ハイガイ	52
꽁치	mackerel pike	秋刀鱼	サンマ	52
꽁치 캔	canned mackerel pike	秋刀鱼罐头	サンマの缶詰	63
꽃꽂이	flower arranging	插花	生け花	129
꽃무늬	flower pattern	花纹	花柄	40
꽃봉오리	bud	花蕾	つぼみ	141
꽃빵	steamed twisted roll	花卷	中国蒸しパン	58
꽃잎	petal	花叶	花びら	141
꽹과리	kkwaenggwari	小锣	鉦 (しょう)	132
꿀	honey	蜂蜜	蜂蜜	63
꿩	pheasant	野鸡	キジ	144
끈	shoestrings	鞋带	紐	43
끌	chisel	凿子	鑿 (のみ)	81
끼어들다	to squeeze into a line of vehicle	插进	割り込む	122

ㄴ

나	I, me, myself	我	私	30
나비	butterfly	蝴蝶	チョウ	145
나쁜	bad	邪恶的	悪い	13
나사	screw	螺丝钉	ねじ	80
나이	age	岁数	歳	28
나일론	nylon	尼龙	ナイロン	41
나침반	compass	指南针	磁石	138
나팔꽃	morning glory	牵牛花	アサガオ	141
낙동강	Nakdong River	洛东江	洛東江	151
낚시	fishing	钓鱼	釣り	128
날개	wings	翅膀	羽	144
남	south	南	南	15
남극	South Pole	南极	南極	149
남대문	Namdaemun	南大门	南大門	153
남동생	younger brother	弟弟	弟	30

남매	brother and sister	兄妹	兄と妹、姉と弟	31
남방	buttondown shirt	衬衫	開襟シャツ	38
남아프리카공화국	Republic of South Africa	南非共和国	南アフリカ共和国	149
남자	man	男人	男	28
남편	husband	丈夫	夫	31
납치	kidnapping	绑架	拉致	155
납품하다	to deliver goods	供货	納品する	98
낮	day	白天	昼	20
내과	internal medicine	内科	内科	101
내부기관	internal organs	内脏器官	内部器官	27
내일	tomorrow	明天	明日	11
냄비	pot	锅	鍋	73
냄비받침	pot stand	锅垫儿	鍋敷き	67
냄비집게	pot lifter	取物夹	鍋つかみ	73
냅킨	napkin	餐巾纸	ナプキン	68
냉면	naengmyeon	冷面	冷麺	56
냉장고	refrigerator	冰箱	冷蔵庫	73
너비	width	宽度	幅	19
너트	nut	螺丝母	ナット	80
네덜란드	the Netherlands	荷兰	オランダ	148
네비게이션	automobile navigation systems	汽车导航器	カーナビ	125
넥타이	necktie	领带	ネクタイ	45
넥타이핀	tie pin	领带夹	ネクタイピン	45
넷째	fourth	第四	4番目	17
노란색	yellow	黄色	黄色	14
노래	singing	唱歌	歌	128
노령산맥	Noryeong Mountains	芦岭山脉	蘆嶺山脈	151
노르웨이	Norway	挪威	ノルウェー	148
노선	line, route	路线	路線	115
노선도	route map	路线图	路線図	115
노선번호	(bus) line number	路线号码	路線番号	114
노약자 보호석	seat reserved for feeble persons	老弱保护席	優先席	117
노인	old person	老人	老人	29
노트북 컴퓨터	laptop	笔记本电脑	ノートパソコン	95
녹차	green tea	绿茶	緑茶	55
녹화방송	filmed television broadcast	录播	録画放送	137
놀랍다	to be surprising	惊人	驚くべきだ	37
놀이	game	游戏	遊び	128
놀이터	playground	儿童游乐场, 游乐场	遊び場	71
농구	basketball	篮球	バスケット	130
농구코트	basketball court	篮球场	バスケットコート	85
농업	agriculture	农业	農業	156
농촌	farm village, farming region	农村	農村	151
높이	height	高度	高さ	19
뇌	brain	脑	脳	27
뇌졸중	stroke	中风	脳卒中	103
누나	elder sister of a man	姐姐	姉	30
눈	snow, eyes	雪, 眼睛	雪、目	12, 24
눈동자	pupil	眼珠	瞳	24
눈썹	eyebrow	眉毛	眉	24
뉴스	news	新闻	ニュース	137
뉴질랜드	New Zealand	新西兰	ニュージーランド	149
느린	slow	慢	遅い	13
느티나무	zelkova tree	榉树	ケヤキ	140
늑대	wolf	狼	オオカミ	143
늙은	old	年迈的	年取った	28
니트	knit	针线衣	ニット	39

ㄷ

| 다리 | leg | 腿 | 脚 | 26 |
| 다리미 | iron | 熨斗 | アイロン | 49 |

다리미판	ironing board	熨斗架	アイロン台	49
다섯째	fifth	第五	5番目	17
다음 주(내주)	next week	下星期	来週	11
다음 페이지	next page	下一页	次のページ	97
다이어리	date book	记事本	ダイアリー	92
다이어트	diet	减肥	ダイエット	63
다큐멘터리	documentary	纪录片	ドキュメンタリー	137
단골	regular customer	常客	得意先	111
단독주택	single-unit housing	单独住宅	1戸建ての家	71
단위	units	单位	単位	18, 19
단풍놀이	an excursion to see autumn tree leaves	赏红叶	紅葉狩り	139
단행본	separate volume	单行本	単行本	87
달	moon	月亮	月	146
달력	calendar	日历	暦	10
달팽이	snail	蜗牛	カタツムリ	145
닭	chicken	鸡	鶏	142
닭고기	chicken (meat)	鸡肉	鶏肉	53
담요	blanket	毯子	毛布	75
답답하다	to be stuffy	烦闷	もどかしい	37
답안지	answer sheet	答卷	解答用紙	88
당구	billiards	台球	ビリヤード	129
당근	carrot	胡萝卜	人参	50
당근주스	carrot juice	胡萝卜汁	キャロットジュース	54
당뇨병	diabetes	糖尿病	糖尿病	103
당면	Chinese noodles	粉丝	春雨	62
당선	election victory	当选	当選	155
당좌수표	check	现金支票	当座小切手	107
당황하다	to be confused	惊慌	あわてている	37
대견하다	to be admirable	了不起	感心だ	35
대구광역시	Daegu Metropolitan City	大丘广域市	テグ広域市	151
대금	daegeum	大琴	韓国固有の横笛	132
대기업	conglomerate	大企业	大企業	91
대기자 번호표	que number, ticket with you number in line	等候票	待合番号	106
대나무	bamboo	竹子	竹	140
대도시	major city	大都市	大都市	151
대동여지도	Daedongyeojido	大东舆地图	大東輿地図	153
대령	colonel	上校	大佐	159
대륙	continent	大陆	大陸	147
대만	Taiwan	台湾	台湾	148
대머리	bald	秃头	はげ頭	25
대문	gate	大门	門	71
대법원	Supreme Court	大法院	大法院(最高裁)	155
대법원장	chief justice of the Supreme Court	大法院长	大法院長	155
대사관	embassy	大使馆	大使館	149
대서양	Atlantic Ocean	大西洋	大西洋	149
대위	captain	大尉	大尉	159
대전광역시	Daejeon Metropolitan City	大田广域市	テジョン広域市	151
대중가요	popular music	大众歌曲	流行歌	133
대중교통	public transportation	公共交通	一般交通手段	115
대추차	jujube tea	枣茶	ナツメ茶	55
대출	book borrowing, loan	借书, 贷款	貸し出し	87, 107
대통령	president	总统	大統領	155
대포	cannon	大炮	大砲	159
대학교	university	大学	大学	89
대학원	graduate school	研究生院	大学院	89
대한민국	Republic of Korea	大韩民国	大韓民国	152
대회	a match	大会	大会	131
댄스	dance	跳舞	ダンス	128
댄스음악	dance music	舞曲	ダンス音楽	133
더위	hot	酷热	暑さ	12

더치 페이	paying separately	AA制	割り勘	23
데스크탑 컴퓨터	desktop computer	台式电脑	デスクトップパソコン	94
덴마크	Denmark	丹麦	デンマーク	148
도	province	道	道	151
도끼	ax	斧头	斧	80
도로 공사중	Road Construction	道路施工	道路工事中	121
도로폭이 좁아짐	Road narrows	两侧变窄	幅員減少	121
도마	cutting board	菜板	まな板	72
도마뱀	lizard	蜥蜴	トカゲ	145
도서	book	图书	図書	86
도서관	library	图书馆	図書館	84, 86
도서명	book title	图书名	書名	86
도시	city	都市	都市	151
도심	city center	市中心	都心	151
도어록	door lock(s)	门锁	ドアロック	125
도움말	Help	帮助	ヘルプ	97
도장	seal, stamp	印章	印鑑	92
독감	influenza	重感冒	インフルエンザ	103
독서	reading	读书	読書	128
독성	Toxic	毒性	毒性	99
독수리	eagle	秃鹫	クロハゲワシ	144
독신	single	独身	独身	28
독일	Germany	德国	ドイツ	148
돈가스	pork cutlet	猪排	豚カツ	59
돋보기안경	reading glasses	花镜	老眼鏡	107
돌아가다	to go back	回去	戻る	123
돌잔치	party marking a baby's first birthday	周岁宴	一歳の誕生日	32
동	east	东	東	15
동갑	of the same age	同岁	同い年	28
동굴	cave	洞	洞窟	147
동대문	Dongdaemun	东大门	東大門	153
동맥	artery	动脉	動脈	27
동메달	bronze medal	铜牌	銅メダル	131
동백	camellia	山茶树	椿	141
동아리	clubs	社团	サークル	89
동아리 방	club room	活动小组房	サークル室	85
동전	coin	硬币	硬貨	22
동전교환기	money changing machine	换铜钱机	コイン両替機	117
동치미	dongchimi	萝卜水泡菜	トンチミ	66
동포	Korean brethren	同胞	同胞	149
돼지	pig	猪	豚	142
돼지고기	pork	猪肉	豚肉	53
되감기	rewind	快倒	巻戻し	136
된장	doenjang	大酱	みそ	63
된장찌개	doenjang jjigae	大酱汤	テンジャンチゲ	56
두건	head towel	头巾	頭巾	79
두꺼비	toad	癞蛤蟆	ヒキガエル	145
두꺼비집	fuse box	熔断器	安全器	81
두꺼운	thick	厚厚的	厚い	13
두렵다	to be afraid of	怕	恐ろしい	37
두부	tofu	豆腐	豆腐	62
두통	headache	头痛	頭痛	102
둘째	second	第二	2番目	17
뒤	rear	后	後ろ	15
드라마	drama	电视剧	ドラマ	137
드라이버	screw driver	改锥	ドライバー	81
드라이어	dryer	吹风机	ドライヤー	111
드럼	drum	架子鼓	ドラム	133
드릴	drill	钻孔机	ドリル	81
든든하다	to be strong, relaible	踏实	心強い	35
듣기시험	listening test	听力考试	聞き取り試験	88

등	back	后背	背中	26
등기	registered mail	挂号邮件	書留	109
등산	mountain climbing	登山	登山	128
등산모자	mountain climbing hat	登山帽	登山帽	44
등산화	mountain-climbing boots	登山鞋	登山靴	43
등심	sirloin	里脊肉	ヒレ	53
디스켓 함	diskette holder	磁盘盒	フロッピーケース	95
디스코 음악	disco	迪斯科音乐	ディスコ音楽	133
디스크	disk	腰间盘突出	椎間板ヘルニア	103
디스크 드라이브	disk drive	磁盘驱动器	ディスクドライブ	94
디자인	design	设计	デザイン	135
디자인하다	to design	设计	デザインする	98
디카폰	phone with digital camera	数码手机	デジタルフォン	93
딱따구리	woodpecker	啄木鸟	キツツキ	144
딱딱한	hard	硬硬的	固い	13
딸	daughter	女儿	娘	31
딸기	strawberry	草莓	イチゴ	51
딸기잼	strawberry jam	草莓酱	イチゴジャム	65
딸기주스	strawberry juice	草莓汁	イチゴジュース	54
땀띠	heat rashes	痱子	あせも	103
때수건	plastic towel for scrubbing	搓澡巾	かすりタオル	77
떡	rice cake	米糕	餅	57
떡국	rice cake soup	米糕汤	トックク (お雑煮)	56
떡볶이	tteokbokki	炒米糕	トッポッキ	57
뚝배기	earthenware bowl	沙锅	土鍋	67
뜨개질	knitting	编织	編み物	129
뜰	yard	庭	庭	71

ㄹ

라디오	radio	收音机	ラジオ	137
라면	ramyeon	拉面	ラーメン	57
라볶이	rabokki	拉面炒年糕	ラボッキ	57
라이터	lighter	打火机	ライター	138
램프	lamp	煤油灯	ランプ	75
랩	rap	说唱	ラップ	133
랩실 (어학실)	language laboratory	语音室	ＬＬ教室	88
러시아	Russia	俄罗斯	ロシア	148
레게	reggae	牙买加的传统音乐	レゲエ	133
레몬	lemon	柠檬	レモン	51
레버	lever	杠杆	レバー	125
레슬링	wrestling	国际摔跤	レスリング	131
레이온	rayon	人造纤维	レーヨン	41
로그아웃	logout	退出	ログアウト	97
로그인	login	登录	ログイン	97
로션	lotion	乳液	ローション	46
록	rock	摇滚乐	ロック	133
롤	roll	卷发筒	ロール	111
리	ri, subdivision of a myeon	里	里	151
리모컨	remote control	遥控器	リモコン	136
린스 (컨디셔너)	conditioner	护发素	リンス (コンディショナー)	76
립스틱	lipstick	口红	リップスティック	46
링거	Ringer's solution	点滴	点滴	100

ㅁ

마	hemp	麻	麻	41
마가린	margarine	人造黄油	マーガリン	63
마늘	garlic	大蒜	にんにく	50
마당	yard	院子	中庭	71
마라톤	marathon	马拉松	マラソン	131
마룻바닥	wooden floor	地板	板の間	74
마른걸레	dry floorcloth	干布	乾いた雑巾	78

마리아	Mary	玛丽亚	マリア	157
마스카라	mascara	睫毛膏	マスカラ	46
마스크	mask	口罩	マスク	45
마요네즈	mayonnaise	沙拉酱	マヨネーズ	62
마우스	mouse	鼠标	マウス	94
마우스 패드	mouse pad	鼠标垫	マウスパッド	94
마을	village, hamlet, neighborhood	村庄	村	151
마을버스	neighborhood bus	小区班车	近隣バス	115
마이크	microphone	麦克风 (话筒)	マイク	137
마파두부	ma po bean curd	麻婆豆腐	マーボ豆腐	58
막걸리	makgeolri	米酒	マッカリ	55
막내	lastborn	老幺	末っ子	31
만둣국	dumpling soup	饺子汤	マンドゥクック (餃子入りスープ)	56
만만하다	to be easy	小看	くみしやすい	37
만족하다	to be satisfactory	满足	満足だ	35
말	horse	马	馬	142
말레이시아	Malaysia	马来西亚	マレーシア	148
맑음	clear	晴天	晴れ	12
망명	defection	亡命	亡命	149
망아지	foal	马驹子	子馬	142
망치	hammer	锤子	かなづち	80
매니큐어	manicure	指甲油	マニキュア	46
매미	cicada	蝉	セミ	145
매실주	apricot/plum brandy	杨梅酒	梅酒	55
매출액	(amount of) sales	销售额	売上高	91
매트리스	mattress	床垫	マットレス	75
매표소	ticket office	售票处	チケット売り場, きっぷ売り場	117, 135
매화	Japanese apricot	梅花	梅	141
맥주	beer	啤酒	ビール	55
머리	head	头	頭	24
머리띠	headband	发带	ヘアバンド	45
머리모양	hair style	发型	ヘアースタイル	25
머리카락	hair	头发	髪の毛	24
머리핀	hairpin	发夹	ヘアピン	45
머큐로크롬	Mercurochrome	红药水	赤チン	105
먼지떨이	duster	掸子	はたき	78
멀미	nausea	晕 (车)	乗り物酔い	103
멀티 탭	multi tab	多用分接头	マルチタップ	94
멍	bruise	淤血	あざ	103
멍게	ascidian	海囊	ホヤ	52
메뉴	menu	菜单	メニュー	64
메뚜기	grasshopper	蚱蜢	トノサマバッタ	145
메리야스	undershirts	针织品	メリヤス	42
메모지	scratch paper	便笺	メモ用紙	92
메밀국수	soba noodles	荞麦面	ざるそば	59
메시지	message	信息	メッセージ	93
메일 주소	mail address	邮件地址	メールアドレス	96
멕시코	Mexico	墨西哥	メキシコ	149
멜빵바지	pants with suspenders	背带裤	つりズボン	38
며느리	daughter-in-law	儿媳妇	嫁	31
면	cotton, myeon, township	棉, 面	綿, 面	41, 151
면 바지	cotton pants	棉裤	綿パン	39
면도기	shaver	剃须刀	みそり	76
면세점	duty free shop	免税店	免税店	127
명소	famous spot, place of interest	名胜古迹	名所	139
명예훼손	defamation of character	损害名誉	名誉毀損	155
명왕성	Pluto	冥王星	冥王星	146
명절	traditional holidays	节日	祝祭日	153
명함	name card	名片	名刺	92
모	fur	毛	毛	41
모기	mosquito	蚊子	カ	145

모니터 (화면)	monitor	显示器	モニター (画面)	94
모뎀	modem	调制解调器	モデム	94
모레	the day after tomorrow	后天	あさって	11
모범택시	deluxe bus	模范出租车	高級タクシー	115
모자	hat	帽	帽子	44
모퉁이	corner	拐角	曲がり角	119
모피코트	fur coat	毛皮大衣	毛皮コート	40
목	neck	脖子	首	26
목 아픔	sore throat	咽喉痛	喉痛	102
목걸이	necklace	项链	ネックレス	45
목구멍	throat	喉咙	喉	27
목도리	winter scarf	围巾	マフラー	45
목련	magnolia	木兰	木蓮	141
목사	minister	牧师	牧師	157
목성	Jupiter	木星	木星	146
목요일	Thursday	星期四	木曜日	10
목욕가운	bathrobe	浴衣	風呂用ガウン	77
목탁	wooden gong	木铎	木魚	157
못	nail	钉子	釘	80
몽골	Mongolia	蒙古	モンゴル	148
무거운	heavy	重重的	重い	13
무관심하다	to be indifferent	无动于衷 (漠不关心)	無関心だ	35
무궁화	Rose of Sharon	无穷花	ムクゲ	141, 153
무늬	pattern(s)	纹儿	柄	40
무대	stage	舞台	舞台	135
무릎	knee	膝盖	膝	27
무선전화기	cordless phone	无线电话机	無線電話機	93
무섭다	to be scary	害怕	怖い	37
무스	mousse	摩丝	ムース	110
무스탕	Mustang	羊皮半大衣	羊皮コート	40
무용	dance	舞蹈	舞踊	135
무용실	dance room	舞蹈室	舞踊室	85
무죄	innocent	无罪	無罪	155
무지개떡	mujigaetteok	彩虹糕	ムジゲトック	57
묵주	rosary	圣珠	ロザリオ	157
문방구	stationery store	文具店	文房具店	85
문어	octopus	章鱼	タコ	52
문자메시지	text message	短信	文字メッセージ	93
문제	question	考题	問題	88
문패	doorplate	门牌	表札	71
문화재	cultural assets / properties	文化遗产	文化財	153
물 티슈	wet tissue	湿巾	ウェットティッシュ	65
물감	water paint	染料	絵の具	134
물걸레	wet floorcloth	湿布	濡れ雑巾	78
물만두	water-boiled dumplings	水饺子	水ギョーザ	58
물방울무늬	polka dotted	水珠纹	水玉模様	40
물뿌리개	sprinkling can	洒水器	じょうろ	81
물수건	wet towel	湿巾	おしぼり	69
물집	blister	水泡	水脹れ	103
물품보관소	left luggage, baggage	存包处	物品保管所	117
뮤지컬	musical	歌舞剧	ミュージカル	135
미국	United States	美国	アメリカ	149
미등	taillight	尾灯	テールライト	124
미사	mass	弥撒	ミサ	157
미사일	missile	导弹	ミサイル	159
미술	art	美术	美術	134
미술관	art gallery, museum	美术馆	美術館	135
미술실	art room	美术室	美術室	85
미안하다	to be sorry	抱歉	申し訳ない	37
미역	brown seaweed	海带	わかめ	62
미용사	beautician	美容师	容師	110

미용실	beauty salon	美容店	美容室	110
미용잡지	beauty magazine	美容杂志	美容雑誌	111
미워하다	to hate	讨厌	憎む	35
믹서	blender	搅拌机	ミキサー	72
민들레	dandelion	蒲公英	タンポポ	141
민박	home stay	农家院	民宿	139
민주주의	democracy	民主主义	民主主義	155
밀가루	flour	白面	小麦粉	62
밑	below	底下	底	15
밑창	sole	鞋底	靴底	43

ㅂ

바가지	dipper, scoop	瓢儿 (葫芦)	ひょうたんで作ったひしゃく	77
바깥쪽	the outside	外边	外側	15
바나나	banana	香蕉	バナナ	51
바다	sea	海洋	海	147
바둑	baduk	围棋	囲碁	129
바바리	trench coat	风雨衣	バーバリーコート	40
바비큐폭찹	barbecue pork chop	烤猪排	ポークチョップ	60
바이러스	virus	病毒	ウイルス	95
바이러스 감염	virus infection	病毒感染	ウイルス感染	97
바이올린	violin	小提琴	バイオリン	133
바지	pants, trousers	裤子	ズボン	38
바코드	bar code	条形码	バーコード	87
밖	outside	外	外	15
반갑다	to be pleased	(见到您) 很高兴	嬉しい	37
반납	book return(ing)	还书	返却	87
반달	half moon	半月	半月	146
반바지	short pants	短裤	半ズボン	38
반송	returned mail	退回	返送	109
반지	ring	戒指	指輪	45
반찬그릇	banchan (side dish) plate	小碟子	おかずの皿	67
반창고	Band-Aid, adhesive bandage	橡皮膏	絆創膏	104
받는 사람	recipient, To:	收件人	受取人	109
받은편지함	inbox	收件夹	受信トレイ	96
발	foot	脚	足	26
발가락	toe	脚指头	足の指	27
발꿈치	heel	脚后跟	かかと	27
발등	the instep of the foot	脚背	足の甲	27
발라드	ballads	叙事曲	バラード	133
발레	ballet	芭蕾舞	バレエ	135
발목	ankle	脚腕	足首	27
발바닥	sole of the foot	脚心	足の裏	27
발신자 (보내는 사람)	From:, sender	发送人	発信者 (送る人)	96
발신자표시창	(display window that shows) caller identification	来电显示窗	発信者表示窓	93
발진	skin rash	出疹子	発疹	103
발찌	ankle bracelet	脚镯	足輪	45
발톱	toenail	脚指甲	足の爪	27
발해	Balhae	渤海	渤海	152
밤	night	夜	夜	20
밥	rice	饭	ご飯	67
밥그릇	rice bowl	饭碗	茶碗	67
밥상	(eating) table	饭桌	食膳	67
밥주걱	rice scoop	饭勺	しゃもじ	67
방광	bladder	膀胱	膀胱	27
방글라데시	Bangladesh	孟加拉国	バングラディシュ	148
방바닥	(bare) floor	地面	部屋の床	75
방사능	radioactive	放射能	放射能	99
방송국	broadcasting station	广播电台	放送局	137

195

방충제	insecticide	防虫剂	防虫剤	79
방향	direction	方向	方向	15
방향 지시등	turn signal	转向灯	方向指示器	124
방향제	aromatic substance	芳香剂	芳香剤	78
배	abdomen, pear	肚子, 梨	腹、梨	27, 51
배구	volleyball	排球	バレーボール	131
배꼽	navel	肚脐	へそ	27
배낭	backpack	背囊	リュックサック	44, 138
배낭여행	backpack travel	背囊旅行	バックパッキング	139
배드민턴	badminton	羽毛球	バドミントン	131
배수구	drain	排水口	排水口	77
배우	actor	演员	俳優	135
배추	Chinese cabbage, pe-tsai	白菜	白菜	50
배탈	stomach upset	坏(拉)肚子	食あたり	103
배터리	battery	电池, 蓄电池	バッテリー	81, 125
백과사전	encyclopedia	百科全书	百科事典	87
백김치	baek kimchi	白泡菜	唐辛子を使わずに漬ける白いキムチ	66
백두산	Mount Baekdu	白头山	白頭山	151
백설기	baekseolgi	白蒸糕	ペクソルギ	57
백신	vaccine	疫苗	ワクチン	95
백제	Baekje	百剂	百済	152
백조	swan	天鹅	ハクチョウ	144
백합	lily	百合	ユリ	141
백화점	department store	百货商店	デパート	112
백화점 카드	department store (credit) card	百货店卡	デパートカード	113
밴드	band	邦迪	バンドエイド	105
밴드스타킹	stockings	长统袜	ガーターストッキング	42
뱀	snake	蛇	ヘビ	145
버너	(gas, oil) burner	燃烧器	バーナー	138
버섯전골	beoseot (mushroom) jeongol	蘑菇火锅	キノコ鍋	56
버스	bus	公交车, 巴士	バス	114
버스 전용	bus lane	公交专用车道	路線バス専用通行帯	121
버스 정류장 (정거장)	bus stop	公交车站	バス停 (停留所)	114
버터	butter	黄油	バター	62
번개	lightening	闪电	稲妻	12
번호	number	学号	番号	88
번호판	license plate	车牌照	ナンバープレート	124
벌	bee	蜜蜂	ハチ	145
범인	criminal	犯人	犯人	155
범죄	crime	犯罪	犯罪	155
범칙금	fine	罚款	罰金	115
범퍼	bumper	保险杠	バンパー	124
법, 법률	law	法律	法、法律	155
법원	court	法院	裁判所	155
법정	court, courtroom	法庭	法廷	154
벚꽃	cherry blossom	樱花	桜	141
벚꽃놀이	cherry blossom viewing party	赏樱花	花見	139
베개	pillow	枕头	枕	75
베란다	veranda	阳台	ベランダ	74
베이컨	bacon	腊肠	ベーコン	53
베인 상처	cut wound	刀伤	切り傷	103
베트남	Vietnam	越南	ベトナム	148
벤치	bench	长椅	ベンチ	85
벨	bell	车门铃	ベル	114
벨기에	Belgium	比利时	ベルギー	148
벨트 (혁대)	belt	腰带	ベルト	45
벽	wall	墙壁	壁	74
변기	toilet	马桶	便器	77
변비	constipation	便秘	便秘	103
변호사	lawyer	律师	弁護士	154
별표	star (on telephone dial)	星号键	星印	93

병사	private	士兵	兵士	159
병실 (입원실)	hospital (room)	病房	病室 (入院部屋)	100
병아리	chick	小鸡	ひよこ	142
병원	hospital	医院	病院	100
보내는 사람	sender, From:	发件人	差出人	108
보낸편지함	outbox	寄件夹	送信トレイ	96
보낼편지함	drafts, unsent mail	草稿夹	下書き	97
보닛	hood	发动机盖	ボンネット	124
보도	pavement, sidewalk	人行道	歩道	119
보드 마카	board marker	白板笔	ボードマーカー	83
보라색	purple	紫色	紫色	14
보름달	full moon	圆月	満月	146
보리	barley	麦	麦	62
보청기	hearing aid	助听器	補聴器	105
보통우편	ordinary post	普通邮件	普通郵便	109
보험료	insurance fee	保险费	保険料	71
보호안경	protective eyewear	保护眼镜	保護メガネ	99
복권	lottery	彩票	宝くじ	107
복도	hallway	走廊	廊下	83
복사실	(photo) copy room	复印室	複写室	87
복숭아	peach	桃	桃	51
복숭아주스	peach juice	桃汁	ピーチジュース	54
복통	stomachache	腹痛	腹痛	102
본관	main building	主楼	本館	85
볼링	bolling	保龄球	ボーリング	131
볼트	bolt	螺栓	ボルト	80
볼펜	ball pen	圆珠笔	ボールペン	88
봄	spring	春	春	11
봉투	envelope	信封	封筒	108
부끄럽다	to be shameful	惭愧	恥ずかしい	35
부대찌개	budae jjigae	什锦汤 (锅)	プデチゲ	56
부동산	real estate	房地产	不動産	156
부드러운	soft	软软的	柔らかい	13
부러워하다	to be envious of	羡慕	うらやましがる	37
부리	beak	喙	くちばし	144
부모	parents	父母	両親	31
부부	married couple	夫妇	夫婦	31
부산광역시	Busan Metropolitan City	釜山广域市	プサン広域市	151
부엉이	owl	猫头鹰	コノハズク	144
부인 (아내, 마누라)	wife	夫人 (妻子, 老婆)	妻	31
부재중 통화	call received while away	未接电话	発信者番号表示	93
부처	Buddha	佛像	仏	157
부츠	boots	靴子	ブーツ	43
부품	parts	零部件	部品	98
북	north, drum	北, 鼓	北、太鼓	15, 132
북극	North Pole	北极	北極	149
분	minute	分	分	20
분리수거 함	garbage can for different classifications of garbage	分装垃圾桶	分別ゴミ回収箱	65
분무기	sprayer	喷水器	噴霧器	49
분수	fractions	分数	分数	19
분수대	fountain	喷水台	噴水	85
분식	snack food	小吃	軽食	57
분실물 센터	lost and found center	失物招领处	紛失物センター	117
분필	chalk	粉笔	チョーク	83
분홍색	pink	粉红色	ピンク	14
불경	scripture	佛经	お経	157
불고기	bulgogi	烤肉	プルゴギ	56
불고기버거	bulgogi burger	烤肉汉堡	プルゴギバーガー	64
불공	mass	佛供	供養	157
불교	Buddhism	佛教	仏教	157

불국사	Bulguk Temple	佛国寺	仏国寺	153
불만스럽다	to be dissatisfactory	不满	不満だ	35
불법	illegality	违法	不法	155
불안하다	to be insecure	不安	不安だ	37
불쾌하다	to be unpleasant	不快	不快だ	35
불편하다	to be uncomfortable	不便	不便だ	35
불행하다	to be unfortunate	不幸	不幸だ	37
붓	writing brush	毛笔	筆	134
붕대	bandage, dressing	绷带	包帯	101
브라질	Brazil	巴西	ブラジル	149
브래지어	bra	胸罩	ブラジャー	42
브레이크	brake	刹车	ブレーキ	125
브로치	brooch	胸针	ブローチ	45
블라우스	blouse	女式衬衫	ブラウス	38
블라인드	blind	遮帘	ブラインド	90
블록	block	街区	ブロック	119
비	rain	雨	雨	12
비극	tragedy	悲剧	悲劇	135
비뇨기과	urology	泌尿科	泌尿器科	101
비누	soap	香皂	石鹸	77
비데	bidet	便洁器	ビデ	77
비둘기	pigeon, dove	鸽子	ハト	144
비디오 카메라	video camera	视频摄像机	ビデオカメラ	136
비디오 플레이어	video player	录像机	ビデオプレーヤー	136
비디오대여점	video rental store	音像店	レンタルビデオ店	137
비디오테이프	video tape	录像带	ビデオテープ	137
비밀번호	password	密码	パスワード、暗証番号	96, 107
비보호	Left Turn Without Signal	非保护	非保護	120
비빔밥	bibimbap	拌饭	ビビンバ	56
비상구	emergency exit	安全出口	非常口	70
비서	secretary	秘书	秘書	91
비수기	slack season	淡季	オフシーズン	139
비스킷	biscuit	饼干	ビスケット	61
비싼	expensive	昂贵的	高い	13
비염	rhinitis	鼻炎	鼻炎	103
비옷	rain clothes	雨衣	雨着	41
비자	visa	签证	ビザ	139
비타민제	vitamin compound	维他命	ビタミン剤	105
비품 보관함	supply cabinet	办公用品保管箱	備品保管箱	91
비프 스테이크 (비후 스테이크)	beef steak	牛排	ビーフステーキ	60
비프커틀릿 (비후가스)	beef cutlet	炸牛排	ビーフカツレツ	60
비행기	airplane	飞机	飛行機	126
빈	empty	空空的	空の	13
빈혈	anemia	贫血	貧血	103
빌라	villa	公寓	(高級な) マンション	71
빗	comb	梳子	櫛	111
빗자루	broom	扫把	ほうき	78
빠른	fast	快	早い	13
빠른우편	express delivery	快速邮件	速達	109
빨간색	red	红色	赤	14
빨래 바구니	laundry basket	洗衣筐	洗濯かご	49
빨래집게	clothes pin	晾衣夹	洗濯バサミ	49
빨랫감	laundry	洗涤物	洗濯物	49
빨랫비누	laundry soap (bar form)	肥皂	洗濯せっけん	49
빨랫줄	clothes line	晾衣绳	洗濯物の干しひも	49
빨리감기	fast forward	快进	早送り	137
빵	bread (pastry)	面包	パン	61
뺨 (볼)	cheek	腮	頬	25
뼈	bone	骨头	骨	27
뿌리	root(s)	树根	根	140

ㅅ

한국어	English	中文	日本語	페이지
사격	shooting	射击	射撃	131
사과	apple	苹果	りんご	51
사기	fraud	欺诈	詐欺	155
사다리 (사다리)	ladder	梯子	はしご	79
사랑하다	to love	爱	愛する	37
사망	death	过世	死亡	33
사무실	office	办公室	事務室	90
사물함	glove compartment	手套箱	私物箱	125
사법부	judicial branch	司法部	司法府	155
사서	librarian	图书管理员	司書	87
사슴	deer	鹿	シカ	143
사용 메일 용량	storage in use	已用空间	使用メールの容量	97
사용 설명서	manual	使用说明书	使用説明書	95
사우디아라비아	Saudi Arabia	沙特阿拉伯	サウジアラビア	148
사위	son-in-law	女婿	婿	31
사이	between	之间	間	15
사이드 미러	sideview mirror	后视镜	サイドミラー	125
사이즈	size	型号	サイズ	41
사자	lion	狮子	ライオン	143
사장실	president's office	经理办公室	社長室	91
사전	dictionary	词典	辞典	83
사진	photograph	照片	写真	135
사진 찍기	photography	拍照	写真を撮る	128
사진기	camera	照相机	カメラ	138
사촌	cousin	堂兄弟	いとこ	31
사탕	candy	糖果	飴	61
산	mountain	山	山	147
산부인과	obstetrics and gynecology	妇产科	産婦人科	101
살균소독기	sterilization device	杀菌消毒器	殺菌消毒機	69
살인	murder	杀人	殺人	155
삼각붕대	triangular bandage	三角绷带	三角巾	105
삼각자	set square, triangle	三角尺	三角定規	88
삼각팬티	briefs	三角内裤	ブリーフ	42
삼겹살	boned rib of pork, samgyeopsal	五花肉	三枚肉	53, 56
삼계탕	samgyetang	参鸡汤	サムゲタン	56
삼국시대	Three Kingdoms Period	三国时代	三国時代	152
삼촌 (숙부)	uncle, younger brother of one's father	叔叔 (叔父)	父の兄弟	31
삽	shovel	铲子	シャベル	80
삽화	illustration	插图	挿絵	135
상의	coat, upper garment	上衣	上着	39
상추	lettuce	生菜	サンチュ	50
상쾌하다	to be refreshing	爽快	爽快だ	35
상품권	gift certificates	商品券	商品券	113
새끼손가락	little finger	小拇指	小指	27
새마을운동	Saemaeul Movement	新农村运动	セマウル運動	152
새벽	dawn	凌晨	明け方	20
새우	shrimp, prawn	虾	エビ	52
새우버거	shrimp burger	虾肉汉堡	エビバーガー	64
색깔	color	颜色	カラー	14
색소폰	saxophone	萨克斯管	サキソホン	133
샌드위치	sandwich	三明治	サンドイッチ	60
샌들	sandals	凉鞋	サンダル	43
샐러드	salad	沙拉	サラダ	60
샘플	sample	样品	サンプル	111
생강차	ginger tea	生姜茶	生姜茶	55
생기 있다	to be animated, lively	有朝气	生き生きとしている	37
생리통	menstrual pain	生理痛	生理痛	103
생머리	straight hair	直发	ストレートヘアー	25
생방송	live broadcast	现场直播	生放送	137

199

한국어	English	中文	日本語	쪽
생산하다	to produce	生产	生産する	98
생선가스	fish cutlet	鱼排	魚フライ	59
생선초밥 (스시)	sushi	寿司	寿司	59
생선회	sashimi	生鱼片	刺身	59
생수	spring water	矿泉水	水	54
생일	birthday	生日	誕生日	28
생일 파티	birthday party	生日宴	誕生パーティー	32
샤워기	shower head	淋浴器	シャワー	77
샤워실	shower room	洗浴室	シャワー室	85
샤워커튼	shower curtain	浴帘	シャワーカーテン	77
샴푸	shampoo	洗发精	シャンプー	76
서	west	西	西	15
서가	bookstack	书架	書架	87
서랍	drawer	抽屉	引き出し	90
서류가방	briefcase	文件包	ブリーフ鞄	44
서류함	filing cabinet	文件箱	書類箱	90
서명, 사인	signature	签字	サイン	107
서비스업	service industry	服务行业	サービス業	156
서예	(East Asian) calligraphy	书法	書道	134
서울특별시	Seoul Metropolis	首尔特别市	ソウル特別市	151
서울 올림픽	Seoul Olympics	首尔奥运会	ソウルオリンピック	152
서점	bookstore	书店	書店	85
석굴암	Seokguram	石窟庵	石窟庵	153
선거	election	选举	選挙	155
선글라스	sunglasses	墨镜 (太阳镜)	サングラス	45
선로	tracks	线路	線路	117
선반	shelf	搁板	棚	72
선생님	teacher	教师	先生	82
선수	athlete	运动员	選手	131
선인장	cactus	仙人掌	サボテン	140
설날	Seollal	春节	元旦	153
설렁탕	seolleongtang	牛杂碎汤	ソルロンタン	56
설사	diarrhea	腹泻	下痢	103
설악산	Mount Seorak	雪岳山	雪岳山	151
설탕	sugar	(食用) 糖	砂糖	63
섬유유연제	fabric conditioner	纤维柔软剂	繊維柔軟剤	49
섬진강	Seomjin River	蟾津江	蟾津江	151
성가대	choir	圣歌队	聖歌隊	157
성경	Bible	圣经	聖書	157
성년식	coming-of-age ceremony	成年仪式	成人式	33
성당	cathedral	教堂	聖堂	157
성수기	high-demand season	旺季	旅行シーズン	139
성악	vocal music	声乐	声楽	133
성인	adult	成人	成人	28
성탄절	Christmas	圣诞节	クリスマス	153
성형외과	plastic surgery	整形外科	成形外科	101
세관	customs	海关	税関	127
세관 직원	customs employee	海关人员	税関職員	127
세면대	washstand	洗面台	洗面台	77
세미나실	seminar room	会议室	セミナー室	85
세숫대야	washbasin, washbowl	洗脸盆	洗面器	77
세일가 (할인가)	sale price	打折价	セール価格 (割引価格)	113
세제	detergent	洗衣粉	洗剤	49
세차장	car wash	洗车场	洗車場	119
세척솔	toilet brush	洗涤刷子	洗浄ブラシ	77
세탁 기호	laundering symbols	洗涤说明	洗濯マーク	49
세탁 망	laundry net	护衣网	洗濯ネット	49
세탁기	laundry machine	洗衣机	洗濯機	49
세트메뉴	set menu	套餐	セットメニュー	65
세트장	a stage / movie set	布景	セット	135
셀프서비스	self service	无服务员餐厅	セルフサービス	69

셋째	third	第三	3番目	17
셔틀버스 승차장	shuttle bus stop	班车站	シャトルバス乗り場	85
소	cow	牛	牛	142
소고기 (쇠고기)	beef	牛肉	牛肉	53
소금	salt	盐	塩	63
소꿉놀이	playing house	儿戏	ままごと	129
소나무	pine tree	松树	マツ	140
소녀	girl	少女	少女	28
소년	boy	少年	少年	28
소독(약)	disinfectant	消毒(药)	消毒(薬)	79, 105
소령	major	少校	少佐	159
소묘	rough drawing	素描	デッサン	135
소백산맥	Sobaek Mountains	小白山脉	小白山脈	151
소비하다	to consume	消费	消費する	98
소시지	sausage	香肠	ソーセージ	53
소아과	pediatrics	儿科	小児科	101
소위	second lieutenant	少尉	少尉	159
소주	soju	烧酒	焼酎	55
소파	sofa	沙发	ソファー	74
소포	package	包裹	小包	109
소풍	picnic	郊游	遠足	89
소형차	compact vehicle	小型车	小型車	119
소형청소기	poterable vacuum	小型吸尘器	小型掃除機	78
소화기	fire extinguisher	消火器	消火器	99
소화전	fire hydrant	消火栓	消火栓	119
소화제	digestive solution	消化剂	消化剤	105
속달	special delivery	快邮	速達	109
속도 계기판	speedometer	速度表	速度計器盤	125
속도측정기	speed measuring (detecting) device	测速器	速度測定器	119
손	hand	手	手	26
손가락	finger	手指头	手の指	26
손녀	granddaughter	孙女	孫娘	31
손등	back of the hand	手背	手の甲	26
손목	wrist	手腕	手首	26
손바닥	palm	手心	手のひら	27
손수건	handkerchief	手绢	ハンカチ	45
손수레	handcart	手推车	手押し車	81, 98
손자	grandson	孙子	(男の)孫	31
손잡이	safety grip	手把	手すり	115
손전등	flashlight	手电筒	懐中電灯	138
손톱	fingernail	手指甲	手の爪	27
손톱깎이	nail cutter	指甲刀	爪切り	46
송아지	calf	牛犊	子牛	142
송편	songpyeon	松糕	ソンピョン	57
숄더백	shoulder bag	挂肩式皮包	ショルダーバッグ	44
수건	towel	毛巾	タオル	76
수교	establish diplomatic relations	建交	修交	149
수녀	nun	修女	修道女	157
수도	capital	首都	首都	151
수도계량기	water guage	自来水计量器	水道計量器	81
수도권	greater capital region	首都圈	首都圏	151
수도꼭지	faucet	水龙头	蛇口	76
수도세	water fees	水费	水道代	71
수동변속	manual transmission	手动变速器	手動変速	125
수두	chicken pox	水痘	水ぼうそう	103
수련회	training gathering	修炼活动	心身鍛錬キャンプ	89
수류탄	grenade	手榴弹	手榴弾	159
수묵화	traditional ink painting	水墨画	水墨画	135
수박	watermelon	西瓜	スイカ	51
수사	investigation	搜查	捜査	155
수상스키	water skiing	滑水运动	水上スキー	131

한국어	English	中文	日本語	Page
수성	Mercury	水星	水星	146
수세미	scrubber	碗刷子	たわし	79
수송하다	to ship (freight)	输送	輸送する	98
수수료	fee	手续费	手数料	107
수술실	surgery room	手术室	手術室	101
수신 확인	confirmation of receipt	回应	受信確認	96
수신자 (받는 사람)	To:, recipient	收件人	受信者 (受け取る人)	96
수영	swimming	游泳	水泳	131
수영복	swimsuit	泳装	水着	41
수영장	swimming pool	游泳馆	プール	85
수요일	Wednesday	星期三	水曜日	10
수저통	spoon stand	餐具盒	箸入れ	68
수제비	sujebi	面片汤	すいとん	57
수줍다	to be shy	害羞	内気だ	35
수채화	watercolor painting	水彩画	水彩画	135
수표	bank check	支票	小切手	23
수하물	baggage	行李	手荷物	126
수하물 찾는 곳	baggage claim area	取行李处	手荷物引渡場	126
수학여행	school excursion	修学旅行	修学旅行	89
숙녀복	(woman's) suit, dress wear	女装	婦人服	40
숙모	aunt, wife of the younger brother of one's father	婶婶 (叔母)	叔母	31
순대	sundae	米肠	スンデ (豚の腸詰め)	57
순두부찌개	sundubu jjigae	嫩豆腐汤	スンドゥブチゲ (豆腐チゲ)	56
숟가락	spoon	勺子	スプーン	67
술	alcoholic drinks	酒	酒	55
숨바꼭질	hide-and-seek	捉迷藏	かくれんぼ	129
숫자 (수)	numbers	数字	数字	16, 17
쉬운	easy	容易的	易しい	13
스님	monk	和尚	お坊さん	157
스무 번째	twentieth	第二十	20番目	17
스웨터	sweater	毛衣	セーター	39
스카프	scarf	丝巾	スカーフ	45
스캐너	scanner	扫描仪	スキャナー	95
스케이트	skating	滑冰	スケート	131
스케치북	sketch book	素描簿	スケッチブック	134
스쿨버스	school bus	学校班车	スクールバス	115
스크린	screen	银幕	スクリーン	135
스키	skiing	滑雪	スキー	130
스키복	ski suit	滑雪运动服	スキーウェアー	41
스킨 (화장수)	skin conditioner	化妆水	スキン (化粧水)	46
스타	a star	明星	スター	135
스터디	study group	小组学习	勉強会	89
스트로 (빨대)	straw	吸管	ストロー	65
스팀기	steamer	蒸汽机	スチーム機	111
스파게티	spaghetti	意大利面	スパゲッティー	60
스파게티 면	spaghetti noodles	意大利面	スパゲッティー (の麺)	62
스패너	wrench	扳手	スパナー	81
스팸메일 차단	spam block	邮件过滤	スパムメール遮断	96
스펀지	sponge	海绵	ポンジ	79
스페어타이어	spare tire	备用轮胎	スペアタイヤ	125
스포츠	sports	体育	スポーツ	130
스프	soup	汤	スープ	60
스프레이	spray	定型剂	スプレー	110
스피커	speaker	音箱	スピーカー	136
슬리퍼	slippers	拖鞋	スリッパ	43
슬립	slip	衬裙	スリップ	42
슬프다	to be sad	悲哀	悲しい	35
습기 제거제	dampness remover	除潮剂	湿気取り(剤)	79
승객	passenger	乘客	乗客	114, 126
승무원	flight attendant	乘务员	乗務員	126

승용차	passenger car	轿车	乗用車	119
승진	promotion	晋升	昇進	33
승차권	passenger ticket	地铁票	乗車券	117
승차권 자동발매기	automated ticket machine	自动售票机	乗車券自動発売機	117
승차문	front door (for entering buss)	上车门	乗車扉	115
승합차	passenger van	面包车	ワゴン車	119
시	hour, city	点, 市	時, 市	20, 151
시간	time	时间	時間	20
시계	watch, clock	手表, 表	時計	45, 75
시골	country, countryside	乡下	田舎	151
시나리오 (희곡)	drama script	剧本	シナリオ (戯曲)	135
시내	downtown	城内	市内	151
시내버스	city route bus	城里公交车	市内バス	115
시럽	syrup	糖浆	シロップ	105
시루떡	sirutteok	蒸糕	シルトック	57
시부모	parents of one's husband	公婆	夫の父母	31
시사회	preview showing	首映式	試写会	135
시아버지	woman's father-in-law	公公	舅	31
시어머니	woman's mother-in-law	婆婆	姑	31
시외	outskirts, outside the city	城外	市外	151
시외버스	inter-city bus	郊区公交车	都市間バス	115
시청자	television viewer	观众	視聴者	137
시트	sheet	床单	シーツ	75
시험	test	考试	試験	88
시험지	test paper	试卷	試験用紙	88
식기세척기	dishwashing machine	洗碗机	食器洗い機	72
식용유	cooking oil	食用油	食用油	63
식초	vinegar	醋	酢	63
식탁	dining table	饭桌	食卓	73
식탁보	tablecloth	饭桌布	テーブルクロス	73
식탁의자	table chairs	饭桌椅子	食卓椅子	73
신나다	to get in high spirits	开心, 兴致勃勃	夢中になる	37
신라	Silla	新罗	新羅	152
신랑	groom	新郎	新郎	28
신문	newspaper	报纸	新聞	87
신문 판매대	newspaper stand	报刊销售亭	新聞販売台	117
신발	footwear	鞋	履物	43
신부	bride, priest	新娘, 神父	新婦, 神父	28, 157
신분증	personal identification	身份证	身分証	107
신사복	(man's) suit	男装	紳士服	40
신용불량	bad credit	信用不良	カード破産	23
신용카드	credit card	信用卡	クレジットカード	23
신입사원	employee without person's first job	新职员	新入社員	91
신장	kidney	肾脏	腎臓	27
신호등	traffic light	信号灯	信号	119
신혼부부	newlywed couple	新婚夫妇	新婚夫婦	28
신혼여행	honeymoon	蜜月旅行	新婚旅行	33
실내등	light	室内灯	室内灯	125
실로폰	xylophone	木琴	木琴	133
실험실	laboratory	实验室	実験室	85
싫다	to be disagreeable	不要 / 不喜欢	嫌いだ	35
심문	examination	审问	審問	155
심심하다	to be bored from inactivity	无聊	退屈だ	37
심야할증	late-night charge	深夜加价	深夜割増し	115
심장	heart	心脏	心臓	27
십자가	cross	十字架	十字架	157
싱크대	sink	水池子	シンク台	72
싼	inexpensive	低廉的	安い	13
쌀	rice	米	米	62
쌀통	rice container, rice dispenser	米桶	米びつ	73
쌍꺼풀	a double-edged eyelid	双眼皮	二重まぶた	24

썬 캡	visor	太阳帽	サンキャップ	44
쓰레기봉투	garbage bag	垃圾袋	ゴミ袋	78
쓰레기통	garbage can, trash can	垃圾桶	ゴミ箱	79
쓰레받기	dustpan	垃圾铲	ちり取り	79
쓸개	gallbladder	胆囊	胆嚢	27
씨름	ssireum, Korean wrestling	摔跤	シルム(韓国の相撲)	130

ㅇ

아가씨	unmarried woman	小姐	未婚の若い女性	29
아군	our forces, friendly forces	我军	我が軍	159
아기	baby	婴儿	赤ちゃん	28
아나운서	announcer	(电视, 广播的)广播员	アナウンサー	137
아동복	children's wear	童装	子供服	40
아들	son	儿子	息子	31
아래	below	下	下	15
아르바이트생	person working temporary, part-timer	打工生	アルバイト	65
아르헨티나	Argentina	阿根廷	アルゼンチン	149
아빠 (아버지)	father	爸爸	お父さん	30
아시안게임	Asian Games	亚运会	アジア大会	152
아이디	ID, username	登录名	ID	96
아이브로펜슬	eyebrow pencil	眼线笔	アイブロウペンシル	46
아이섀도	eye shadow	眼影	アイシャドー	46
아이스크림	ice cream	冰淇淋	アイスクリーム	61
아일랜드	Ireland	爱尔兰	アイルランド	148
아쟁	ajaeng	雅筝	7本の弦からなる弦楽器の一種	132
아저씨	ajeossii, adult man	大叔	おじさん	29
아줌마	ajumma, middle aged woman	阿姨	おばさん	29
아침	morning	早晨	朝	20
아카시아	acacia	金合欢树	アカシア	140
아코디언	accordion	手风琴	アコーディオン	133
아토피	atopy	敏感性皮肤病	アトピー	103
아파트	apartment	公寓	マンション	70
아파트 관리비	apartment management fees	公寓管理费	アパート管理費	71
아홉째	ninth	第九	9番目	17
악보	music score, sheet music	乐谱	楽譜	133
악어	crocodile	鳄鱼	ワニ	145
안	inside	里	中	15
안개	fog, mist	雾	霧	12
안경	eyeglasses	眼镜	眼鏡	45
안과	ophthalmology	眼科	眼科	101
안내데스크	information desk	接待处	案内カウンター	113
안내책자	information pamphlet	旅行手册	ガイドブック	139
안대	eye patch	眼罩	眼帯	105
안심	lead beef	牛筋间肉	ロース	53
안심하다	to be relieved	放心	安心する	37
안전 작업 기호	work safety signs	安全作业记号	安全作業のマーク	99
안전마스크	safety mask	安全口罩	安全マスク	99
안전모	safety helmet	安全帽	ヘルメット	99
안전벨트	seat belt	安全带	安全ベルト	125
안전선	safety line	安全线	安全線	117
안전장화	safety boots	安全靴子	安全長靴	99
안전조끼	safety vest	安全坎肩	安全チョッキ	99
안전지대	safety zone	安全地带	安全地帯	118
안쪽	the inside	里边	内側	15
안테나	antenna	天线	アンテナ	125
알레르기	allergy	过敏性反应	アレルギー	103
알밥	rice topped with fish roe	鱼仔拌饭	丼	59
알약	pill	药丸	錠剤	105
알츠하이머병	Alzheimer's disease	老年性痴呆症	アルツハイマー病	103
암	cancer	癌症	癌	103
압박붕대 (탄력붕대)	compress, elastic bandage	压力绷带	サポーター	105

앞	front	前	前	15
앞 유리	windshield	前挡风玻璃	フロントガラス	124
앞지르다	to pass (another vehicle)	超车	追い越す	123
앞치마	apron	围裙	プロン	79
애국가	national anthem	爱国歌	愛国歌	153
애플파이	apple pie	苹果派	アップルパイ	65
액세서리	accessories	首饰	アクセサリー	45
액셀러레이터	accelerator	油门	アクセル	125
앵무새	parrot	鹦鹉	オウム	144
야구	baseball	棒球	野球	131
야구모자	baseball cap	棒球帽	野球帽子	44
야근	night duty, working late	夜班	夜勤	91
야외음악당	outdoor music venue	露天音乐堂	野外音楽堂	85
야유회	picnic party	郊游	ピクニック	89
야자수	palm tree	椰子树	ヤシの木	140
약과	yakgwa	药果	ヤッカ	57
약국	pharmacy	药店	薬局	104
약사	pharmacist	药师	薬剤師	104
약지	ring finger	无名指	薬指	27
약혼식	engagement ceremony	订婚礼	婚約の式	33
얇은	thin	薄薄的	薄い	13
양	lamb	羊	羊	142
양궁	(Western-style) archery	射箭	アーチェリー	131
양념	seasonings, marinades, condiments	调料	薬味	63
양념통	condiment jar	调料盒	調味料容器	68
양동이	(metal) bucket	白铁罐	バケツ	79
양로원	retirement home	养老院	老人ホーム	71
양말	socks	袜子	靴下	45
양배추	cabbage	卷心菜	キャベツ	50
양보	Yield the right of way	减速让行	先行優先	121
양복	suit	西服	洋服	40
양식	Western food	西餐	洋食	60
양장피	liang zhang pi	凉皮	両張皮	58
양쪽	both sides	两边	両側	15
양치 컵	cup for toothbrushing	漱口杯	うがいコップ	77
양파	onion	洋葱	玉ねぎ	50
어깨	shoulder	肩膀	肩	26
어려운	difficult	艰难的	難しい	13
어린	(very) young (child age)	年少的	幼い	28
어린이, 아이	child	儿童, 小孩	子供	28
어린이날	Childrens' Day	儿童节	子供の日	153
어린이집	day care center	托儿所	子供の家	71
어묵	eomuk	鲜鱼凉粉	かまぼこ	57
어업	fishery	渔业	漁業	156
어제	yesterday	昨天	昨日	11
어촌	fishing village	渔村	漁村	151
억울하다	to feel mistreated	冤枉	悔しい	35
언니	elder sister of a woman	姐姐	姉	30
얼굴	face	脸	顔	24
얼룩말	zebra	斑马	シマウマ	143
엄마 (어머니)	mother	妈妈	お母さん	30
엄지	thumb	拇指	親指	27
엉덩이	buttocks	臀部	尻	26
에스컬레이터	escalator	自动扶梯	エスカレーター	113
에스파냐/스페인	Spain	西班牙	スペイン	149
에어백	airbag	安全气囊	エアバック	124
에어컨	air conditioner	空调	エアコン	74
에어컨디셔너	air conditioner	空调设备	エアコン	125
엑셀	Excel	电子表格	エクセル	95
엘리베이터 (승강기)	elevator	电梯	エレベーター	70, 113
엘리베이터 안내원	elevator operator	电梯服务员	エレベーターガール	113

여관	yeogwan, Korean inn	旅馆	旅館	139
여군	female soldier	女兵	女性軍人	159
여권	passport	护照	旅券	139
여덟째	eighth	第八	8番目	17
여동생	younger sister	妹妹	妹	31
여드름	pimple	粉刺	にきび	25, 103
여름	summer	夏	夏	11
여름 방학	summer vacation	暑假	夏休み	89
여섯째	sixth	第六	6番目	17
여우	fox	狐狸	キツネ	143
여자	woman	女人	女	28
여행경비	travel expenses	旅行经费	旅行経費	139
여행사	travel agency	旅行社	旅行社	139
역도	weight lifting	举重	重量挙げ	131
역무원	station official	服务员	駅員	117
연고	ointment	软膏	軟膏	105
연극	a play	戏剧(话剧)	演劇	135
연기	acting	演技	演技	135
연날리기	kite flying	放风筝	凧揚げ	129
연료 계기판	gas gauge	燃料表	燃料計器盤	125
연립주택	row houses	连排住宅	テラスハウス	71
연봉	annual salary	年薪	年俸	91
연상	older	年长	年上	28
연습장	notebook	练习本	練習帳	83
연예인	star, entertainment figure	演艺人	芸能人	137
연주회	concert	演奏会	演奏会	135
연차	annual paid hoilday	年休	年次	91
연체료	late fee	滞纳金	延滞料	137
연출	directing	编导	演出	135
연필	pencil	铅笔	鉛筆	88
연하	younger	年少	年下	28
열 번째	tenth	第十	10番目	17
열람실	reading room	阅览室	閲覧室	87
열매	fruit, nuts, berries	果实	果実	140
열선	heating wires	热线	熱線	125
열쇠	key	钥匙	キー	125
염려하다	to worry	担心	心配する	37
염색약	dying agent	染发剂	ヘアカラーリング剤	111
염소	goat	山羊	ヤギ	142
염주	rosary, string of beads	佛珠	数珠	157
엽서	postcard	明信片	はがき	109
영국	Britain	英国	イギリス	148
영남	Yeongnam region	岭南	嶺南	151
영사기	movie projector	放映机	映写機	135
영수증	receipt	发票	領収書	23
영화	movie	电影	映画	134
영화 감상	watching movies	电影欣赏	映画鑑賞	128
영화배우	movie actor	电影演员	映画俳優	135
영화제	film festival	电影节	映画祭	135
옆	next to	旁边	横	15
예금	deposit, savings	存款	預金	107
예방주사	inoculation	预防针	予防注射	103
예배	worship service	礼拜	礼拝	157
예선전	preliminary match	预赛	予選	131
예수	Jesus	耶稣	イエス	157
예술	art	艺术	芸術	135
예술가	artist	艺术家	芸術家	135
예술제	art festival	艺术节	文化祭	89
예약석	reserved seat	预约席	予約席	69
오늘	today	今天	今日	11
오디오	stereo	音响	オーディオ	74

오렌지	orange	橙子	オレンジ	51
오렌지주스	orange juice	橙汁	オレンジジュース	54
오르간	organ	风琴	オルガン	133
오르막경사	Steep ascend	上陡坡	上り急勾あり	121
오른쪽	right	右	右	15
오리	duck	鸭	アヒル	142
오리고기	duck (meat)	鸭肉	カモ肉	53
오보에	oboe	双簧管	オーボエ	133
오븐	oven	烤箱	オーブン	73
오빠	elder brother of a woman	哥哥	兄	30
오스트레일리아 / 호주	Australia	澳大利亚	オーストラリア	149
오이	cucumber	黄瓜	きゅうり	50
오이소박이	oi sobagi	黄瓜泡菜	キュウリの中に具を詰めたキムチ	66
오전	morning	上午	午前	20
오징어	cuttlefish	鱿鱼, 墨斗鱼	イカ	52
오케스트라	orchestra	管弦乐	オーケストラ	133
오토바이	motorcycle	摩托车	オートバイ	119
오페라	opera	歌剧	オペラ	135
오한	chills	恶寒	悪寒	103
오후	afternoon	下午	午後	20
옥상	rooftop	楼顶	屋上	71
옥수수	corn	玉米	とうもろこし	50
올림픽	Olympics	奥运会	オリンピック	131
옷감	cloth types, textures	衣料	生地	41
옷걸이	hanger	衣架	ハンガー	49
옷장	wardrobe	衣柜	洋服ダンス	75
와이셔츠	(dress) shirt	男衬衫	ワイシャツ	38
와이퍼	windshield wipers	雨刮器	ワイパー	125
완전 삭제	delete permanently	永久删除	完全削除	97
외과	surgery	外科	外科	101
외교	diplomacy	外交	外交	149
외교관	diplomat	外交官	外交官	149
외국	foreign country	外国	外国	149
외롭다	to be lonely	孤单	寂しい	37
외삼촌	(maternal) uncle	舅舅	母方のおじ	31
외숙모	wife of one's (maternal) uncle	舅妈	母方のおじの妻	31
외할머니 (외조모)	maternal grandmother	姥姥	母方の祖母	30
외할아버지 (외조부)	maternal grandfather	姥爷	母方の祖父	30
왼쪽	left	左	左	15
요구르트	yogurt	酸奶	ヨーグルト	54
요금	fare	车费	料金	115
요금 미터기	fare meter	标价器	料金メーター	115
요금함	fare box	收费箱	料金箱	114
요일	days of the week	星期(周)	曜日	10
요통	lumbago	腰痛	腰痛	102
욕실	bathroom	浴室	浴室	76
욕실 슬리퍼	bathroom slippers	浴室拖鞋	風呂用スリッパ	77
욕실용 세제	restroom cleanser	卫浴洁净剂	浴室用洗剤	79
욕조	bathtub	浴缸	浴槽	77
용의자	suspect	嫌疑犯	容疑者	155
우동	udon	乌冬面	うどん	59
우물정	pound button (on telephone dial)	井字键	シャープ	93
우산	umbrella	雨伞	傘	138
우승	victory	优胜	優勝	131
우울하다	to be depressed	忧郁	憂鬱だ	37
우유	milk	牛奶	牛乳	54
우족	beef feet	牛蹄	牛の脚	53
우좌로 이중굽은도로	Winding road	右(左)侧绕行	右(左)つづら折りあり	121
우체국	post office	邮局	郵便局	109
우체국 소인	postmark	邮局印章	郵便局の消印	108
우체부	letter carrier	邮递员	郵便配達人	109

우체통	mailbox	邮箱	郵便ポスト	109
우편번호	postal code	邮编	郵便番号	108
우편함	mailbox	邮件箱	郵便受け	71
우표	stamp	邮票	切手	108
우표 수집	stamp collecting	集邮	切手収集	129
우회전 금지	No Right Turn	禁止右转	右折禁止	120
우회전하다	to turn right	右转弯	右折する	122
운동장	playground	操场	運動場	85
운동화	sneakers, sports shoes	运动鞋	運動靴	43
운동회	clubs sports tournament	运动会	運動会	89
운반하다	to transport (objects)	搬运	運搬する	98
운전기사 (운전사)	driver	驾驶员	運転手	114
울	wool	毛	ウール	41
울다	to cry	哭	泣く	35
울면	ulmyeon	温面	五目あんかけソバ	58
울산광역시	Ulsan Metropolitan City	尉山广域市	ウルサン広域市	151
웃다	to smile	笑	笑う	35
워드 프로세서	word processor	文字编辑器	ワープロ	95
워셔액	washer fluid	洗涤液	ウォッシャー液	125
워크맨	Walkman	随身听	ウォークマン	136
원	won	元	ウォン	22
원고	plaintiff	原告	原告	154
원숭이	monkey	猴子	サル	143
원피스	one-piece dress	连衣裙	ワンピース	38
원형 컨베이어	carousel	圆形输送机	円形コンベアー	126
원형 테이블	round table	圆桌	円形テーブル	91
월	month	月	月	10, 11
월급	monthly salary	月薪	月給	91
월드컵	World Cup	世界杯	ワールドカップ	131
월요일	Monday	星期一	月曜日	10
월차	monthly day off	月休	月次	91
웨딩드레스	wedding dress	婚纱	ウエディングドレス	38
위	above, stomach	上, 胃	上, 胃	15, 27
위생복	disinfected overgarment, gown	卫生服	生服	111
위성방송	satellite broadcast	卫星电视	衛星放送	137
위치	location	位置	位置	15
위험	Danger	注意危险	危険	120
유괴	abduction (usually a child)	诱拐	誘拐	155
유교	Confucianism	儒教	儒教	157
유니폼	uniform	制服	ユニホーム	41
유도	judo	柔道	柔道	131
유리 세정제	window washing fluid	玻璃清洁剂	ガラスクリーナー	79
유부남	married man	有妇之夫	既婚男性	28
유부녀	married woman	有夫之妇	既婚女性	28
유부초밥	inari sushi	油腐寿司	いなり寿司	59
유산슬	sea cucumber with shrimp and beef	溜三丝	溜三絲	58
유선전화기	wired telephone	有线电话	有線電話機	93
유아	infant	幼儿	乳児	28
유아놀이방	children's play area	幼儿房	お遊戯広場	69
유아복	clothing for infants	婴儿服装	乳児服	40
유자차	citron tea	柚子茶	ゆず茶	55
유죄	guilty	有罪	有罪	155
유치원	kindergarten	幼儿园	幼稚園	89
유턴 금지	No U Turn	禁止掉头	転回禁止	120
유화	an oil painting	油画	油絵	135
육개장	yukgaejang	细丝牛肉汤	ユッケジャン	56
육교	land bridge	天桥	陸橋	118
육군	army	陆军	陸軍	159
육지 (땅)	land	陆地	陸地 (土地)	147
은메달	silver medal	银牌	銀メダル	131
은하계	galactic system	银河系	銀河系	146

은행	bank	银行	銀行	106
은행나무	gingko tree	银杏树	イチョウ	140
은행원	banker, bank employee	银行职员	銀行員	106
음량 (볼륨)	volume	音量	音量 (ボリューム)	137
음료	beverages	饮料	飲み物	54
음성메시지	voice message	留言	音声メッセージ	93
음악	music	音乐	音楽	132
음악 감상	listening to music	音乐欣赏	音楽鑑賞	128
음악실	music room	音乐室	音楽室	85
응급실	emergency room	急诊室	救急室	101
응급처치	emergency care	应急措施	応急処置	104
응급치료상자	first aid kit	急救用箱子	救急箱	104
의료보험카드	medical insurance card	医疗保险卡	医療保険カード	101
의사	doctor	大夫	医者	100
의자	chair	椅子	椅子	82, 90
이	teeth	牙齿	歯	25
이라크	Iraq	伊拉克	イラク	148
이력서	resume	履历表	履歴書	91
이름	name	姓名	名前	88
이름표	name tag	名签	名札	65
이마	forehead	额头	額	24
이모	(maternal) aunt	姨妈	母の姉妹	31
이모부	husband of one's (maternal) aunt	姨夫	母の姉妹の夫	31
이민	immigration and emigration	移民	移民	149
이발사	barber	理发员	理髪師	111
이발소	barbershop	理发店	理髪店	110
이번 주 (금주)	this week	这星期	今週	11
이불	(Korean) bedclothes, quilt	被子	布団	75
이비인후과	ENT	耳鼻喉科	耳鼻咽喉科	101
이스라엘	Israel	以色列	イスラエル	148
이쑤시개	toothpick	牙签	爪楊枝	69
이어폰	earphone	耳机	イヤホン	136
이자	interest	利息	利子	107
이전 페이지	previous page	上一页	前のページ	97
이집트	Egypt	埃及	エジプト	149
이착륙 모니터	arrival and departure monitor	航班消息显示板	離着陸モニター	127
이탈리아	Italy	意大利	イタリア	148
인도	India	印度	インド	148
인도네시아	Indonesia	印度尼西亚	インドネシア	148
인도양	Indian Ocean	印度洋	インド洋	149
인라인 스케이트	inline skates	溜旱冰	インラインスケート	128
인류	humanity	人类	人類	149
인삼차	ginseng tea	人参茶	人参茶	55
인절미	injeolmi	糯米糕	インヂョルミ	57
인종	race	人种	人種	149
인주	red stamping ink for traditional seals	印泥	朱肉	92
인천광역시	Incheon Metropolitan City	仁川广域市	インチョン広域市	151
인터넷 뱅킹	internet banking	网络银行	インターネットバンキング	107
인화물질	Flammable material	易燃物	引火物質	99
일	day	日	日	10
일곱째	seventh	第七	7番目	17
일방통행	One Way	单行路	一方通行	120
일본	Japan	日本	日本	148
일시불	payment in full	一次付清	一回払い	23
일시정지	Stop and yield the right of way	停车让行, 暂停	一時停止	121, 137
일식	Japanese food	日餐	日本料理	59
일요일	Sunday	星期日	日曜日	10
일제강점기	Japanese colonial period	日本殖民地	日帝植民地期	152
임산부	pregnant woman	孕妇	妊婦	28
임시보관함	draft	临时保管箱	臨時保管庫	97
임업	forestry	林业	林業	156

입	mouth	嘴	口	25
입국심사	entrance inspection	入境检查	入国審査	127
입금 신청 용지	deposit slip	存款申请表	入金申請用紙	107
입대	entering the military	当兵	入隊	33
입법부	legislative branch	立法部	立法府	155
입사	entering a company	进公司	入社	32
입술	lips	嘴唇	唇	25
입학	school admittance	入学	入学	83
입학식	ceremony marking entrance to a new school entrance ceremony	入学典礼	入学式	32
잇몸	gums	牙龈	歯茎	25
잎 (잎사귀)	leaf	树叶(叶子)	葉	140

ㅈ

자	ruler	尺子	物差し	88
자기소개서	written personal introduction	自我介绍书	自己推薦書	91
자동 현금인출기	automated teller machine	自动取款机	自動現金引き出し機	107
자동응답기	answering machine	电话留言机	留守番電話	93
자동이체	automated transfer (wire)	自动转账	自動振込	107
자동차 정비소	auto repair shop	汽车维修店	自動車整備士	119
자동차세	auto tax	汽车税	自動車税	71
자동판매기	automatic vending machine	自动售饮机	自動販売機	85
자랑스럽다	to be proud	骄傲	誇らしい	35
자료실	data (material) room	资料室	資料室	86
자루걸레	mop	拖把	モップ	79
자리, 좌석	seat	座位	席、座席	115
자막	subtitles	字幕	字幕	135
자매	sisters	姐妹	姉妹	31
자식 (자녀)	child	儿女(子女)	子供	31
자신 있다	to be confident	有信心	自信がある	37
자외선 차단제	sun block	防晒霜	紫外線カット剤	46
자장면	jajangmyeon	炸酱面	ジャージャー麺	58
자전거	bicycle	自行车	自転車	119
자정	midnight	午夜	夜中の12時	20
작업복	work clothes	工作服	作業服	41
작은	small	小小的	小さい	13
잔돈	small change	零钱	おつり	23
잠금장치	lock	关闭装置	ロック装置	125
잠수함	submarine	潜水艇	潜水艦	159
잠옷	sleepwear	睡衣	寝巻き	41
잠자리	dragonfly	蜻蜓	トンボ	145
잡지	magazine	杂志	雑誌	87
잡채밥	chop suey rice	什锦饭	チャプチェパプ	58
잡탕밥	rice mixed with fish and vegetables	汤泡饭	チャプタンパプ	58
장	intestines	肠	腸	27
장갑	gloves	手套	手袋	45
장갑차	armored vehicle	装甲车	装甲車	159
장관	minister	长官(部长)	長官(大臣)	155
장구	janggu	长鼓	チャング	132
장군	general	将军	将軍	159
장기	janggi	象棋	将棋	129
장남 (큰아들)	first son	长子	長男	31
장례식	funeral	葬礼	葬式	33
장모	man's mother-in-law	岳母	義母	31
장미	rose	玫瑰	バラ	141
장어	eel	鳗鱼	ウナギ	52
장어구이	broiled eel	烤鳗鱼	ウナギの蒲焼	59
장인	man's father-in-law	岳父	義父	31
장화	boots	长筒鞋	長靴	43
재다이얼	redial	重播	リダイアル	93
재떨이	ashtray	烟灰缸	灰皿	69

재미없다	to be uninteresting	没趣儿	つまらない	35
재미있다	to be interesting	有趣儿	面白い	35
재산세	property tax	财产税	財産税	71
재즈	jazz	爵士乐	ジャズ	133
재판	trial	裁判	裁判	155
잼	jam	果酱	ジャム	63
쟁반	tray	盘子	お盆	68
저녁	evening	晚上	夕方	20
저울	scale	秤	秤	109
저자명	author's name	著作名	著者名	86
저혈압	low blood pressure	低血压	低血圧	103
적군	the enemy	敌军	敵軍	159
적금	installment savings	定期储蓄	積立金	107
전광판	electric billboard	电光板	電光掲示板	106
전구	light bulb	电灯泡	電球	74
전국	the whole country	全国	全国	151
전기 면도기	electric shaver	刮胡刀	かみそり	111
전기밥솥	electric rice cooker	电饭锅	電気炊飯器	73
전기세	electricity fees	电费	電気代	71
전기위험	Electric hazard	电危险	電気危険	99
전기테이프	electric tape	绝缘胶布	電気用絶縁テープ	81
전기통신	telecommunications	电子通讯	電気通信	156
전등	electric light	电灯	電気	75
전라남도	Jeollanam-do	全罗南道	全羅南道	150
전라북도	Jeollabuk-do	全罗北道	全羅北道	150
전선	electric wire	电线	電線	81
전술	tactics	战术	戦術	159
전시회	exhibition	展览会	展示会	135
전원 스위치	power switch	电源开关	電源スイッチ	94
전자레인지	microwave oven	微波炉	電子レンジ	73
전자사전	electric dictionary	电子词典	電子辞典	83
전자정보실	computer room	电子信息室	電子情報室	87
전쟁	war	战争	戦争	159
전조등	headlights	前照灯	ヘッドライト	124
전진하다	to move forward	前进	前進する	123
전철	subway	地铁	電車	117
전체 메일 용량	total storage available	邮箱总容量	メールボックスの容量	97
전통차	traditional tea	传统茶	伝統茶	55
전투	combat, battle	战斗	戦闘	159
전투기	jet fighter	战斗机	戦闘機	159
전학	transfer schools	转学	転校	83
전화	telephone	电话	電話	93
전화기	telephone	电话机	電話機	91
전화세	telephone fees	电话费	電話代	71
절	temple	寺庙	寺	157
절도	larcenist	盗窃	窃盗	155
절편	jeolpyeon	切糕	チョルピョン	57
젊은	young	年轻的	若い	28
점	mole	痣	ほくろ	25
점퍼	jumper	夹克	ジャンパー	38
접시	plate, dish	盘子	皿	67
젓가락	chopsticks	筷子	箸	67
젓갈	salted fish	鱼籽浆	塩辛	63
정기 간행물실	periodicals room	期刊阅览室	定期刊行物室	87
정기권	(period specific) prepaid ticket	定期票	定期券	117
정당	political party	政党	政党	155
정맥	vein	静脉	静脈	27
정문	main gate	正门	正門	85
정부	government	政府	政府	155
정상가 (정가)	regular price	定价	標準価格 (定価)	113
정상회담	summit talks	首脑会谈	首脳会談	149

정수기	water purifier	净水器	浄水器	69
정신과	psychiatry	神经科	精神科	101
정오	noon	中午	正午	20
정원	garden	庭园	庭	71
정월 대보름	Jeongwol Daeboreum	元宵节	正月15日	153
정장	formal wear	正装	正装	40
정지	stop	停止	停止	137
정지선	stop line	停止线	停止線	118
정지하다	to stop	停止	停止する	122
정차하다	to stop	停车	停車する	123
정치권	the political world	政治圈	政界	155
정치인	politician	从政人	政治家	155
정형외과	orthopedics	正骨科	整形外科	101
제대	discharge from the military	退伍	除隊	32
제동등	brakelights	制动灯	ブレーキライト	124
제목	subject	题目	題名	96
제비	swallow	燕子	ツバメ	144
제사	ancestral rites	祭礼	祭祀	33
제작자	producer	制片人	製作者	135
제조업	manufacturing	制造行业	製造業	156
제조하다	to manufacture	制造	製造する	98
제주도	Jeju Province	济州道	済州道	151
젤	jell	定型液	ジェル	110
조각	sculpture	雕刻	彫刻	135
조개	shellfish	贝	貝	52
조깅	jogging	慢跑	ジョギング	131
조끼	vest	坎肩	チョッキ	38
조리대	kitchen table, kitchen counter	烹调台	調理台	73
조립라인	assembly line	组装线	組み立てライン	98
조명	lighting	照明	照明	135
조미료	artificial seasoning	调味料	調味料	63
조선	Joseon	朝鲜	朝鮮	152
조연	supporting actor	配角	助演	135
조종사	pilot	驾驶员	操縦士	126
조카	nephew, niece	侄子	甥、姪	31
조퇴	leaving early	早退	早退	83
족발	pettitoes	猪蹄	豚足	53
졸리다	to feel sleepy	困 (倦)	眠い	37
졸업	graduation	毕业	卒業	83
졸업식	graduation ceremony	毕业典礼	卒業式	32
졸업여행	graduation trip	毕业旅行	卒業旅行	89
종아리	calf	小腿	ふくらはぎ	27
종업원	employee	服务员	店員	69
종이접기	origami	折纸	折り紙	129
종이타월	paper towel	厨房纸巾	紙タオル	73
종점	last stop	终点站	終点	115
종지	small bowl	小碗	調味料容器	67
종착역	terminus	终点站	終着駅	117
종합병원	general hospital	综合医院	総合病院	101
좋다	to be good	好	良い	35
좋아하다	to like	喜欢	好む	37
좌약	a suppository	栓剂	座薬	105
좌측면통행	Pass obstacle on the left	靠左侧道路行驶	指定方向外進行禁止	121
좌회전하다	to turn left	左转弯	左折する	122
죄수	prisoner	犯人	罪人	155
주	week	星期(周)	週	10
주가	stock prices	股价	株価	156
주근깨	freckle	雀斑	そばかす	25
주말	weekend	周末	週末	10
주문대 (계산대)	counter	收银台	カウンター	65
주문하다	to order	订购	注文する	98

주방	kitchen	厨房	キッチン	72
주방장	head chef	厨师长	コック長	69
주사	injection	注射	注射	101
주소록	contacts	通讯录	住所録	96
주식	shares, stocks	股票	株式	156
주식회사	stock company	股份公司	株式会社	91
주유소	petrol station	加油站	ガソリンスタンド	119
주인	owner	主人	主人	69
주인공 (주연)	main character	主角	主人公(主演)	135
주전자	kettle	水壶	やかん	73
주제어	keyword	主题词	キーワード	87
주중	during the week	本周内	週の半ば	10
주차 금지	No Parking	禁止停车	駐車禁止	120
주차 단속원	parking enforcement officer	交通管理员	駐車取り締まり員	119
주차 안내원	parking attendant	停车管理员	駐車案内員	113
주차권	parking ticket	停车卡	駐車券	113
주차장	parking lot	停车场	駐車場	71
주차하다	to park	停车	駐車する	123
주행거리 계기판	odometer	里程表	走行距離計器盤	125
주황색	orange	朱黄色	だいだい色	14
준결승전 (4강전)	semifinal (final 4)	四强赛	準決勝戦	131
준준결승전 (8강전)	quarter final (final 8)	八强赛	準々決勝戦	131
줄기	trunk	树干	幹	140
줄무늬	striped	条纹	縞柄	40
줄자	measuring tape	卷尺	巻尺	80
중계방송	relay, hook-up	转播	中継	137
중국	China	中国	中国	148
중년의	middle aged	中年的	中年の	28
중량초과 요금	overweight charge	超重费	重量超過料金	127
중령	lieutenant colonel	中校	中佐	159
중소기업	medium-sized company	中小企业	中小企業	91
중식	Chinese food	中餐	中国料理	58
중위	first lieutenant	中尉	中尉	159
중절모	soft hat, felt hat	礼帽	中折れ帽子	44
중지	middle finger	中指	中指	27
중학교	middle school	初中	中学校	89
즐겁다	to be pleasant	愉快	楽しい	35
증거	evidence	证据	証拠	155
증권거래소	securities exchange	证券交易所	証券取引所	156
증명서 자동 발급기	automated document-issuing machine	电脑开证机	証明書発給機	85
증상	symptom	症状	症状	102
증인	witness	证人	証人	154
지각	arriving late	迟到	遅刻	83
지갑	wallet	钱包	財布	23, 45
지게차	forklift	铲车	フォークリフト	98
지구	earth	地球	地球	146
지구본	globe	地球仪	地球儀	82
지난주	last week	上星期	先週	11
지도	map	地图	地図	83, 138
지렁이	worm	蚯蚓	ミミズ	145
지로용지	giro form	储蓄存款凭证	振込用紙	107
지루하다	to be boring	乏味	退屈だ	37
지리산	Mount Jiri	智异山	智異山	151
지방	region, provinces, district	地方	地方	151
지방도	provincial highway	地方道	県道	119
지방자치제	regional autonomy	地方自治制	地方自治体	155
지시봉	pointer	指挥棒	指示棒	83
지우개	eraser	橡皮	消しゴム	88
지운편지함	trash	回收站	削除済みトレイ	96
지중해	Mediterranean	地中海	地中海	149
지진	earthquake	地震	地震	147

한국어	English	中文	日本語	페이지
지폐	paper money	纸币	紙幣	22
지하도	underground passageway	地下通道	地下道	117
지하철	subway	地铁	地下鉄	117
지하철 출구	subway station exit	地铁出口	地下鉄出口	117
지하철노선도	subway map	地铁路线图	地下鉄路線図	117
지휘자	conductor	指挥	指揮者	133
직원 (판매원)	employee (salesperson)	销售员	職員(販売員)	113
직진 금지	Must Turn	禁止直行	直進禁止	120
직진 및 좌회전	Straight Or Left Turn	直行和向左转弯	左折及び直進	120
직행하다	to drive straight	直行	直進する	122
진달래	azalea	杜鹃花	カラムラサキツツジ	141
진맥	pulse taking	号脉	診脈	101
진찰실	examination room	门诊室	診察室	101
진통제	pain killer	镇痛剂	鎮痛剤	105
질병	disease	疾病	疾病	102
질투하다	to be jealous	嫉妒	嫉妬する	35
집	house, home	房子	家	71
집게	tongs	夹子	ヘアクリップ	111
집들이	housewarming party	乔迁宴	引っ越し祝い	32
징	jing	锣	どら	132
짜증나다	to become annoyed	烦躁	苛立つ	37
짝	desk mate	伴儿	ペア	83
짧은 머리	short hair	短发	ショートヘアー	25
짬뽕	jjamppong	大杂烩面	チャンポン	58
쫄면	jjolmyeon	劲道面	チョルミョン	57
찜질팩	massage pack	热敷带	温湿布	105

ㅊ				
차	tea, automobile	茶, 汽车	お茶、車	55, 115
차고	garage	车库	車庫	125
차높이제한	Maximal height 3.5 meters	限制高度	高さ制限	121
차도	roadway	行车道	車道	118
차림표 (메뉴)	menu	菜单	メニュー	68
차선	lane	车道	車線	119
차중량제한	Mass at most 5.5 tons	限制质量	重量制限	121
착한	good (character)	善良的	良い	13
찬송가	hymn	赞颂歌	賛美歌	157
찬장	pantry, cupboard	厨具柜	食器棚	72
참고 열람실	reference bookstack room	参考阅览室	参考閲覧室	87
참기름	sesame oil	香油	ごま油	63
참새	sparrow	麻雀	スズメ	144
참외	chamoe, oriental melon	香瓜	マクワウリ	51
참치 캔	canned tuna	金枪鱼罐头	シーチキンの缶詰	63
창고	warehouse	仓库	倉庫	98
창구	teller window	窗口	窓口	106
창문	window	窗户	窓	74
창피하다	to be embarrassed	羞愧	恥ずかしい	35
채널	channel	频道	チャンネル	137
채팅	chatting	网上聊天	チャット	97
책	book	书	本	83
책가방	book bag	书包	学生かばん	83
책꽂이	bookstand	书架	本立て	90
책상	desk	书桌, 办公桌	机	82, 90
책장	bookcase	书柜	本棚	74
챔피언	champion	世界冠军	チャンピオン	131
처방전	prescription	处方	処方箋	104
처벌	punishment	处罚	処罰	155
천왕성	Uranus	天王星	天王星	146
천장	ceiling	天花板	天井	74
천주교	Catholicism	天主教	カトリック教	157
철로	tracks	铁路	鉄路	117

첨부파일	attachment	附件	添付ファイル	97
첫째	first	第一	1番目	17
청년	young man	青年	青年	29
청록색	blue green	青绿色	黄緑色	14
청바지	blue jeans	牛仔裤	ジーンズ	39
청소기	vacuum cleaner	吸尘器	掃除機	78
청소년	juvenile	青少年	青少年	28
청와대	Cheong Wa Dae	青瓦台	青瓦台	155
청진기	stethoscope	听诊器	聴診器	101
체	strainer	筛子	ふるい	73
체스	chess	国际象棋	チェス	129
체온계	thermometer	体温表	体温計	101
체육관	gymnasium	体育馆	体育館	85
체육대회	clubs sports tournament	运动会	体育大会	89
체조	gymnastics	体操	体操	130
체중계	scale	体重称	体重計	77
체크무늬	checkered	格纹	チェック	40
체크인 카운터	check-in counter	登记手续窗口	チェックインカウンター	127
체포	detain	逮捕	逮捕	155
첼로	cello	大提琴	チェロ	133
초	second	秒	秒	20
초고속 인터넷	high speed internet	超速因特网	超高速インターネット	95
초등학교	elementary school	小学	小学校	89
초록색	green	绿色	緑色	14
초상화	portrait	肖像画	肖像画	135
초승달	new moon	新月	三日月	146
초인종 (벨)	doorbell	门铃	呼び鈴 (ベル)	71
초조하다	to feel anxious	焦急	いらだっている	37
초콜릿	chocolate	巧克力	チョコレート	61
총	gun	枪	銃	159
총각김치	chonggak kimchi	小萝卜泡菜	チョンガーキムチ	66
총리	prime minister	总理	総理	155
촬영	filming, photography	摄影	撮影	135
최고속도제한	Speed Limit 50kph	最高限速标志	最高速度50(km/h)	120
최저속도제한	Minimum speed 30kph	最低限速	最低速度	120
추석	Chuseok	中秋节	お盆	153
축구	soccer	足球	サッカー	130
축제	festival	联欢节	大学祭	89
출국심사	exist inspection	出境检查	出国審査	127
출금 신청 용지	withdraw slip	取款申请表	引き出し申請用紙	107
출발역	station at end of line	出发站	始発駅	117
출산	giving birth	分娩	出産	33
출생	birth	出生	出生	32
출석	attendance	考勤	出席	83
출입국 신고서	exit and departure card	出入境填表	出入国申告書	127
출장	business trip	出差	出張	91
출판사명	publisher's name	出版社名	出版社名	86
충청남도	Chungcheongnam-do	忠清南道	忠清南道	150
충청북도	Chungcheongbuk-do	忠清北道	忠清北道	150
취소	cancel	取消	取り消し	97
치과	dentistry	口腔科	歯科	101
치마	skirt	裙子	スカート	39
치매	dementia	痴呆	痴呆	103
치약	toothpaste	牙膏	歯磨き粉	76
치즈	cheese	奶酪	チーズ	63
치즈버거	cheese burger	奶酪汉堡	チーズバーガー	64
치즈스틱	cheese stick	奶酪条	チーズスティック	65
치킨	chicken	炸鸡	チキン	65
치킨버거	chicken burger	鸡肉汉堡	チキンバーガー	65
치통	toothache	牙痛	歯痛	102
친척	relative	亲戚	親戚	31

칠부 바지	knickers	七分裤	七分ズボン	38
칠판	blackboard	黑板	黒板	82
칠판지우개	blackboard eraser	黑板擦儿	黒板消し	83
칡차	arrowroot tea	葛茶	くず茶	55
침	acupuncture needle	唾液	針	101
침낭	sleeping bag	睡袋	寝袋	138
침대	bed	床	ベッド	75
침대커버	bedspread	床罩	ベッドカバー	75
침착하다	to be composed	沉着	落ち着いている	37
칫솔	toothbrush	牙刷	歯ブラシ	76

ㅋ

카네이션	carnation	康乃馨	カーネーション	141
카드	card	卡片	カード	109
카드 메일	email greetings card	电子贺卡	カードメール	97
카드놀이	card game	玩牌	カード遊び	129
카드단말기	card reader	终端机	カード端末機	114
카디건	cardigan	开襟毛线衣	カーディガン	40
카레라이스	curry rice	咖喱饭	カレーライス	60
카세트 플레이어	cassette player	磁带录音机	カセットプレーヤー	136
카세트테이프	cassette tape	磁带	カセットテープ	137
카센터	auto supply shop	汽车服务中心	カーセンター	119
카펫	carpet	地毯	カーペット	74
칼	knife	菜刀	包丁	72
칼국수	kalguksu	切面	カルグクス (韓国式手打ちうどん)	56
캐나다	Canada	加拿大	カナダ	149
캐리어	luggage carrier	行李车	キャリア	126
캐미솔	camisole	背心式女内衣	キャミソール	42
캐비닛	cabinet	橱柜	キャビネット	90
캐스터네츠	castanets	响板	カスタネット	133
캐주얼	casual wear	便装	カジュアル	40
캔버스	canvas	帆布 (印花布)	キャンバス	134
캠프파이어	camp fire	篝火	キャンプファイヤー	138
캠핑	camping	野营	キャンピング	139
캡	cap	电热帽	キャップ	111
캡슐약	capsule	胶囊	カプセル薬	105
캥거루	kangaroo	袋鼠	カンガルー	143
커튼	curtain	窗帘	カーテン	74
커피	coffee	咖啡	コーヒー	54
커피메이커	coffee maker	咖啡机	コーヒーメイカー	72
커피자판기	coffee vending machine	自动饮料机	コーヒー自動販売機	69
컨베이어 벨트	conveyer belt	组装带	ベルトコンベア	98
컴퍼스	compas	圆规	コンパス	88
컴퓨터	computer	电脑	パソコン, コンピューター	90, 94
컴퓨터 게임	computer game	电脑游戏	コンピューターゲーム	129
컴퓨터 그래픽	computer graphics	电脑图表	コンピューターグラフィック	135
컴퓨터 기사	computer technician	电脑技师	コンピューター技師	95
컵	cup	杯子	コップ	65, 68
컵 라면	cup ramyeon	杯装拉面	カップラーメン	63
컷	cut	剪	カット	111
케냐	Kenya	肯尼亚	ケニア	149
케이블 포트	cable port	电缆端口	ケーブルポート	95
케이블 TV	cable television	有线电视	ケーブルテレビ	137
케이크	cake	蛋糕	ケーキ	61
케첩	ketchup	番茄酱	ケチャップ	62
코	nose	鼻子	鼻	24
코 막힘	stuffed nose	鼻塞	鼻づまり	103
코끼리	elephant	大象	ゾウ	143
코브라	cobra	眼镜蛇	コブラ	145
코뿔소	rhinoceros	犀牛	サイ	143
코스모스	cosmos	大波斯菊	コスモス	141

코알라	koala	树袋熊	コアラ	143
코치	coach	教练	コーチ	131
코트	coat, overcoat	大衣	コート	40
콘 샐러드	corn salad	玉米沙拉	コーンサラダ	65
콘도미니엄	condominium, time-share vacation apartment units	度假村	コンドミニアム	139
콘서트	concert	演唱会	コンサート	135
콘택트렌즈	contact lenses	隐形眼镜	コンタクトレンズ	77
콜택시	call taxi	呼叫出租车	呼び出しタクシー	115
콤팩트	compact (case)	粉饼	コンパクト	46
콧구멍	nostril	鼻孔	鼻の穴	25
콩	bean	豆	豆	50
콩나물	bean sprouts	大豆芽	豆もやし	50
쿠션	cushion	软垫儿	クッション	74
쿠키	cookie	饼干	クッキー	61
크레파스	pastel crayon	蜡笔	クレパス	135
크림	cream	面霜	クリーム	46
큰	large	大大的	大きい	13
큰아버지	uncle, elder brother of one's father	伯父	伯父	31
큰어머니	aunt, wife of the elder brother of one's father	伯母	伯母	31
클라리넷	clarinet	单簧管	クラリネット	133
클래식	classic music	古典音乐	クラシック	133
클러치	clutch	离合器	クラッチ	125
키보드 (자판)	keyboard	键盘	キーボード	94

ㅌ

타악기	percussion instrument	打击乐器	打楽器	133
타월장	towel cabinet	毛巾柜	タオル棚	77
타이	Thailand	泰国	タイ	148
타이어	tire	轮胎	タイヤ	124
타일	tile	瓷砖	タイル	77
타임클록 (시간기록시계)	time clock	打卡机	タイムクロック	98
타조	ostrich	鸵鸟	ダチョウ	144
탁구	table tennis	乒乓球	卓球	131
탁상용 달력	desktop calendar	台式月历	卓上カレンダー	92
탁자	table	茶桌, 写字台	テーブル	74, 82
탈수기	drying machine	甩干机	脱水機	49
탈의실	changing room, locker room	脱衣室	脱衣室	85
탑승	boarding	搭乘	搭乗	126
탕수육	sweet-and-sour pork	糖醋肉	酢豚	58
태권도	Taekwondo	跆拳道	テコンドー	130
태극기	Taegeukgi	太极旗	太極旗	153
태백산맥	Taebaek Mountains	太白山脉	太白山脈	151
태양	sun	太阳	太陽	146
태양계	solar system	太阳系	太陽系	146
태평양	Pacific Ocean	太平洋	太平洋	149
택시	taxi	出租车	タクシー	115
택시 승차장	taxi stand	出租车站	タクシー乗り場	115
탤런트	television star, performer	演员	タレント	137
탬버린	tambourine	铃鼓	タンバリン	133
탱크	tank	坦克	タンク	159
터널	tunnel	隧道	トンネル	120
터미널	terminal	总站	ターミナル	115
터키	Turkey	土耳其	トルコ	148
턱	chin	下颌	あご	25
턱수염	beard	三洋胡子	あごひげ	25
턱시도	tuxedo	(男) 礼服	タキシード	39
털	(facial) hair	毛	毛	25
털모자	fur hat	毛线帽	毛皮の帽子	44
테니스	tennis	网球	テニス	131

한국어	English	中文	日本語	페이지
테니스코트	tennis court	网球场	テニスコート	85
테이블	table	餐桌	テーブル	68
텐트	tent	帐篷	テント	138
토끼	rabbit	兔	ウサギ	142
토마토	tomato	番茄	トマト	50
토마토주스	tomato juice	番茄汁	トマトジュース	54
토성	Saturn	土星	土星	146
토스터	toaster	烤面包机	トースター	73
토요일	Saturday	星期六	土曜日	10
톱	saw	锯	のこぎり	81
통근버스	commute bus	通勤班车	通勤バス	115
통일신라	Unified Silla	统一新罗	統一新羅	152
통장	bankbook	存折	通帳	106
통장 정리기	machine that updates bankbook	存折处理机	通帳記入機	107
통조림	canned foods	罐头	缶詰	63
통쾌하다	to be gratifying	痛快	痛快だ	37
통행권	road pass	通行券	通行券	119
통행료	road use fee	通行费	通行料	119
통화중	busy, call in progress	通话中	通話中	93
투기	speculation	投机	投機	156
투표	voting	投票	投票	155
투피스	two-piece dress	套装	ツーピース	39
튤립	tulip	郁金香	チューリップ	141
트라이앵글	triangle	三角铁	トライアングル	133
트럼펫	trumpet	小号	トランペット	133
트렁크	trunk	后背箱	トランク	124
트렁크 팬티 (사각팬티)	boxer shorts	平口内裤	トランクス	42
트레이닝복 (운동복)	sweat suit, sportswear	运动服	トレーニングウェア, 運動着	41
트렌치코트	trench coat	防水衣	トレンチコート	40
트로트 (뽕짝)	trot	快步舞曲	演歌	133
트롬본	trombone	长号	トロンボーン	133
특별시	metropolis, special city	特别市	特別市	151
특별채용	special hiring	特别录用	特別採用	91
특산물	products unique to a region	土特产	特産物	139
티셔츠	T-shirt	T血衫	Tシャツ	38

ㅍ

한국어	English	中文	日本語	페이지
파	green onion	葱	ネギ	50
파김치	pa kimchi	葱泡菜	ネギのキムチ	66
파란색	blue	蓝色	青	14
파리	fly	苍蝇	ハエ	145
파마 머리	perm	卷发 (烫发)	パーマヘアー	25
파스	poultice	派司	貼り薬	104
파스텔	pastels	彩色蜡笔	パステル	134
파우더	powder	散粉	パウダー	46
파운데이션	foundation	粉底液	ファンデーション	46
파워포인트	Power Point	(电脑) 图形软件	パワーポイント	95
파이	pie	派	パイ	61
파이프	pipe	钢管	パイプ	81
파일 폴더	file folder	文件夹	ファイルホルダー	91
파자마	pajamas	睡衣裤	パジャマ	40
파출부	maid	小时工	派出婦	79
파카	parka	派克	パーカー	40
파키스탄	Pakistan	巴基斯坦	パキスタン	148
파티션	partition	隔板	パーティション	90
판결	judgment	判决	判決	155
판다	panda	熊猫	パンダ	143
판사	judge	审判官	判事	154
판탈롱 스타킹	knee-highs	短袜	ショートストッキング	42
판화	(a) print	版画	版画	135
팔	arm	胳膊	腕	26

팔꿈치	elbow	胳膊肘儿	肘	27
팔만대장경	Palman Daejang Gyeong	八万大藏经	八万大蔵経	153
팔보채	ba bao cai	八宝菜	八宝菜	58
팔찌	bracelet	手镯	腕輪	45
팝송	(foreign) pop music	流行歌曲	ポップソング	133
팥빙수	patbingsu, red-bean sherbet	冰粥	カキ氷	54, 65
팩	pack	面膜	パック	46
팩스	fax machine	传真机	ファックス	91
팬	pan	平锅	ファン	73
팬티	underpants	内裤	パンツ	42
팬티스타킹	pantyhose	连裤丝袜	パンティーストッキング	42
퍼머넌트, 펌	permanent, perm	卷发	パーマ	111
퍼센트	percent	百分比	パーセント	19
퍼즐 맞추기	doing puzzles	拼图	ジグソーパズル	129
펀드	a fund	基金	ファンド	156
페루	Peru	秘鲁	ペルー	149
페인트	paint	油漆	ペイント	81
페인트롤러	paint roller	油漆滚棒	ペイントローラー	81
페인트붓	paint brush	油漆刷子	ペイント筆	81
페티코트	petticoat	衬裙	ペチコート	42
펜션	pension	租赁木屋	ペンション	139
펜싱	fencing	击剑	フェンシング	131
펜치	pliers	铁钳	ペンチ	81
펭귄	penguin	企鹅	ペンギン	144
편안하다	to be peaceful	舒服	安らかだ	37
편지	letter	信	手紙	108
편지 찾기	email search	查邮件	メール検索	97
편지쓰기	compose	写邮件	メールを書く	96
편지읽기	open, read mail	读邮件	メールを読む	96
편지함	mailbox	邮件夹	メールボックス	97
편하다	to be comfortable	方便	便利だ	35
평일	weekday	平日	平日	10
포도	grape	葡萄	ブドウ	51
포도주	grape wine	葡萄酒	葡萄酒	55
포도주스	grape juice	葡萄汁	ブドウジュース	54
포르투갈	Portugal	葡萄牙	ポルトガル	149
포스터	poster	海报/宣传画	ポスター	135
포스트잇	post-it	便条	ポストイット	92
포장	wrapping	包装	包装	65
포장센터	gift wrapping	包装中心	包装センター	113
폭풍	storm	暴风	嵐	12
폰뱅킹	phone banking	电话银行	テレバンク	107
표 (티켓)	ticket	票 (入场券)	券 (チケット)	135
표지판	road sign	标志牌	標識板	119
프라이드치킨	fried chicken	炸鸡	フライドチキン	60
프랑스	France	法国	フランス	149
프렌치프라이	French fries	炸署条	フライドポテト	65
프린터	printer	打印机	プリンター	95
플래시라이트	flashlight	手电筒	フラッシュライト	81
플랫폼	platform	站台	プラットホーム	117
플로피 디스크	floppy disk	软盘	フロッピーディスク	95
플루트	flute	长笛	フルート	133
피고	defendant, accused	被告	被告	154
피곤하다	to be tired	疲倦	疲れている	37
피리	pipe	笛子	笛	133
피부	skin	皮肤	皮膚	27
피부과	dermatology	皮肤科	皮膚科	101
피아노	piano	钢琴	ピアノ	133
피자	pizza	比萨饼	ピザ	60
피해자	victim	被害者	被害者	155
핀	pin	发卡	ピン	111

필기도구	writing utensils	笔记用具	筆記用具	88
필기시험	written test	笔试	筆記試験	88
필름	film	胶卷 / 影片	フィルム	135
필리핀	the Philippines	菲律宾	フィリピン	148
필통	pencil case	笔筒	筆箱	83

ㅎ

하늘	sky	天空	空	147
하늘색	azure	天蓝色	空色	14
하드디스크	hard disk	硬盘	ハードディスク	95
하마	hippopotamus	河马	カバ	143
하사관	noncommissioned officer	下士	下士官	159
하이힐	high heels	高跟鞋	ハイヒール	43
하차문	rear door (for exiting bus)	下车门	下車扉	115
학과 사무실	department office	教研室	学科事務室	85
학교 신문사	school newspaper	校报社	学校の新聞社	85
학생	student	学生	学生	82
학생 상담소	student counseling	学生咨询处	学生相談所	85
학생식당	student cafeteria	学生食堂	学生食堂	84
학생증	student identification	学生证	学生証	87
학생활동	student activities	学生活动	学生活動	89
학생회	student association	学生会	学生会	89
학생회관	student center	学生会馆	学生会館	85
학예회	art festival	艺术节	学芸会	89
학위 논문실	dissertation room	学位论文室	学位論文室	87
한강	Han River	汉江	漢江	151
한라산	Mount Halla	汉拿山	漢拏山	151
한복	Korean clothing, hanbok	韩服	韓服	40
한식	Korean food	韩餐	韓国料理	56
한약	Oriental medicine	韩药	漢方薬	101
한의원	Oriental medicine clinic	韩医院	漢方医院	101
할머니 (조모)	grandmother	奶奶 (祖母)	おばあさん (祖母)	30
할부	installment	分期付款	分割払い	23
할아버지 (조부)	grandfather	爷爷 (祖父)	おじいさん (祖父)	30
할인	discount	优惠	割引	111
할인쿠폰	discount coupon	优惠券	割引クーポン	113
합승	sharing a taxi	合乘	相乗り	115
핫도그	hot dog	热狗	ホットドッグ	65
항생연고제	antibiotic ointment	抗生软膏	抗生物質軟膏	105
해 (년)	year	年	年	10
해 (태양)	sun	太阳	太陽	12
해군	navy	海军	海軍	159
해바라기	sunflower	向日葵	ヒマワリ	141
해산물	marine products	海产物 (水产品)	海産物	52
해삼	trepang	海参	ナマコ	52
해열제	fever remedy	退烧药	解熱剤	105
해왕성	Neptune	海王星	海王星	146
해외	overseas	海外	海外	149
해외여행	overseas travel	国外旅行	海外旅行	139
해일	tidal wave	海啸	津波	147
해킹	hacking	黑客侵入	ハッキング	95
해파리냉채	cold dish of jellyfish	凉拌海蜇	クラゲの冷菜	58
핸드 브레이크	parking brake	手闸	ハンドブレーキ	125
핸드백	handbag	手提包	ハンドバッグ	44
핸드볼	handball	手球	ハンドボール	131
핸드폰	mobile phone	手机	携帯(電話)	93
핸들	steering wheel	方向盘	ハンドル	125
햄	ham	火腿	ハム	53
햄버거	hamburger(s)	汉堡包	ハンバーガー	65
행복하다	to be happy	幸福	幸せだ	37
행정부	executive branch	行政部	行政府	155

향수	perfume	香水	香水	46
허리	waist	腰	腰	26
허벅지	inside of the thigh	大腿	内もも	27
허파	lung	肺	肺	27
헌법재판소	Constitutional Court	宪法裁判所	憲法裁判所	155
헤드폰	headphone	头戴式耳机	ヘッドホン	136
헤어 드라이기	hair dryer	吹风机	ドライヤー	77
헬기	helicopter	直升机	ヘリコプター	159
혀	tongue	舌头	舌	25
현금	cash	现金	現金	23
현금카드	cash card	储蓄卡 (现金卡)	キャッシュカード	23
현악기	stringed instrument	弦乐器	弦楽器	133
현충일	Memorial Day	显忠日	顕忠日	153
혈압계	blood pressure gauge	血压计	血圧計	101
혐오하다	to hate	厌恶	嫌う	35
형	elder brother of a man	哥哥	兄	30
형광등	fluorescent lamp	日光灯	蛍光灯	74
형제	brothers	兄弟	兄弟	31
혜성	comet	彗星	彗星	146
호남	Honam region	湖南	湖南	151
호떡	hotteok	烙饼	ホットック	57
호랑이	tiger	老虎	トラ	143
호른	horn	圆号	ホルン	133
호박	squash	南瓜	かぼちゃ	50
호수	lake	湖	湖	147
호스	hose	胶皮管 (水龙)	ホース	81
호텔	hotel	宾馆	ホテル	139
호흡마스크	mask with air filter function	呼吸口罩	呼吸マスク	99
홍수	flood	洪水	洪水	12
홍역	measles	麻疹	麻疹	103
홍차	black tea, Western tea	红茶	紅茶	55
홍합	sea mussel	贻贝	イガイ	52
화가	painter	画家	画家	135
화나다	to be angry	生气	腹が立つ	35
화물차	freight truck	货车	貨物車	119
화물차 통행 금지	No Large Trucks	禁货运汽车通行	貨物自動車等通行止め	120
화분	flowerpot	花盆	植木鉢	74
화산	volcano	火山	火山	147
화성	Mars	火星	火星	146
화요일	Tuesday	星期二	火曜日	10
화이트보드	white board	白板	ホワイトボード	82
화장대	makeup stand, dressing table	化妆台	化粧台	75
화장솜	cotton	化妆棉	コットン	46
화장지	toilet paper	卫生纸	トイレットペーパー	76
환갑, 회갑	60th birthday	花甲	還暦	33
환경 설정	settings / preferences	背景设置	環境設定	97
환승역	transfer station	换乘站	乗り換え駅	117
환율	exchange rate	汇率	為替相場	156
환자	patient	病人	患者	100
환전소	money change booth	换钱处	両替所	127
환풍기	ventilation fan	排气扇	換気扇	73
활주로	runway	跑道	滑走路	126
회색	gray	灰色	灰色	14
회식	eating out with coworkers	公司聚餐	会食	91
회원카드	membership card	会员卡	会員カード	65
회의실	meeting room	会议室	会議室	91
회화	a painting	绘画	絵画	135
횡단보도	crosswalk	人行横道	横断歩道	119
효도관광	filial piety tourism	孝道旅行	両親に旅行をプレゼントすること	139
후문	rear gate	后门	裏門	85
후보자	candidate	候选人	候補者	155

Korean	English	Chinese	Japanese	Page
후식	dessert	甜食	デザート	63
후진하다	to go in reverse	倒车	後進する	123
후춧가루	ground pepper	胡椒粉	コショウ	63
훈련	training	训练	訓練	159
훈민정음	Hunmin Jeongeum	训民正音	訓民正音	153
휠캡	hubcap	(车) 毂	ホイールキャップ	124
휴가	vacation	休假	休暇	91
휴강	(a teacher) skipping a lecture	停课	休講	83
휴게실	lounge	休息室	休憩室	86
휴대용 가스레인지	portable gas stove	携带用煤气灶	携帯用ガスコンロ	69
휴지통	wastepaper basket	垃圾桶	ゴミ箱	91
흐림	cloudy	阴天	曇り	12
흙손	trowel	泥刀	こて	81
희극	comedy	喜剧	喜劇	135
흰색/하얀색	white	白色	白	14
히터	heater	加热器	ヒーター	125

기타

Korean	English	Chinese	Japanese	Page
0 영 (공)	zero	零	0	16
1 일 (하나)	one	一	一 (一つ)	16
1,000 천	one thousand	一千	千	17
1,000,000 백만	one million	一百万	百万	17
1,000,000,000 십억	one billion	十亿	十億	17
10 십 (열)	ten	十	十 (とお)	16
10,000 만	ten thousand	一万	一万	17
100 백	one hundred	一百	百	17
100,000 십만	one hundred thousand	十万	十万	17
10월	October	十月	10月	11
11 십일 (열하나)	eleven	十一	十一	16
11월	November	十一月	11月	11
12 십이 (열둘)	twelve	十二	十二	16
12월	December	十二月	12月	11
13 십삼 (열셋)	thirteen	十三	十三	16
14 십사 (열넷)	fourteen	十四	十四	16
15 십오 (열다섯)	fifteen	十五	十五	16
16 십육 (열여섯)	sixteen	十六	十六	16
17 십칠 (열일곱)	seventeen	十七	十七	16
18 십팔 (열여덟)	eighteen	十八	十八	16
19 십구 (열아홉)	nineteen	十九	十九	16
1월	January	一月	1月	11
1학기	the first semester	一学期	一学期	89
2 이 (둘)	two	二	二 (二つ)	16
20 이십 (스물)	twenty	二十	二十	16
2002 월드컵	2002 World Cup	2002世界杯	2002ワールドカップ	152
2월	February	二月	2月	11
2학기	the second semester	二学期	二学期	89
3 삼 (셋)	three	三	三 (三つ)	16
3.1 운동	March 1st Movement	3.1运动	3.1運動	152
3.1절	Independence Day	三一节	三一節	153
30 삼십 (서른)	thirty	三十	三十	16
3월	March	三月	3月	11
4 사 (넷)	four	四	四 (四つ)	16
4.19 혁명	March 19 Revolution	4.19革命	4.19革命	152
40 사십 (마흔)	forty	四十	四十	16
4월	April	四月	4月	11
5 오 (다섯)	five	五	五 (五つ)	16
50 오십 (쉰)	fifty	五十	五十	16
5월	May	五月	5月	11
6 육 (여섯)	six	六	六 (六つ)	16
6.25 전쟁	Korean War, June 25 War	6.25战争	6.25戦争	152
60 육십 (예순)	sixty	六十	六十	16

6월	June	六月	6月	11
7 칠 (일곱)	seven	七	七 (七つ)	16
70 칠십 (일흔)	seventy	七十	七十	16
7월	July	七月	7月	11
8 팔 (여덟)	eight	八	八 (八つ)	16
8.15 해방	Liberation	8.15解放	8.15解放	152
80 팔십 (여든)	eighty	八十	八十	16
8월	August	八月	8月	11
9 구 (아홉)	nine	九	九 (九つ)	16
90 구십 (아흔)	ninety	九十	九十	16
9월	September	九月	9月	11
ARS 퀴즈	telephone quiz	ARS 智力竞赛	視聴者クイズ	137
CD	CD	CD	CD	95
CD 플레이어	CD player	CD 机	CDプレーヤー	136
CD ROM	CD rom	CD光驱	CD ROM	95
DVD 플레이어	DVD player	DVD播放机	DVDプレーヤー	137
DVD ROM	DVD rom	DVD光驱	DVD ROM	95
E-mail	E-mail	电子邮件	E-mail	96
L (대)	large	大	L(大)	41
M (중)	medium	中	M(中)	41
MP3 플레이어	MP3 player	MP3	MP3プレーヤー	136
MP3폰	phone with MP3 function	MP3手机	MP3フォン	93
MT	group retreat	MT	合宿	89
PDA	PDA	掌上电脑	PDA	95
S (소)	small	小	S(小)	41
T자형교차로	T-junction ahead	T形交叉	T形道路交差点あり	121
TV	television	电视	TV	136
U턴하다	to make a U-turn	掉头	ユーターンする	122
UN 안전보장이사회	United Nations Security Council	联合国安理会	UN安全保障理事会	149
WTO	World Trade Organisation	WTO	WTO	149
XL (특대)	extra large	特大	XL(特大)	41
XS (특소)	extra small	特小	XS(極小)	41

About the Author

Kang Hyoun-hwa

Ph.D. (Yonsei Univ)
Professor, Department of Korean Language, Kyunghee University
Head of GK Kyunghee University Specialization Project

Editorial Board Member of The Applied Linguistics Association of Korea
Research Board Member of The International Association for Korean Language Education
Editorial Board Member of The Korea Association of Foreign Languages Education

[Books]
A Study of Korean Verb-Verb Constructions (1998), Hankookmunhwasa Publishing
A Study in Contrasitive Analysis (2003), Yeokrak Publishing
Korean; an Intermediate Textbook (2003), Kyunghee University Press
How to Think & Write (2004), Kyunghee University Press
A Study of Korean As A Foreign Language (2004), Pagijong Press
A Study of Korean as a Foreign Language Education (2005), Korea National Open University Press
Learner's Dictionary of Korean (2005), Sinwon Prime

Assistant Author : **Kim Yu-mi** (Kyunghee University)

Korean Picture Dictionary

Written by	Kang Hyoun-hwa
Translated by	Peter Schroepfer, Piao Wenzi, Ogoshi Naoki
Illustrated by	Kim Moon-su, Joo Young-keun
First Published	November, 2006
2nd Printing	June, 2007
Publisher	Chung Hyo-sup
Editor	Lee Suk-hee, Lee Eun-ju, Jang Byung-sik
Designer	Son Hye-jung, Choi Young-ran
Cover Designer	Kang Sung-ae

DARAKWON Published by Darakwon Inc.
509-1 Munbal-ri, Gyoha-eup, Paju-si
Gyeonggi-do, Korea 413-756
Tel : 02-736-2031 Fax : 02-732-2037
(Marketing Dept. ext.: 113,114 Editorial Dept. ext.: 412)

Copyright©2006, Kang Hyoun-hwa

This book is published and distributed
by Darakwon Inc.
All right reserved.
Reproduction in whole or on part
without written permission is prohibited.

Price : 18,000 won

ISBN : 978-89-5995-756-9 13710

http://www.darakwon.co.kr

※ Visit the Darakwon homepage to learn about our other publications and
promotions, and to download the contents of the CD in MP3 format.